Robert Jamieson

The Inspiration of the Holy Scriptures

Being the Baird Lecture for 1873

Robert Jamieson

The Inspiration of the Holy Scriptures
Being the Baird Lecture for 1873

ISBN/EAN: 9783337813970

Printed in Europe, USA, Canada, Australia, Japan

Cover: Foto ©Lupo / pixelio.de

More available books at **www.hansebooks.com**

THE INSPIRATION

OF

THE HOLY SCRIPTURES

BEING

The Baird Lecture for 1873

BY

ROBERT JAMIESON, D.D.

MINISTER OF ST PAUL'S PARISH CHURCH, GLASGOW

WILLIAM BLACKWOOD AND SONS
EDINBURGH AND LONDON
MDCCCLXXIII

EXCERPT *from the* DEED OF TRUST *by* JAMES BAIRD, ESQ., *in favour of the Trustees of the* 'BAIRD TRUST.'

'Whereas, at the Meeting of the General Assembly of the Church of Scotland, held in May 1872, I declared my intention to found a Lectureship, to be called "The Baird Lecture," for the illustration and the defence of the vital truths hereinbefore referred to, as well as for the promotion of Christian knowledge and Christian work generally, and for the exposure and refutation of all error and unbelief, under which foundation the Reverend Robert Jamieson, D.D., lately Moderator of the General Assembly, was to be the first Lecturer, and that for the spring of the year 1873; Therefore, and for the endowment of the said Lectureship, I appoint my said Trustees to hold an annual sum of £220 out of the revenue of the funds under their charge for the purposes of said Lectureship; and I direct that the following shall be the conditions and terms on which my said Trustees shall carry out my foundation of said Lectureship :—

'1. The Lecturer shall be a minister of the foresaid Church of Scotland who shall have served the cure of a parish for not less than five years, or a minister of any other of the Scottish Presbyterian Churches who shall have served as pastor of a congregation for a similar period in his own Church; and in making the appointment, care shall be taken by the Trustees to choose a man of piety, ability, and learning, and who is approved and reputed sound in all the essentials of Christian truth, as set forth in the statement hereinbefore written of what is meant by sound religious principles.

'2. The Lecturer shall be appointed annually in the month of April by my said Trustees, and the appointment shall be made at a meeting of the Trustees to be called for the purpose, and held in Glasgow.

'3. The Lecturer shall deliver a course of not less than Six Lectures on any subject of Theology, Christian Evidences, Christian Work, Christian Missions, Church Government, and Church Organizations, or on such subject relative thereto as the Trustees shall from year to year fix in concert with the Lecturer.

EXCERPT FROM DEED OF TRUST.

'4. The Lectures shall be duly advertised to the satisfaction of the Trustees, at the cost of the Lecturer, and shall be delivered publicly at any time during the months of January and February in each year, in Glasgow, and also, if required, in such other one of the Scottish University towns as may from time to time be appointed by the Trustees.

'5. The Lectures of each year shall be published, if possible, before the meeting of the next General Assembly, or at latest within six months of the date when the last of the course shall have been delivered. Such publication to be carried out at the sight and to the satisfaction of the Trustees, but by the Lecturer at his own cost and risk, and to the extent of not less than 750 copies, of which there shall be deposited, free, two copies in the Library of each of the Universities of Glasgow, Aberdeen, Edinburgh, and St. Andrews, two copies in the Library of the General Assembly of the Church of Scotland, and one copy in each of the Theological Libraries connected with the said Universities, and twenty copies shall be put at the disposal of the Trustees. The price of publication to be regulated by the Trustees in concert with the Lecturer.'

PREFACE.

THESE Lectures, which were orally delivered in the early part of the year, are now given to the public in a printed form. The author was not laid under any of the restrictions as to the time of publication which have been laid down since in Mr. Baird's Deed of Bequest; and various circumstances, which it is unnecessary to mention, have occasioned its postponement till this date.

The choice of a subject was left entirely to the judgment and taste of the Lecturer; and being the first of a series intended to expound and establish the great fundamental truths of Christianity, it appeared to him that no theme could be so appropriate as a short treatise on the divine character and authority of the Book which forms "the only rule that God has given to teach us what we are to believe concerning Him, as well as what is the duty He requires of man." Besides, a condensed view of the arguments which prove the Scriptures to be the inspired word of God is greatly needed in the present day, when the public mind is, from various causes, agitated on religious matters, and the foundations of old beliefs are eagerly examined; and it is hoped that some aid may be afforded by the following Lectures to honest and anxious inquirers, who long to rest their faith in the inspiration of the Scriptures on a sound and solid basis.

The Author deems it a high honour that he was requested to commence a Lectureship which, he fondly trusts, will in the future series reflect credit on Scotland, by contributing to stimulate the study of Theology amongst her clergy, and thereby to promote the cause of Christ.

GLASGOW, *December* 1873.

CONTENTS.

	PAGE
LECTURE I.	1
LECTURE II.	61
LECTURE III.	156
LECTURE IV.	247
LECTURE V.	303
LECTURE VI.	344
NOTES	377

THE INSPIRATION

OF

THE HOLY SCRIPTURES.

LECTURE I.

Titles of the Bible—Supreme Importance of its Contents—Loftiness of its Character and Tone—Hereditary Reverence for the Scriptures—Happy Influence of them—Assaults of Infidelity—Peculiar Character of Scepticism in the Present Day—Inspiration a Subject of Vital Interest and Importance—Word of God existed in the World before it was embodied in a Written Form—Meaning of Inspiration—Necessity of Inspiration—Inspiration of the Scriptures collectively—Evidence furnished by the Faithful Custody of the Old Testament by the Jews—And of the New by the Early Christians—Evidence of their Inspiration given by the Testimony of Christ and of the Apostles—Meaning of Canon—Formed by Ezra—Account of the Old Testament Books by Josephus—Charge against Christ and the Apostles of speaking regarding the Scriptures in accommodation to the Prejudices of their Countrymen—Groundlessness of such a Charge—All Scripture given by Inspiration—Doubts regarding some Books, as Esther and Song of Solomon—Objections answered—Infallible Authority arising from Inspiration—Scriptures an Organic Whole.

THE Bible is a communication from God to man; and the transcendent importance of its contents is significantly indicated by the various titles applied to it. This sacred volume is called "the Bible," *i.e.* the Book, and the Scriptures, *i.e.* the Writings, as being incomparably more valuable than all the volumes which, in a written as well as printed form, have ever appeared in the world. It is called also "the oracles of God," as containing heavenly responses on matters of highest concern to man's peace and happiness, and "lively oracles," as pointing out the way to his enjoyment of spiritual and eternal life; "the word of reconciliation," as holding out the hope as well as the means of securing favour and acceptance with his greatly offended Maker; "the word of truth," as affording clear and certain information for guidance in faith and practice; and "the word of God," as, though conveyed in the language of man, it was divine in its origin, and carries a divine authority along with it. These different names describe the distinctive properties of the Bible, which occupies the same high rank amongst books as did the sheaf of Joseph, to which the sheaves of his father and brethren were seen to bow. The Scriptures are distinguished from all other books, not only by containing a greater mass and variety of matter than is to be found within the same compass in any other book, but by the character of their contents. They are the most ancient of all books in the world, and tell us of events and transactions in the earliest ages of which we can obtain the knowledge from no other source. But it is not their venerable antiquity, their oriental dress, their picturesque delineation of patriarchal manners, that form their great value, or that recommend them pre-eminently to our notice. It is because they communicate information on matters of surpassing interest and importance; matters bearing directly on the welfare of man, both in this world and that which is to come. Moreover, the slightest acquaintance with them is sufficient to show that they are unique in their character, and, viewed generally, bear so little resemblance to any known productions of man, as to create a strong presumption that he is not the author. The style is so much more dignified and commanding than the greatest or boldest of mortals would have dared to assume; the discoveries made in the Scriptures stretch forward in a direction so remote from the course which all human researches have uniformly taken; the principle that pervades them is so humiliating to the native pride of man, and the whole of the details are of a kind, to the invention of which the natural powers of humanity are so manifestly unequal, that every intelligent and reflecting person must be convinced that it has had a higher than human origin. Moreover, considered in their internal character and leading aim, the Scriptures are found to breathe a spirit of such exalted purity; they display such stern opposition to every form and degree of iniquity and vice; they make such an effectual provision for the banishment of all evils, and for the growth and establishment of all true excellence; their tendency is so strong and so well fitted to elevate this fallen world to the pure condition of heaven, and to renew man in conformity to the moral image of God, as affords conclusive evidence that they contain His revealed scheme of grace for the moral and spiritual regeneration of the human race.

In this land of Christian knowledge and observance, we are born and bred with a feeling of hereditary reverence for the Scriptures. This book awakens in the minds of all far other sentiments than those connected with a venerable antiquity; and though it presents only the same common appearance, and is composed of the same common materials with other books, its very name is a symbol of sacredness, greater than what is attached to any of the highest productions of human genius or learning. Nor is this feeling of veneration confined only to classes of people who may be actuated by blind superstition on the one hand, or pietistic enthusiasm on the other. It is a sentiment which animates the inhabitants of this country generally, the origin of the popular belief being traceable to the influence of early impressions. And happy it is that this idea is engraven on the tablets of the youthful mind; that the persuasion is intertwined with its tenderest associations; and that the first elements of knowledge imbibed are usually those simple but sublime and interesting truths, that are taught as the leading principles of the sacred volume. I say, happy it is that childhood and youth are imbued with such strong prepossessions in favour of the divine character and authority of the Scriptures; for every intelligent and candid observer will admit that the use of the Bible for centuries in our national system of education has been one main cause of the superior intelligence that distinguishes our countrymen generally. In numberless instances it must have produced a beneficial influence in training the pupils to the love and practice of good; and while the remembrance of its precepts and solemn sanctions must have exercised a secret but powerful restraint on the passions of many who were not accustomed to take it as their governing principle of action, multitudes who drank its spirit, and cherished its benign influence, have looked to it as their polar star in regulating the daily course of their lives; and felt that, to part with it, would be to deprive themselves of a hope and belief essential to their comfort, and inwrought into their very being. By its direct and indirect influence amongst all classes, it has long moulded the national faith; and the happy effects of it upon the people are seen in all the pursuits of social life and the arrangements of civil society, making them high in civilisation, advanced in the cultivation of the arts and sciences, refined in their manners, correct in their morals, pure in the administration of justice, and always in a state of progress. It must needs be, however, that offences come; and persons whose attachment to the Scriptures has grown with their growth, and strengthened with their strength, are liable to have their cherished feelings frequently shocked by the assaults that are made on what they have been taught to regard and are accustomed to revere as sacred. At all times there have been secret or open enemies, who have doubted or denied the claims of the Bible, from the determined infidel who scouts the idea of an external revelation through a book, deeming the inward light of reason and conscience sufficient, up to the rationalist who, while admitting the Scriptures to contain the will of God, subjects all its statements to the ordeal of reason. The age in which we live is no exception: for although the virulent spirit with which the Deistical controversy was last century waged has long ago ceased; although a Voltaire and a Paine have happily no imitators in the present day, their place has been occupied by successors like Strauss and Renan, whose philosophical or romantic theories are as wild and mischievous as the scoffing cavils of the one or the vulgar ribaldry of the other. The old hypothesis, indeed, which represented the sacred books as forgeries has been abandoned as untenable, its abettors having been discomfited by force of superior learning and well-applied argument. But although knowledge has changed the mode of warfare, and refinement tempered the asperity of opposition, infidelity is so far from being extirpated, that from special causes, connected chiefly with the scientific character and critical tendencies of the age, a quiet but settled scepticism prevails to a wide extent among the higher class of society; and it has been reserved to the present day to witness the strange phenomenon of professed Christians declaring their conviction that the Bible is a merely human production. While recognising the fact of a supernatural revelation having been given, they assert that the men who received the communication gave an honest account of it so far as they knew, understood, or remembered it, but that, through national prejudices or personal frailties, misapprehending or misstating its meaning, their records are so imperfect, erroneous, often self-contradictory and false, that no confidence can be placed in them; and that even where they are correct and coherent, the grains of divine truth are so blended with a mass of poetical myths, of legendary fables, and popular traditions, that reason and the higher criticism must be employed to test the credibility of the narrative, and admit only what approves itself to the moral intuition. This habit of thought, which has long prevailed in Germany, and given rise to a large proportion of the errors into which the divines of that country have fallen, has been imported into Britain, and is producing its natural fruits. The old recognised boundaries of inspiration have been broken down: some contend for a partial inspiration; others reject the idea of inspiration altogether as unreasonable, or reduce it to a minimum. So that the dignity and authority of the divine sanction are almost wholly withdrawn from the sacred volume; and critics feel themselves at liberty to discuss both the Bible itself, and the contents of its various books, with no other restraint than they would feel in the examination of the most ordinary publication. How greatly does it tend to lower the character and destroy all confidence in the sacred volume, when, instead of receiving implicitly its statements as the word of God, an active and constant exercise of judgment is required to extract the precious ore from the earthly accretion with which it is encrusted—to select the divine from the human, and to determine in what portions God is addressing us! How directly does it tend not only to destroy the feeling of veneration due to the pure and holy word of God, but to keep the mind of the reader in a state of painful doubt and uncertainty as to whether, in the portion accepted, his faith is resting on the word of man or the word of God! In these circumstances, the subject of inspiration is invested with immense importance. It has become one of the vital questions of the times; and while it may be expedient to examine the grounds of our faith generally, as we are living in an age when the foundations of all old beliefs are being upturned and sifted, it is imperatively necessary, from its bearing upon all our religious principles and practice, to have full confidence in the breadth and solidity of the basis on which we rest our persuasion of the divine character and supreme authority of the Scripture.

To set before you the evidences of this momentous fact, that the Scriptures of the Old and New Testaments are the revealed word of God, and the only supreme rule of faith and manners, is the object of the following Lectures. But before entering upon the discussion of this subject, it may be proper to premise, that in one point of view the word of God long preceded the Bible. For the gracious declaration of God concerning a Redeemer of fallen man was announced in substance many centuries before the earliest of the sacred writers was born. The antediluvian patriarchs, Adam, Enoch, Noah, and others, as well as the first post-diluvian patriarchs, Shem, Melchizedek, and Job, Abraham, Isaac, and Jacob, were not in possession of a Bible. And yet they had the word of God, communicated to them in various ways, and containing the essence of "the gospel which is now preached unto us." Nay, the very day that man became a sinner, the word of God came to him, convincing him of sin, and relieving his despondency or despair by the announcement of a remedial scheme of salvation which divine grace had provided. That word, thus early given, was repeated by peculiar manifestations to many good men, and maintained in the world for a while by oral tradition, till, in the course of time, the revelations it embraced, and what information relating to the origin and early condition of mankind would be subservient to their religious instruction, were embodied in the permanent form of a book. That book has during four thousand years been wonderfully preserved amid the greatest vicissitudes; and while myriads of other books, once well known and held in high estimation, have become entirely obsolete, or been long ago lost in the gulf of oblivion, it still continues abreast, or rather in advance of the age,—as suitable to the character and condition of mankind in the nineteenth century as in the earliest times. If, then, God has spoken of Himself and His purposes of grace to our fallen humanity, what He has said must be authoritative, and all our speculations on these subjects must be superseded by the transcendent utterances of the divine oracle. But to the mind of every intelligent and reflecting person, it must appear that, in such a case, the proper initiative is to satisfy ourselves that the Scripture is the word of the Most High God; and then, with that "as a light that shineth in a dark place," to explore our way into the regions of faith and duty.

Now all that constitutes Christianity as a scheme, separate from all other religious systems ever known in the world, is contained in this book, which sets forth its distinctive peculiarities in a series of facts, doctrines, and duties, accompanied with a record of miraculous interpositions, which are God's attestations to those truths and duties. Assuming, as on the present occasion we must do, that the record is authentic and genuine, we lay down, and shall endeavour to establish, the position that it is also inspired. In other words, our purpose is to show that the Bible, though consisting of matter written in the language and traced by the pen of mortals, frail and fallible as other men, yet bears the impress of a divine origin and character; consequently, is of supreme, infallible authority. Inspiration signifies "a breathing into;" and although it is not, strictly speaking, a scriptural term, the phraseology is borrowed from the act of the

Creator, who breathed into the nostrils of the newly formed man the breath of life; and the same act was repeated by our Lord after His resurrection, when He breathed on His disciples, saying, "Receive ye the Holy Ghost." By this significant act, He announced to them in a metaphorical way that a power was imparted to them, by which they were to be supernaturally enlightened in the knowledge and guided in the exhibition of divine truth,—a power exercised over them by the Holy Ghost, which caused the things which they wrote to be of absolute authority. It might or might not be accompanied by a revelation of facts, or of principles of truth previously unknown; but in either case, inspiration was equally needed. For else, how could a man, however holy or wise, write authoritatively? and how could he rightly know what should be a record conducive to the instruction and profit of God's people in all ages? In the course of our Lectures, we propose to consider the subject first in reference to the Scriptures collectively, and afterwards to the separate books, taking up in succession, though not formally, such points as the following: What is the kind as well as amount of evidence which can be adduced to prove the inspiration of the Bible? Does this supernatural quality characterize the whole Scriptures? Does it pervade the sacred volume in an equal degree throughout; or does a higher degree attach to some portions, while an inferior measure only is imparted to others? Is the nature and extent of this inspiration sufficient to stamp upon the Bible the broad seal of divine and infallible authority, as the only standard of faith and duty? This summary of topics seems sufficiently comprehensive to cover the whole field of inquiry relating to the subject; and we are persuaded that a candid, enlightened, and full consideration of them will lead to the important result of establishing the Scriptures to be the word of God.

Now, with regard to the inspiration of the Old Testament, where can we look for the evidence of the fact so naturally and properly, as to the people who were appointed to be the depositaries of the divine will, and who executed their important trust with a fidelity worthy of the highest praise? It does not appear that the Almighty gave any written declaration of His will until He had separated the Jewish people from the rest of the nations for a time, to be His witnesses, and at the same time custodiers of the various revelations which were to be made in the progressive development of His scheme of grace. From the commencement of their national history, they were placed under the superintendence of a human leader, who had received a divine legation, and who, in discharging the duties of his high mission, was admitted to the privilege of frequent and direct communication with his Divine Master, for the purpose of receiving instructions how he should introduce and establish that system of polity which was designed for the government of the people. During the whole existence of their peculiar economy, God was pleased to maintain a close and constant superintendence of the Jewish people by extraordinary messengers, sent from time to time to communicate His will; and although numbers of false prophets appeared, who counterfeited the true, and by their artful address gained a temporary ascendency in deluding and misleading the people, certain plain and palpable criteria were given, by which all classes might easily determine the character of the men who spoke to them in the name of the Lord. The tests of a false prophet were these—the speedy failure of his predictions, or the infliction upon himself[1] of some sudden judgments of Heaven; and by the application of those marks the youngest and simplest might have been enabled to decide whether and how far the persons who appeared amongst them assuming the prophetic character were worthy of confidence. As the special dispensation which God established with that nation necessitated His frequent and direct interposition in their affairs, so that miraculous incidents were occasionally intermingled with the ordinary course of their history, we are prepared to expect a class of inspired men who were ambassadors of God in communicating His will; and by this divinely contrived system of agency, the light of truth was preserved in the land which God had chosen to put His name there. Nor was this all; for oral discourses would have produced a very transient impression on a rude and ignorant people, and therefore some permanent means were provided for the religious instruction of the people. The communications which Moses received from God he was commanded to record in a book, which was deposited, not only for perfect security, but as the protest against the national breach of the covenant in future times by idolatry, beside the

[1] Jer. xxviii. 17.

ark in the sanctuary.[1] This book was increased by successive additions made in the progress of the Jewish nation, such as the record of Joshua,[2] and other portions of the Scripture,[3] with a collection of Proverbs, and perhaps of Psalms.[4] At a later period, "the book of the Lord" is mentioned by Isaiah as a general collection for religious instruction;[5] and "the book of the law," "the former prophets," and "the books," are referred to by Zechariah and Daniel.[6] The popular belief of the Jewish church ascribed to Ezra, on the return from the Babylonish captivity, the honourable undertaking of collecting the isolated books of Scripture for the use of the resuscitated Jewish church. That protracted exile led to a complete revolution of the Jewish mind; for, from that time, the Jews being effectually cured of their infatuated propensity to idols and idolatry, began to cherish a devoted reverence for the God of their fathers, and an adherence to the religious institutions of their native country. The church was reorganized; and to aid the celebration of public worship, the sacred canon of the Old Testa-

---

[1] Deut. xxxi. 25; 1 Kings viii. 9; 2 Kings xxii. 8.
[2] Josh. xxiv. 26.   [3] 1 Sam. x. 25.   [4] Prov. xxv.
[5] Isa. xxix. 18.   [6] Zech. vii. 12; Dan. ix. 2.

B

ment was formed under the auspices of Ezra and "the great synagogue," so that part of the divine word was read every Sabbath-day in the synagogue, and the people acquired thereby a feeling of reverential regard for it, which time tended only to deepen and confirm. This was the great advantage of the Jews, that " to them were committed the oracles of God," and their whole subsequent history showed how highly they prized the sacred treasure. No lapse of time, no distance of place, no reverse of fortune, could cool their zeal or superinduce a spirit of indifference about the preservation of the sacred books. At home or abroad, in freedom or in exile, in Judea no less than in Babylon or Persia, in times of national independence, or during the prevalence of Roman ascendency, their conservative tenacity to the Scriptures formed one of the prominent features of the Jewish character. Amid all the aberrations and crimes with which the Jews were chargeable, an imputation of treachery in the guardianship, or of designs upon the integrity, of the sacred books was never raised against them; and rather than surrender them at the mandate of a persecuting tyrant, they were prepared to encounter death in its most revolting forms. Nay, even though destitute for the most part of a right apprehension of their meaning, and strangers to their spirit, they cherished a superstitious veneration for the letter of the Scriptures; and it rests upon the clearest historical testimony, that they maintained a constant jealous vigilance over their sacred books, extending their scrupulous care even to an enumeration of the words and letters contained in each book, — a bibliolatry which has often been the occasion of exposing them to ridicule. Indeed, it is very remarkable that, divided as they were, in our Lord's time, into several hostile sects, there never was any difference amongst them respecting the character and status of the Scriptures, even though these Scriptures were unsparing in condemnation of their ways. In fact, it is the grand redeeming feature in the character of this singular people, that they watched with such unvarying scrupulosity over the written word; and the transmission of the sacred books from age to age, pure, uncorrupted, and unmutilated, affords to the church a satisfactory guarantee not only for the authenticity and genuineness, but for the divine origin and authority, of the Old Testament.

As the books of the Old Testament were committed to the Jews, so were those of the New committed to the Christians; and although they were not deposited in the inaccessible crypt of a sanctuary, they were kept in the secure custody of churches or societies of pious servants of Christ, who set the highest value upon them as sacred treasures. As no part of the ancient Scriptures existed in a written form till the providence of God had selected a nation to preserve them, so no book of the later Scriptures was brought out in a permanent form till the organization of churches, in which they were carefully kept. And as the Old Testament existed in separate books till an advanced period in the history of the Jewish nation, when they were formed into a general collection; so the Gospel histories of Christ, and the Epistles of counsel and pastoral direction, were in private circulation a considerable time before the New Testament catalogue was made out as at present. Some of them were compiled in particular localities, and some of the epistles were addressed to churches or private individuals, so that they were not generally known to the church. But wherever writings were found, and ascertained on thorough inquiry to be the work of apostolic men, they were recognised by the Christians as sacred books. Amid all the heresies and corruptions which rose with such rank luxuriance in the first centuries, the books which were inspired were universally received by the churches without a dissentient voice. If doubts were entertained respecting some of them, and a strict investigation made into their origin, these very circumstances contributed to establish their character as the compositions of apostolic writers, and diffused throughout the church a settled opinion in their favour. Their inspired character was certified by the common consent of the most intelligent Christians, who were very numerous in the second century, and not by the decision of an ecclesiastical council; for the Council of Laodicea, held in 363, which was not of extensive authority, "rather declared," as Paley remarks, "than regulated the public judgment on the subject of the New Testament canon."

The word canon denotes a rule; and, applied to the Bible, signifies that the books comprehended in the Old and New Testaments were regarded as an authoritative rule for regulating faith and practice. The canon of the Old Testament was, as we have seen, according to the uniform tradition of the Jewish church, formed by the united counsels of Ezra, Haggai, Zechariah, and Malachi, at a time when the spirit of inspiration had ceased, and the minds of the people, instead of anxiously looking for new revelations, were directed exclusively to the anticipated advent of the great Messiah. As these four men were prophets, who were each honoured to take a prominent part in the reorganization of the church or the rebuilding of the temple after the restoration, as well as to contribute independent portions to the volume of Scripture, their pious labours in carefully collecting, arranging, and revising a general edition of the sacred books, were received by their countrymen as a work of inspired authority, binding them to receive it as comprising a series of precious revelations with which their nation had been favoured from the God of their fathers. From that time the Old Testament was regarded as the standard of the national religion, the confession of the Jewish faith, the liturgy of the Jewish church, the venerable authority to which the Jews appealed for the origin and sanction of their peculiar polity and distinctive institutions. We learn from Josephus that it consisted of precisely the same contents, book for book, and word for word, as are found in the copies of the Old Testament possessed by ourselves. "Every one," says he, "is not permitted of his own accord to be a writer, nor is there any disagreement in what is written; they being only prophets that have written the original and earliest accounts of things, as they learned them of God Himself by inspiration; and others have written what hath happened in their own times, and that in a very distinct manner also. For we have not an innumerable multitude of books among us, disagreeing from and contradicting one another (as the Greeks have), but only twenty-two books, which contain the records of all the past times, which are justly believed to be divine. And of them five belong to Moses, which contain his laws, and the traditions of the origin of mankind till his death. This interval of time was little short of three thousand years. But as to the time from the death of Moses till the reign of Artaxerxes King of Persia, who reigned after Xerxes, the prophets who were after Moses wrote down what was done in their times in thirteen books. The remaining four books contain hymns to God, and precepts for the conduct of human life. It is true, our history has been written since Artaxerxes very particularly, but has not been esteemed of the like authority with the former by our forefathers, because there hath not been an exact succession of prophets since that time; and how firmly we have given credit to these books of our own nation, is evident from what we do: for, during so many ages as have already passed, no one has been so bold as either to add anything to them, or to take anything from them, or to make any change in them; but it is become natural to all Jews, immediately and from their very birth, to esteem these books to contain divine doctrines, and to persist in them, and if occasion be, willingly to die for them. For it is no new thing for our captives, many of them in number, and frequently in time, to be seen to endure racks and deaths of all kinds upon the theatres, that they may not be obliged to say one word against our laws, and the records that contain them."[1] The Old Testament then appears, on the testimony of the Jewish historian, to have been exactly the same in his day as it is in ours; and as the canon was formed by the authority of prophets who were

---

[1] Josephus, *Contra Apion*, vol. iv. Book i. sec. 8, Whiston's translation. See Note A.

universally acknowledged to be inspired messengers of God, it must be regarded as inspired also.

Similar remarks are applicable to the canon of the New Testament. Without entering into the detailed history of its formation, which is too complicated a narrative to be undertaken here, it may suffice to say, that although the three first Gospels were compiled for the use, and for a considerable time known within the confines, of particular localities only; although many of the Epistles, which occupy a large portion of the New Testament, were occasional and fragmentary, the collection of these isolated documents to an extent that forms a complete system of doctrine, duty, and discipline, exhibits a striking proof of the watchful providence which presided over the development of the early Christian church. Doubts were entertained respecting some of the epistles, viz. that to the Hebrews, 2 Peter, 2 and 3 John, and Jude. But the researches of many learned and pious fathers, who earnestly and patiently traced out their apostolic origin, established the claims of these epistles to be the genuine productions of the authors whose names they bear; and the general consent with which all the western churches especially have united in recognising the canon of the New Testament, is a fact which must be considered as tantamount to an acknowledgment of its inspiration. Now, such an acknowledgment rests upon the basis of tradition, and may be considered on that account as a doubtful or unsound conclusion. But it is one thing to recognise the use of tradition as authoritative; it is a totally different thing to admit it in the way of testimony; and while we decidedly object to the elevation of ecclesiastical tradition to a place of authority in regulating our faith, we value it exceedingly, when it is pure, uninterrupted tradition, as attesting a historical fact of great importance, viz. the unanimity of the early church in ratifying the canon of the New Testament.

We have now advanced the first stage in our treatment of the subject of these Lectures. For, considering the persons by whom, as well as the grounds on which, the canon both of the Old and the New Testaments was constituted, the admission of any book into the number of the canonical books is a virtual recognition of its inspiration. *Canonical* becomes synonymous with inspired; and every one book which has obtained a place amongst the sacred books, is presumably worthy to constitute a component part of the word of God, and to demand the faith and submission of believers.

But canonical authority, though a strong, is only a presumptive, argument in favour of inspiration; and therefore we proceed to adduce " a nobler Witness still," in the person of our Saviour, followed by His apostles, who bore the most unequivocal testimony to the divine character and authority of the Old Testament. In His frequent rebukes of the lifeless formalities and gross corruptions of His age, as well as in His exposition of the principles and blessings of the gospel dispensation, our Lord was necessarily led to speak of the Scriptures; and whether the strain of His discourse required Him to appeal to them in support of an argument or in fulfilment of a prophecy, He represented these sacred books as containing the will of God, and constituting the only authoritative standard of truth. When He exhorted His hearers to "search the Scriptures," or, as it is sometimes rendered, commended them for doing so, He referred to the collection of religious documents which, according to the testimony of Josephus, the Jews held to be of divine authority. When He put to them the question, Did ye never read in the Scriptures, The stone which the builders despised, the same is made the head of the corner? He meant the Scriptures which were publicly read in their synagogues, and contained in these words an inspired prediction of His rejection as Messiah. When, in His memorable conversation with the disciples at Emmaus, He expounded to them in all the (Old Testament) Scriptures the things concerning Himself; and when, on a later occasion, He said to them, "These are the words which I spake unto you while I was yet with you, that all things must be fulfilled which are written in the law of Moses, and in the Prophets, and in the Psalms, concerning me,"—He described the Old Testament according to that triple arrangement of the sacred books which popular usage had introduced. When He appealed to "Moses and the prophets," and to "all the law and the prophets," as containing the fundamental principles of pure and undefiled religion, He was employing another common and familiar form of speech for the Old Testament Scriptures, and appealing to them as the tribunal to which all controversies about doctrine and practice must be brought. Nay, He not only bore testimony to the inspired character of the Old Testament in general, but at different times, and in different ways, vouched for the inspiration of the writers separately. He attested the truth and divine authority of the books of Moses;[1] of the books of Samuel;[2] of the books of Kings and Chronicles;[3] of the book of Psalms;[4] of the prophets generally;[5] of the book of Isaiah;[6] of the book of Daniel;[7] of the book of Hosea;[8] of the book of Jonah;[9] of the book of Micah;[10] and of the book of Malachi.[11] These and several others of the prophets were quoted by our Lord as possessing in their writings the authority of the word of God. Perhaps no higher attestation to the divine character of the ancient Scriptures was given than what is furnished by the fact, that the weapons with which He encountered and vanquished the tempter in the wilderness were taken from the armoury of the Old Testament; and it

[1] Matt. v. 17, 18, xv. 1–6, xxii. 31, xxiii. 1, 2; Mark vii. 8–13, xx. 26; Luke xvi. 29, 31, xx. 37; John iii. 14, v. 45, 47.
[2] Matt. xii. 1–5; Luke vi. 3, 4.
[3] Cf. 1 Kings x. 1–13, 2 Chron. ix. 1–12, with Matt. xii. 42.
[4] Cf. Ps. viii. 2 with Matt. xxi. 15, 16, and Ps. cx. 1 with Matt. xxii. 41–46, Mark xii. 35–37.
[5] Luke xxiv. 44–46.
[6] Matt. xiii. 13–15, xv. 7–9, xxi. 13; Mark vii. 6, 7; Luke iv. 17–21.
[7] Matt. xxiv. 15; Mark xiii. 14.
[8] Cf. Hos. vi. 6 with Matt. ix. 13, xii. 9.
[9] Matt. xxii. 39–41, xvi. 4; Luke xi. 29–32.
[10] Cf. Mic. vii. 6 with Matt. x. 35, 36.
[11] Cf. Mal. iii. 1, iv. 5, 6, with Matt. xi. 10, Luke vii. 27.

may be noticed that the last act in the tragic scene of the crucifixion was the fulfilment of the only remaining prophecy connected with His personal history: "My tongue cleaveth to my jaws, and in my thirst they gave me vinegar to drink."[1] Nay, further, He has ratified that class of facts which appear to human reason to stand most in need of confirmation, and are pronounced by rationalistic critics fatal to the idea of inspiration. The deluge, the overthrow of Sodom, the fate of Lot's wife, the burning bush, the brazen serpent, and the manna; these miracles He authenticated as actual facts, and inferentially bore testimony not only to their truth, but to the inspired character of the books which narrated them.

In like manner, the apostles bore testimony to the divine authority of the Old Testament Scriptures collectively. "When Paul, according to his custom, went into the synagogue of Thessalonica, and reasoned three successive Sabbaths out of the Scriptures," the book referred to was, of course, those ancient writings of "Moses and the prophets," for which those foreign Jews professed so great a regard, and to which, in common with that people,

---

[1] Ps. xxii. 15, lxix. 21; John xix. 28.

the apostle appealed as his divine authority for his Christian teaching.[1] When Paul reminded the Corinthians of the fundamental principle of his gospel, that Christ died, was buried, and rose again, according to the Scriptures,[2] he virtually claimed inspiration for those ancient books, which so truly predicted those great crises in the Saviour's history. When this apostle, in his pastoral letter to Timothy, alluded to his young friend having known the Holy Scriptures from his childhood, there could be no doubt that he was referring to those Scriptures which were universally received by the Jews, and to which was ascribed the divine quality of "making wise unto salvation through faith in Christ Jesus." And when another apostle ranked the Epistles of Paul with "the other Scriptures," and employed terms of severe rebuke to those ignorant and unstable men who "wrested both to their own destruction," he drew a line of demarcation around the books of the sacred volume, that separated them from all literary productions of ordinary men, as the cordon that was drawn around the base of Sinai separated its holy heights from all earthly objects around. While the apostles thus bore testimony to the

[1] Acts xvii. 2. [2] Isa. liii. 6, 12; Dan. ix. 26; Ps. xvi. 10.

divine authority of the Scriptures collectively, they also spoke in the same strain of the sacred writers separately. Thus Paul says:[1] "The Scripture, foreseeing that God would justify the heathen through faith, preached before the gospel unto Abraham, saying, In thee shall all nations be blessed." The same apostle writes:[2] "The Scripture saith, Thou shalt not muzzle the ox that treadeth out the corn,"—referring to a precept in the book of Deuteronomy, and to that book as one of divine authority. The author of the Epistle to the Hebrews[3] refers to Ps. xcv. 7 in this manner: "Wherefore, *as the Holy Ghost saith*, Today, if ye will hear His voice, harden not your hearts." The same author says:[4] "*God*, who at sundry times, and in divers manners, *spake* in time past to the fathers by the *prophets*." Peter, in a discourse spoken in the primitive church,[5] said, in allusion to Ps. xvi., "Men and brethren, let me freely speak unto you of the patriarch *David*, that being a *prophet*, he seeing this before, spake of the resurrection of Christ, that His soul was not left in *Hades*, neither did His flesh see corruption." This apostle says:[6] "The prophets inquired

---

[1] Gal. iii. 8.   [2] 1 Tim. v. 18.   [3] Heb. iii. 7.
[4] Heb. i. 1.   [5] Acts ii. 29–31.   [6] 1 Pet. i. 10–12.

and searched diligently, who prophesied of the grace that should come unto you; searching what, or what manner of time, the *Spirit of Christ which was in them* did signify, when it (the Spirit of Christ which was in them) testified beforehand the sufferings of Christ, and. the glory that should follow." And this same apostle declares in a similar strain:[1] "Prophecy came not in old time by the will of man, but holy men of God spake as they were moved by the Holy Ghost."[2]

The writers of the New Testament themselves adopt the same style as the ancient prophets in claiming submission to their instructions as the word of God;[3] and their claim to inspiration also was attested by our Lord,[4] who, by various expressions of His, virtually and absolutely gave the sanction of His high authority to their instructions, whether in oral discourses or in writings. Such, then, is the claim to inspiration made for the writers of the Old and New Testaments; and resting, as that claim does, on the unchallengeable testimony of our Lord, as

[1] 2 Pet. i. 21.
[2] See other passages: Rom. iii. 2; 2 Tim. iii. 16, 17; 1 Pet. iii. 19-21.
[3] 1 Cor. vii. 40; 1 Thess. iv. 6, 8; 2 Pet. iii. 1-4, 16; 1 John iv. 6.
[4] Luke xii. 12; John xiv. 17, 26.

well as their own high character as men of truth and piety, it would be sufficient, independently of all other considerations, to entitle them to our faith and confidence. It is an attestation to the divine authority of the Old Testament, of the most positive, unqualified nature; and, therefore, all who recognise the unerring authority of the New Testament, will admit the full weight and value of such a declaration, made by Him whom all Christians regard as "the Prophet of the Highest." But this conclusion is not universally assented to; for those modern critics who deny the genuineness and authenticity of several portions of the Old Testament, and at the same time profess their faith in the Christian Scriptures, do not hesitate, in order to evade the irresistible force of evidence derived from the testimony of Christ and His apostles, to characterize their declarations as a mere accommodation to Jewish errors and prejudices. "They maintain," to use the words of an excellent writer, "from Le Clerc downwards, that it formed no part of the mission of Christ and His apostles to instruct the Jews in matters of criticism; not considering that, though they may not have been teachers of criticism, yet they were certainly, as Witsius remarks, 'teachers of truth,'[1] and of criticism too,—if the term is allowable,—when the current criticism and interpretation were opposed to truth. How utterly unsupported this pretended accommodation is, must be evident to every impartial reader who considers the passages adduced above, and particularly John v. 46, 47, where belief in the *writings of Moses* and in Christ's own words is so intimately related, that the divinity of the Redeemer's mission is so connected with the divine authority of the law, as to constitute with it one whole."[2] In short, this is a line of argument which no sincere and enlightened Christian can for a moment adopt. To maintain that our Lord, in the course of His sermons and conversations, was in the habit of accommodating His language and views to the reigning notions of His country and age, is at variance with the whole character of His ministry; to concede that He possessed no better knowledge than the rest of His countrymen, is a dishonour to the character of Him to whom "the Spirit was given without measure;" to suppose that, through the mere influence of traditional impres-

---

[1] *Miscell. Sac.* 115.
[2] Macdonald, *Introduction to the Pentateuch,* i. 366.

sions, He represented books as worthy of credit which comprised only a collection of legends, false miracles, forged prophecies, and gross exaggerations of real events, is a libel on Him who is emphatically called "the Truth;" above all, to allow that He was fallible, or mistaken in applying passages from the Old Testament as inspired predictions of His advent and ministry, would naturally lead to the conclusion that He was equally liable to err in His interpretation of other parts of Scripture, and thus, by throwing doubt and uncertainty upon all the texts He cited as evidences of His Messiahship, the inevitable result would be a disturbance of that complete harmony between the Old and New Testaments, on which depends the truth of Christianity as the fulfilment of the old covenant. Such are the consequences which apparently follow from the hypothesis that Christ "shared the common views of the Jews in His day, in regard to points ethically and doctrinally unimportant."[1] To adopt it, therefore, as a way of determining the value and extent of His testimony to the divine authority of the Old Testament, and to represent Him as speaking of that early portion of the Bible

[1] Davidson's *Introduction*.

in conformity with the current notions of His time, is a perilous argument, from which all sound Christians will shrink. His attestation must be regarded as that of the great infallible Prophet of the Church; and although a certain class of critics have declared against its enlistment into this argument, as inconsistent with the principles of scientific criticism, believers must receive His verdict as decisive upon the point.

The apostles were in this respect, as in all others, "the followers of Christ;" and being endowed with an extraordinary effusion of His Spirit, they acted upon the same principle of appealing to the Old Testament as a divine authority. So far from showing a loose and temporizing accommodation to the prejudices of their countrymen in their interpretation and application of the ancient Scriptures, they assumed a firm and unyielding attitude in maintaining that "they spake none other things than Moses and the prophets did say should come;" and the language of Paul, "Though we or an angel from heaven preach any other doctrine than that which has been preached unto you, let him be accursed," would have been that employed by all his apostolic brethren in reference to any party who should have asserted that the gospel which they taught was not the just development of the scheme of grace which had been progressively revealed in "the law and the prophets." This conclusion is expressed by Paul in the classical passage in the Epistle to Timothy,—"All Scripture is given by inspiration of God,"—a passage containing an affirmation which, according to the direct literal import of the words as they stand, is applicable to the whole contents of the sacred volume. The correctness of the translation, however, has been called in question, and various renderings have been proposed and supported. One of these, "Every Scripture divinely inspired is also profitable," is strenuously espoused by the opponents of plenary inspiration, as it implies that there are some parts not inspired. Another, "the whole Scripture divinely inspired," limits it to the books which the Jews received as canonical, founding on the assumed position that, at the time when the apostle wrote to Timothy, no part of the New Testament had been published. But that is a mistaken idea; and hence Coleridge, with a manly frankness that did him honour, made this declaration: "Here I renounce any advantage I might obtain for my argument against plenary inspiration, by restricting our Lord's and the apostle's words to the Hebrew canon. I admit the justice, I have long felt the force, of the remark, 'We have all that the occasion allowed.' And if the same awful authority does not apply so directly to the evangelical and apostolical writings as to the Hebrew canon, yet the analogy of faith justifies the transfer. If the doctrine be less decisively scriptural in its application to the New Testament or the Christian canon, the temptation to doubt it is likewise less."[1] The fact is, to translate the passage in the manner proposed, not only does violence to the grammatical structure of the sentence, but to the course of argument pursued by the apostle, who, having urged Timothy to adhere to the teaching of the Holy Scriptures, by ascribing to them the noblest of all powers, viz. being "able to make wise unto salvation," lest he might be charged with an exaggerated eulogium, reminds his beloved son in the faith, that every part of them is inspired of God. "Every portion of them," says Bengel, "is inspired of God,[2] *i.e.* not merely when written,

---

[1] Coleridge's *Confessions*, p. 30. See Note B.
[2] θεόπνευστος.

God breathing through the writers, but also when read, God breathing through the Scriptures, and the Scriptures breathing Him." This famous passage, in which the divine inspiration of the Scriptures is dogmatically asserted on the high authority of an apostle, may seem decisive on the point; and were there no other from which we could discover the real character and claims of the Bible, this declaration of Paul, it might be supposed, would be considered final and conclusive in determining that the book is divine in its origin, and possessed of infallible authority. But critics of no mean name and authority contend, that to view it as susceptible of so unlimited application, is to extend it beyond the range which the circumstances of the case will warrant. They allege, that as the word "all" is used frequently by the sacred writers in a restricted sense, "all" Scripture must be considered as so limited here; and that especially, as there is reason to believe that interpolations have been made by later hands on the original text of the historical books, it falls within the legitimate province of reason to separate what is divine from what is merely human, or to winnow the spurious matter that may have been intermixed with the text. And they maintain further, that as there is no catalogue of the canonical books, nor any express declaration made in the sacred volume concerning the inspiration of each particular book, it is quite possible that there may be some books which, although undoubtedly genuine and authentic, may possess but slight or doubtful claims to be regarded as written under the influences of the Holy Spirit, and forming a part of the rule of faith. In the number of such disputed works they place the book of Esther and the Song of Solomon; the former of which is noted for the extraordinary omission of the name, or any allusion to the name, of God from beginning to end,—an omission unaccountable, if this book emanated from a divine source; and the latter of which abounds with strange scenes and indelicate images, while it is pervaded throughout by a strain of gross and undisguised sensuousness, which it is impossible to adapt to the purposes of moral and religious edification. These books, it is alleged, are little in accordance with the rest of the Old Testament; and their title to be regarded as inspired productions is by no means so clear or strong as that it should be required of all Christians, under a penalty of ostracism as heretics, to believe in their inspiration. To all such objections satisfactory answers are at hand. Admitting that a few chronological or archæological explanations were inserted by Ezra or his prophetic colleagues in the historical books, the addition of such supplementary notes is never considered as affecting the intrinsic character or value of the original composition; and so far as relates to the integrity of the Old Testament books, and the fact of their comprising the identical sameness of contents as of old, the extreme scrupulosity of the Jews, and the jealous vigilance of their rival sects, afford the fullest guarantee for their inviolable purity before the destruction of Jerusalem. Since that momentous era there has been no opportunity, from the opposing attitude of both Jews and Christians, of attempting, had the wish been cherished, any corruptions on the state of the Old Testament text. The Christians who appeal to the writings of Moses, the Prophets, and the Psalms, in proving that Jesus of Nazareth was the promised Messiah, would not have permitted the Jews to lay the daring hand of innovation upon any portion of them; while the Jews, on the other hand, inheriting the reverential feelings of their ancestors for the letter of Scripture, still cling with fond tenacity to "the oracles of God which were committed to them," and thus unconsciously exhibit the most extraordinary instance which the history of the world presents, of a whole people preserving with marvellous fidelity national documents which hold up continually before their veiled eyes the great sin which was the occasion of their ruin and dispersion. With regard to the book of Esther, the omission of the divine name may be considered as sufficiently accounted for by its being an excerpt from the Persian archives. The design of it is to record one of the most signal deliverances which the providence of God ever wrought for His imperilled people; and on this account, it has not only been incorporated with the history, but forms an indispensable link in the chain of records that pertain to the captivity of the ancient church. It is a book, therefore, of great importance. Its canonical authority was never doubted; and the Jews, who valued it next to the Pentateuch, placed it amongst the Chetubim or Hagiographa, *i.e.* "Holy Writings," which constituted the first in their threefold division of the Old Testament. The objection to the Song of Solomon is the amatory strain of the poem, which seems incongruous with the character of the divine word. But it has always formed a portion of the sacred canon; and the Christian church has, from the beginning, regarded it as a divine allegory, descriptive of the mutual love that is cherished between Christ, the heavenly Bridegroom, and the church, which is the Bride, the Lamb's wife. The figure which pervades the book is a favourite one with the sacred writers; for the books of Ezekiel and Hosea, particularly the forty-fifth Psalm, which is descriptive of the glories of Messiah, furnish eminent examples of the same luxuriant imagery. The leading idea of the Song is the exhibition of religion as a divine affection, a lively union between Christ and His people, with all the sentiments, emotions, and warm language expressive of human attachment. It is entirely in unison with Oriental taste to represent moral and religious truths in such a figurative garb; so that, however strange it appears to our European views of propriety and taste, the strain of this Song exactly accords with the style of sentiment and feeling that prevails in the countries of the East. However mystical it may be, and difficult to apply in the way of spiritual improvement, that obscurity is no reason in itself against the inspiration of the book, any more than against parts of Ezekiel, Daniel, and the Revelation. It may be expected to become clearer and better understood as time rolls on, just as light has been thrown on various portions of the sacred volume in these latter days. Upon the whole, the objections urged against these two books, as well as against some parts of others, cannot outweigh the uniform testimony of the church, which has always regarded them as included in the sacred canon. As they formed part of the Scriptures which were read in the synagogues every Sabbath-day, we must consider them as constituting a portion of divine truth; and we lay it down as a fundamental principle in the exercise of Christian judgment, that every book in the Old Testament must be considered inspired, if there is clear historical evidence that it was ranked amongst the Jewish Scriptures at the time when our Lord set His seal on them. The fact that "all Scripture is given by inspiration of God" stamps it as divine truth, and at the same time invests it with infallible authority. Such authority is indispensable in the matter of revealed religion, otherwise the benefits it was intended to confer will not be realized. If God was pleased to give to man a special revelation of His will, and yet allowed the agents He selected for communicating it to the world to make it known in what manner and terms they pleased, mankind must have been involved in painful doubt and uncertainty whether they really possessed a true and perfectly reliable expression of the divine mind—whether in matters of the greatest interest and importance they were informed of the exact truth, or whether it might be safe for them to follow the counsels of men, who, however wise, were liable to err, and however benevolent, might undesignedly mislead. But the assurance that we have in the Scriptures, not only a revelation of the divine will, comprising all that we are to believe concerning God, and all the duty He requires of us, but an unerring record of that revelation, imparts an incomparable value to that sacred volume, and raises the authors of its several books to a supremacy above all other instructors of the world. It was not by the force of their natural talents, nor by means of profound study and extensive erudition, nor even through the influence of rare advancement in piety, they became what they were. Not one, nor all these qualities combined, could have placed them above the condition of fallible men, and enabled them to speak the momentous truths of religion without some admixture of error. Many learned and good men have been raised up in different ages of the church to undertake the office of religious teachers, —Augustine, Calvin, Luther, and a host of others in early as well as later times,—who, by their oral discourses, performed good service while living, and left behind them in their published writings, memorials of their zeal and usefulness, by which, though "being dead, they yet speak." None of them, however, were free from error, can be followed implicitly as guides, or were possessed of authority to demand submission. But when we go to the writers of the Scriptures, we have instructors and guides in whom we can repose the fullest confidence, and who were possessed of commanding authority. And how were they so pre-eminently qualified? Who or what enabled them to teach the highest doctrines and duties of religion unmixed with error? It was because they spoke and wrote "by the inspiration of God;" because they were favoured with such extraordinary and supernatural measures of light and assistance, as made them fully instructed in all the truth which they required themselves to know, or were called to communicate to others—the truth, the whole truth, and nothing but the truth. But it is not doing justice to the penmen of the Scriptures, to represent them in the light merely of teachers or guides to the discovery of truth. The extraordinary messengers, or ambassadors of God, furnished with credentials of a divine mission, they professed to declare truths which men could not discover by their natural faculties, and to be the bearers of intelligence which could be known only through their testimony. They made no pretensions to penetration or foresight superior to other men, or claimed credence on the ground of extensive knowledge and conscious intellectual and moral greatness. The only claim to the attention and confidence of men they put forth, was that they were the messengers of God; and appealing, in support of that claim, to the preternatural powers with which they were endowed, they demanded the reception due to men who, by the miracles they wrought, gave unequivocal evidence that "they were teachers come from God." They did not propound the doctrine which they taught as recommended by the prestige of illustrious names, or accordant with the principles of sound philosophy: they rested it exclusively on the ground that it was divine, and urged it on the acceptance of men, not because it was true and good, and therefore, as might be reasonably thought, came from God, but because it came from God, and therefore was true and good. This was the uniform tone they assumed, the authoritative manner in which they spoke. They laid no stress on their personal characters and positions as entitling them to attention, but put all their claim to confidence on the fact that they were commissioned legates, who uttered the words which God had bidden them.

Thus each of the sacred writers performed his allotted part; and as "God at sundry times and in divers manners spake unto the fathers by the prophets," those various revelations were adapted with divine wisdom to the state and capacities of the church in successive ages, being clearer and fuller as the people were able to bear them. If Moses wrote his laws, and Isaiah recorded his evangelical predictions, if David indited his devotional songs, and Paul his pastoral epistles, they contributed, along with their prophetic and apostolic brethren, to the completion of the sacred volume. There is no evidence that they had received any revelation beyond what is embodied in the Scriptures; and there is good reason for concluding that they were favoured with none: for if any new or unknown truths had been communicated to one or another of those men of God, the knowledge of which would have proved beneficial to the church, we may be assured that they would have been incorporated with "the volume of the book." But the era of sensible manifestations, or revelations in visions and dreams, has long ago passed away; the spirit of inspiration has been withdrawn; and since John, in the Apocalypse, completed what Moses began, there is every reason to believe that we have the mind of God as fully disclosed in the Scriptures as it was His pleasure that it should be in the present state and economy of providence. The Spirit, indeed, is still with the church, and we have a divine assurance that He will permanently abide with her. But instead of pouring His supernatural light directly into the minds of Christians now, as He did of old into those who were the chosen agents in revealing the will of God, He shines with beams reflected from the pages of the written word; and while we anticipate that, in the church of the future, religious knowledge will be greatly increased by the development of latent and yet unperceived truths lying in the Bible, just as men have become richer in the world since its mineral wealth has been discovered, and chemical science has shown us the method of applying its products to the useful and liberal arts, no new revelation is to be expected beyond what is contained in the Scriptures of the Old and New Testaments. These comprehend the whole word of God, which has been revealed for our salvation. There is an entire harmony between them as to the main purpose of revelation: the one is the germ, the other is the full-grown plant; the one is the promise, the other the fulfilment; the one is the dawn of the early or advancing morn, the other the light of the full day; the one gives the history of the preparation for the kingdom of God, while the other exhibits its establishment. In this view there is a close and indissoluble connection between the Old and New Testaments,— the one is incomplete and disjointed without the other; and an enlightened perception of the relative importance of the various books of Scripture, as well as of their collective bearing on the system of divine truth, is indispensable to a full appreciation of the value of the revealed word. So remarkable is the unity of the Scriptures, so strongly are the same great characteristics impressed upon them, that the wondrous drama which it contains, beginning in Eden, and closing with the New Jerusalem, though divided into various scenes, consisting of many successive and diversified acts, is one organic whole. The *dramatis personæ*, if we may say so, are the same throughout. Thus the opening scene describes God as having created all things in the world very good: Adam formed out of the earth, and Eve taken from his side; the serpent in paradise; man tempted,—seduced from his allegiance to his Maker, and exiled from Eden; the way of the tree of life guarded by a flaming sword; and a gracious promise made most seasonably to the fallen pair, "that the seed of the woman should bruise the serpent's head." The closing scene bears a striking correspondence to the opening portion of the book. The objects that were withdrawn from view after the fall are reproduced upon the scene; paradise is regained, the ends of the sacred history are united, and the glorious circle of revelation completed. The tree of life, whereof there were but faint reminiscences in all the intermediate time, again stands by the river or water of life, but no longer an interdicted object, and access to it guarded by a flaming sword. God is there seated on His throne, and represented as the object of universal adoration; Christ the second Adam, and Eve in the character of the church, His bride; the dragon, that old serpent, in the deadly contest with whom Christ had been wounded in the heel (His humanity), and slain; but He "liveth for evermore, and hath the keys of hell and of death;" He has now bruised the serpent's head; and having chained him, opens the bottomless pit, and casts him into the lake of fire and brimstone, there to remain for ever. But though there is this unity between the early and the concluding scenes of the wondrous drama of this world's history as contained in the Scriptures, "a great advance has been made during the interval. Even the very differences of the forms under which the heavenly kingdom reappears are characteristic, marking, as they do, not merely that all is won back, but won back in a more glorious shape than that in which it was lost, because won back in the Son. It is no longer paradise, but the New Jerusalem,—no longer the *garden*, but now the *city* of God, which is on earth. The change is full of meaning: no longer the garden, free, spontaneous, and unlaboured, even as man's blessedness in the state of a first innocence would have been; but the city, costlier indeed, more stately, more glorious, but at the same time the result of toil, labour, and pain, occupied not by a single human pair, but by a vast multitude, 'whom no man can number,' reared into a nobler and more abiding habitation, yet with stones which, after the pattern of 'the elect corner-stone,' were each in his time laboriously hewn and painfully squared for the places which they fill." (Trench.)

Such is the completed form of the divine scheme of grace that is revealed in the Scriptures; and when we consider its nature and provisions, the manner in which it was given out by small and detached communications, and the lengthened period occupied in its progressive development, till the mystery hid from ages was disclosed, we must perceive the absolute necessity there was, that the men successively employed in announcing it should be inspired. How would an earthly government do, in conducting a diplomatic correspondence with a foreign state, when about to transmit a despatch on some delicate and important matter that has disturbed or broken their amicable relations? Would they entrust the preparation of the document that contains their proposals of adjustment to inferior persons, who should be at liberty to communicate it in whatever manner they chose? Would not the master mind of the ruler, if he did not dictate the precise terms, take good care that it should accurately and fully convey the views entertained by himself or cabinet? And when God, in the fulness of His mercy and love to His fallen and sinful creatures, provided a scheme of grace which He chose special ambassadors to announce to man, in the language of man, would not the same paternal wisdom and goodness guard against error in a case of such moment to their highest interests, by guiding His messengers to speak the truth, the whole truth, and nothing but the truth? We are thus led on by the principles of reason to believe in the *necessity* of inspiration. And when we look to the character of the Scriptures,—their veracity, their fidelity, their spirit of purity, their penetrating foresight and comprehensive wisdom,—we are led to believe also in the *fact* of inspiration: the Scripture is a witness of its own inspiration. Were a rude and ignorant peasant to produce a work of profound intelligence, such as Butler's *Analogy*, elucidating the profoundest subjects in the philosophy of religion, we should revert to his antecedents, and consider how far they justified a belief that he was equal to so great an intellectual achievement. And in reviewing all that history, observation, or experience has taught us of what men have done, what they are or have been, is there the smallest ground for believing that they were, by their unaided powers, equal to the composition of a Bible which Carlyle has pronounced "the greatest work of literature in the world"? And then, when we take into account its fitness for its purpose, its precious truths, its supernatural doctrines, its insight into the hearts of men, its selection of subjects, its manner of teaching them, its complete adaptation to the character and wants of men, together with the miraculous testimony it bears to its own truth, and the numerous prophecies to be found in every part of the Bible,—many of them fulfilled, some in the course of fulfilment, and others remaining to be fulfilled,—what are all these, but cumulative proofs of the heavenly origin, the divine inspiration of the sacred books which constitute the Scriptures? In this view, the Scriptures, in their collective capacity, appear to be the word of God; and their authority does not depend on the fact whether this prophet or that wrote a particular book or parts of a book; whether a certain portion was derived from the Elohist or Jehovist; whether Moses wrote the close of Deuteronomy, Solomon was the author of Ecclesiastes, or Paul of the Epistle to the Hebrews; but on the fact that a prophet, an inspired man, having the credentials of his high commission, wrote them, and that they bear the stamp and impress of a divine origin. Since this, then, is the general character of the Scriptures, it sufficiently exposes the folly and presumption of Rationalism, the object of which is to eliminate everything of a supernatural character from the sacred volume, by denying all miracles and prophecy, and even expunging from the historical records every fact and incident different from the natural course of things, as the fabulous legends of an ignorant and a credulous age. But those who allow themselves thus to decide what are the truths which it is fit for God to reveal, and what it is worthy of human reason to receive, invest their fallible judgment with an authority to which it is totally inadequate, and for which it never was designed. In assuming this high prerogative, they are chargeable with daring presumption; they act on the supposition that they are perfectly capable of judging as to the nature and degree of that illumination which God may be pleased to communicate, and that He will not reveal any truths to His intelligent offspring, whose meaning is not obvious to their comprehension. But the Bible is the record of revelation,—of a scheme of grace for the pardon and salvation of sinful men, who can obtain the knowledge of it from no other source; it exhibits the hand of Jehovah, announcing, superintending, and directing the development of this scheme in all ages of the church. It must therefore be received, not as men may think it ought to be, but as the Revealer Himself has described it in the Scriptures; and the only way to know this is to search the Scriptures, endeavouring to discover the import of their language according to the most approved principles of interpretation. Most invaluable is the knowledge they communicate; for from this book, and from it alone, we obtain information on the most important subjects which it concerns us to know and believe,—on the origin of man, the introduction of sin into the world, the method of redemption, the reality and retributions of a future world, the pure society and the perfect form of God's moral government there.

Of these and numerous other subjects,—which are of the highest interest and of vital importance to man, and utterly beyond the reach of our natural means of intelligence, nay, respecting which we do not possess the means of forming even a faint conjecture without the guiding light of revelation, —we know nothing, and have not the means of knowing anything, except they be shown to us by the Revealer. Those who acknowledge the Scriptures to be the word of God, are bound to bow to their sovereign authority in all matters of faith and duty. It is the only divine and perfect standard by which the value of all things in the world is determined; by which all characters are judged, all actions are weighed, and the lawfulness or excellence of all pursuits is tried. It is the common source from which all sects derive their distinctive principles, the ultimate tribunal to which all sects appeal for the settlement of their differences. On every work which emanates from the mind of a mere human author, we may sit in judgment with perfect propriety,— may canvass its principles or reject its conclusions at pleasure. But towards a book which bears the stamp and impress of a heavenly origin, we are bound to cherish no other sentiment than that of reverence for its character, as well as submission to its authority; and, yielding to the supremacy of its utterances in all matters beyond the grasp of our reason, the language of our hearts should be, "Let God be true, and every man a liar."

We have thus endeavoured to show the inspiration of the Scriptures collectively, first, from the testimony of the ancient Jewish church, which reckoned the same books of the Old Testament as we have in their sacred canon; secondly, from the repeated appeals to them made by our Lord and His apostles as the word of God; and thirdly, from the internal evidence of their contents. The testimony of our Lord, independently of all other considerations, is, or ought to be, a decisive authority; for it is the testimony of Him who spoke with perfect and infallible knowledge, and therefore it would be the height of presumption to subjoin evidence additional to His for the purpose of confirming the position that the Scriptures are given by inspiration of God. But it may be interesting and useful to trace the application of this principle in the separate books or classes of books of Scripture; and this we purpose to do in the following two Lectures.

LECTURE II

A large Portion of the Old Testament in the Form of History—Sources of Information, Divine and Human—All the Historical Books connected as a Whole—Composed under Inspiration—Leading Characteristics of Sacred History.—I. Religious—Selection of Subjects and pervading Spirit entirely different from ordinary Human History—A Record of God's Providence and His Moral Government.—II. Typical—The Old Testament Dispensation foreshadowed the New — In Persons, Institutions, Events. — III. The Element of the Promise — The Stream of History directed through the Channel of Seth's Descendants — Definite Renewal of the Promise to Abraham—Separation of the Heirs of the Promise —Poetical Books—Prophetical Books—Religious Teaching the Stated Work of the Prophets — Writings — Predictive Element—Insulated Prophecies—Prophecies relative to the Jews, and the Nations connected with them — Progressive Prophecies concerning Christ.

A LARGE proportion of the Old Testament is historical; and the information contained in it might be obtained by the writers from monuments, from public archives, or from their personal knowledge of the facts they relate. Whatever views we may entertain of the manner in which the spirit of inspiration operated on the minds of the sacred penmen, one thing is clear, that it did not supersede the exercise of their natural faculties with regard to matters within the reach of human knowledge; and hence we may conclude that Moses, the author of the opening history, would be left at liberty to avail himself of such oral testimony or written documents as might be accessible to him. In regard to his account of creation and the fall of man, that must have been a divine communication, being probably derived by tradition from Adam, whose knowledge of the origin of himself, as well as of all creatures and all things, was doubtless communicated to him by a heavenly instructor; and though it would be presumptuous to affirm anything with dogmatic confidence upon the subject, it appears in the highest degree reasonable to believe, that the imparted intelligence regarding the order and results of the creative process, given by his condescending Maker in conversations with the primeval man, is embodied in the early chapters of Genesis. Accordingly it may be safely asserted, that the first portion of that book contains a condensed epitome of aboriginal history, which no forger, no late compiler, could have invented; and consequently that its very originality is a pledge of its divine origin and inspired truth. With regard to the later details of this book, relating to the increase, degeneracy, and dispersion of mankind, together with the most striking dispensations of providence during the first two thousand years, Moses doubtless derived his materials from human sources that were accessible to him. Writers of history avail themselves of every means and opportunity of obtaining reliable information, whether from oral testimony, ancient monuments, public archives, or private journals; and according to the zeal, assiduity, and judgment with which they ransack latent stores of knowledge, and consult the most proper authorities upon their subject, will their work contain a collection of trustworthy and varied facts, and themselves be esteemed interesting and valuable historians. Moses acted in this manner. His history in the first ten chapters is evidently derived from tradition, for it bears all the characteristics of that kind of knowledge which is limited to some striking or memorable facts; and considering that, from the longevity of the antediluvian and early post-diluvian patriarchs, the tradition must have passed through a very few hands, the source whence the knowledge of those facts he has recorded came to Moses, independently of divine superintendence, was direct and pure. When he comes down to the time of Abraham, there is a manifest change on the character of the history, which becomes much more copious and connected, descending into minute and circumstantial details, and recording incidents in personal and family experience, of which there is no similar trace in the earlier portion of the book. A still greater change appears in the tenor of the history when the narrative is brought down to the time of the exodus; for it then assumes the character and form of a journal, containing a record of the chief and most important transactions of the passing time. It was not a voluntary labour that Moses thus imposed upon himself; for, however natural and interesting it might have been for the leader of a young and independent nation to keep a record of the events that marked its early history, this duty was not left to his own option or sense of its utility. It was enjoined upon him by the high authority that invested him with his divine legation; and by the successive additions made to this public register, as the human incidents occurred, or the divine communications were made, the document rose to the magnitude it attained at the close of the great legislator's career, comprising in its chequered pages narratives of the natural intermingled with the supernatural, as might be expected to characterize a history of the establishment of a divine economy amongst the chosen people.[1] This is the Pentateuch, the first portion of the sacred history. The book of Joshua follows. It holds an indispensable place in the sacred canon, as it is the only authoritative document which shows the faithfulness of God in accomplishing His promises made to the patriarchs and to Moses, by giving that people a permanent possession of the land; and it was stamped, in the eyes of the Hebrew people, with great value, as recording the original distribution of property among the tribes of Israel, and the early provision made for the ordinances of the true religion. Joshua was called by the express authority of God to undertake the command of the Hebrew people in the war of invasion which was about to commence in Canaan; and having been their leader in the conquest of the promised land, it is natural to think that he would preserve a record of all the great occurrences and acquisitions that marked so memorable a period in

[1] Deut. xxxi. 10, 11, 26, 27, xvii. 14, 18; Ex. xxiv. 7; Deut. xxviii. 58-61.

the national history of God's people. Several circumstances lead to the conclusion that it was composed by Joshua himself, or under his direction.¹ It was *added by him to the book of the law of the Lord*, and it is frequently alluded to as a sacred book in other parts of Scripture.² The succeeding book of Judges is not to be considered a regular and complete history of the period, but only as a link connecting the narrative of Joshua with the historical books which follow, and furnishing selected details in proof of its leading object, which was to show that, whenever the Israelites apostatized from God, they were overtaken by war or fell into servitude, and, on the other hand, whenever they returned to His service, and continued in dutiful allegiance, they enjoyed a course of national peace and prosperity. Its author is, on good grounds, believed to have been Samuel, and various references are made to it both in the Old and New Testaments.³ Ruth was regarded by the ancient church as a part of Judges, and the importance of the book consists

---

[1] Josh. v. 1, xxiv. 26.
[2] 1 Kings xvi. 34; Ps. xliv. 2, lxviii. 12; Hab. iii. 12; Acts vii. 45; Heb. xi. 30, 31; Jas. ii. 25.
[3] 1 Sam. xii. 9; 2 Sam. xi.21; Ps. lxxxiii. 11, xcvii. 5; Matt. ii. 23; Acts xiii. 20; Heb. xi. 32.

in contributing to show the ancestry of David, and consequently the genealogy of a greater than David. The books of Samuel are exceedingly interesting, as they abound with circumstantial and varied details relative to the religious and political state of the Israelites under the two last judges and the two first kings; especially as they show the preservation of the church of God amidst all the vicissitudes of the Jewish government, the promises made to David respecting the continuance of the royal authority in his family, and Solomon's peaceful reign as a type of Messiah's universal kingdom, the establishment of the national worship on Mount Zion, and the permanent erection of God's temple in Jerusalem. Facts and statements in these two books are referred to in many portions of the Scriptures. The two books of Kings comprise a succinct account of the reigns of the later kings of Israel and Judah. The subjects they relate are of great interest and importance, such as the building and dedication of the temple, the partition of the nation into the two separate kingdoms of Israel and Judah, the introduction and prevalence of idolatry, the ministrations of many prophets, the Egyptian and Assyrian invasions, and the captivity, first of Israel, afterwards of Judah. Repeated allusions are made to these books in the New Testament;[1] and the allusions which our Lord, as well as the Apostle James, has made to the wonderful miracles they relate, and to the prophecies they contain, particularly that relating to Josiah,[2] attest their divine inspiration. The books of Ezra and Nehemiah relate occurrences that fell under their observation, and of which they took respectively a leading direction. But the movements which they commenced or conducted were manifestly under the guidance of Providence; and therefore the books which relate those occurrences are so essential to the progressive development of the state of things which was to bring about "the fulness of time," when the true oracle, "the WORD," and the great High Priest, was to appear, that the insertion of both forms important links in the chain of the sacred history. Of Esther we have taken notice already; and it remains only to say a few words regarding the two books of Chronicles. They comprise genealogical lists, which must have been regarded as of great interest after the cap-

---

[1] Matt. i. 7–12, vi. 29, xii. 42; Luke iv. 25–27; Acts ii. 29, vii. 47–50; Jas. v. 17, 18.
[2] 1 Kings xiii. 2.

tivity; details of the governments of David and Solomon, which throw great light on the succinct accounts contained in the books of Samuel and Kings; and also of the dismemberment of the kingdom under Rehoboam, and of many transactions relating to the two severed portions of the kingdom, the history of Judah being minutely recorded. The object of the sacred historian was, by dwelling particularly on the peculiarities of the national constitution,—such, for instance, as related to the temple worship, together with the prosperity which would lighten up the country by a faithful adherence to the service of the true God, and the public calamities that would be entailed by apostasy,—to furnish a directory, after the restoration from the captivity, for the instruction and guidance of the people. That they were compiled after the period of exile had terminated, is evident from references made to facts connected with the return of the exiles, particularly the decree of Cyrus, which, from the conclusion of the book, and some peculiar forms of expression, betoken that the writer had been in the habit of using the Chaldee language. The two books of Chronicles, which are essentially one, form a most important addition to the sacred writings. They were the latest in being introduced into the ancient canon; and though they are allowed by scholars to be the most corrupted in point of text, they are of the greatest use for obtaining an accurate knowledge of the tribal or family history of the Jews. Moreover, they are of a character which fully harmonizes with the other sacred books: for, amid the somewhat dry details of genealogical and geographical facts, there are interspersed many passages containing narratives, discourses, parables, and prayers, which no reader of sensibility, and, above all, of piety, can read without emotion and lively interest.

All these books are separate and in themselves complete compositions, yet they form a continuous and progressive chain of historical information relating to the character and condition of the Jewish people during the greater part of their temporary dispensation; and they are so closely connected, that here, as well as elsewhere, "the Scripture cannot be broken." They do not, however, constitute a series of books, like those of a cabinet or family library, in which portions of literary work are assigned to different contemporary authors, and the volumes, prepared and issued in succession, form a general collection, which is designed to embrace the whole range of a nation's history. The Old Testament histories were written by men who lived in times widely remote, and their several contributions describe diversified periods in the progress of the Jewish Church and State. But the writers, with one exception, begin their respective works with a formula which clearly intimates that what they drew up was to be conjoined, as an integral part, with the sacred books which the Holy Ghost had moved others before them to compose. The copulative conjunction, *And*,[1] is the link by which each author unites his book with those of preceding Scriptures. And as such a particle, or its equivalent, serves the same purpose in all languages,— that of being the means or sign of connection,— the systematic use of it by the Old Testament historians demonstrates that their several narratives were intended to form one connected whole. It joins the second, third, and fourth books of Moses to the first,—the last being only a recapitulation of the former; it continues the history through Joshua, Judges, Ruth, the books of Samuel and Kings; and though the seventy years' captivity made a long interruption, the historical

---

[1] Sometimes in our translation rendered *Now*.

thread is resumed, and Ezra, Nehemiah, and the writer of Esther commence their post-exilian narratives precisely in the same manner as the preceding historians. The books of Chronicles occupy an exceptional position: for, being filled chiefly in the early part with genealogical registers, which begin with the first man, Adam, and supplying in the later portions many things which were omitted in the former books of the sacred history, they did not make a contribution of new and additional matter; and therefore, though serving the purpose of appendices to the books of Samuel and Kings, they could not be introduced as a sequel to the preceding books. It is evident, then, that so remarkable a uniformity in the style of commencing these histories indicates design on the part of the authors; and their common employment of the connecting particle which in all languages serves to join things together, can be regarded in no other light than as signifying that all these books constitute one continuous history.

The authors of these books must have been dependent upon testimony for the facts they narrate, and they are very free and unreserved in their reference to the documentary sources whence they derived the information which they embody in their narratives. Thus, both Joshua and Samuel quote the book of Jasher,[1] an anthology, or collection of national songs. Frequent appeals also are made to the narratives of Nathan, Ahijah, and Iddo,[2] of Jehu,[3] and others, who wrote memoirs of detached periods and annals of successive reigns; for in the courts of Israel and Judah, as in those of all Oriental countries, there was a recorder, or historiographer, whose special duty it was to register the most interesting and prominent occurrences of every passing day. Accordingly, no documents are more frequently referred to than the books of the chronicles of the kings of Israel and Judah;[4] and, in fact, the later historical books of the Old Testament are to a great extent an abridgment of, or extracts from, the records made by those royal secretaries. Now it cannot, in the mind of an intelligent and reflecting person, affect the character of the sacred history, that the materials of which it consists have been derived from many different sources, and compiled from private records or public archives. There is not a more erroneous idea than to conceive of the books

---

[1] Josh. x. 13 ; 2 Sam. i. 18.   [2] 2 Chron. ix. 29.
[3] 2 Chron. xx. 34.
[4] 1 Kings xiv. 19 ; 1 Chron. xxvii. 24 ; also Esth. vi. 1.

of Scripture as containing nothing but matter that has been directly revealed. For although, in common and familiar language, the Scripture is called the volume of revelation, because it contains all that God has been pleased to reveal of His will to man, it comprehends also a great variety of subjects that are of merely human origin and secondary importance. All Scripture, therefore, is not *revelation*, but all Scripture is given by inspiration of God. Let its contents have been derived from sources ever so diversified,—from the direct and immediate communications of God, from the suggestions or cogitations of the authors, from ancient traditions, from private memoirs or national registers,—yet, having been accepted by the Spirit of truth, and incorporated in that Book which expresses the divine mind, they have been brought under the influence of inspiration, have been appropriated to divine purposes, and must be regarded as bearing the stamp and impress of truth. In other words, it is an inspired history. This is a principle of the greatest importance, and we propose to expound it at length in the present lecture, by directing attention to the leading characteristics of the sacred history, religious, typical, and pervaded by the element of a divine promise.

I. *Religious.*—Between the Scripture historians and the ordinary historians of the world, there is a remarkable difference in the subjects they select, in the characters that figure at full length in their pages, and which they respectively hold up to the esteem and admiration of their readers. In the one, it is the statesmen who have guided the counsels of the senate, the warriors who have fought the battles of their country, the monarchs who have swayed the sceptre of a powerful and extensive empire,—whose hands have held the balance of power between rival states, and whose government has given a tone and character to their age. In the other, the characters held up to our view are those who, though moving in the vale of private or buried in the obscurity of humble life, were yet the sincere and devoted servants of God,—those who, by their faithfulness and fortitude, maintained the cause of truth, who spent their lives in diffusing the knowledge and influence of religion, or were bright exemplars of the virtues and graces of piety. In the one, the records given in full detail of the men of power, science, or military renown, have been often made to lend a false splendour to other qualities which have no claims on our moral esteem. In the other, while faults and blemishes are delineated with a faithful and impartial hand, the deeds of humble piety, the achievements of faith, the power of religion, are always brought conspicuously before us. In the one, though genius has strained her utmost efforts, and eloquence poured forth her noblest strains, to perpetuate the memory of great men and ensure them a deathless fame, they have in time either been consigned to total oblivion, or they have remained but the empty shadows of a name. In the other, the ancient worthies of the church are preserved in the Bible, as in an ark, from all the destructive ravages of time; and when its records of eternal truth shall be diffused over the whole world, "that which they did shall be everywhere spoken of as a memorial of them." In the one, the object aimed at is, to narrate the doings of man in his individual or collective capacity; to describe the progress of society, the discoveries of science, the inventions in art, the measures adopted to develope the material resources of a country, or to reform and improve the political institutions of a nation. In the other, the grand pervading object is to reveal the character and the will of God. All the other matter which the

Scriptures contain is subordinate to this design,—has been introduced merely from being connected in some way or other with the progress or extension of true religion in the world, or from its being calculated to illustrate and enforce its provisions. So that, in order to perceive the character and enter into the spirit of the Scriptures, one must ever keep in mind the *peculiar* design for which they were written. And just as, in perusing a work of any human author, we must direct our minds, amid the occasional notices of other things we may meet with in the volume, to the principal subject on which it professes to give information; as, in taking up a medical book, for instance, we are prepared, from its character, to obtain from it chiefly an account of the symptoms and treatment of disease; or, in reading a history of Scotland, we expect to find, amid incidental allusions to foreign powers, with whom it may have been in amicable relations, that the main stream of the narrative will be directed towards the affairs and institutions of our native country; so, in reading that book which was dictated by the Spirit, and which pre-eminently claims to give an historical detail of the progressive development of the scheme of grace for the recovery of fallen man, we are led to consider particularly the character of Him who provided and announced this peculiar method for the moral and spiritual education of the world. The sacred history gives us an account of His dealings with that people whom He selected for a time to be the depositaries of His will; and in the establishment of that people in the land of promise, as well as in the direct and constant superintendence He maintained over them, we have an instructive view of the maintenance of a divine providence over all the course of the world and the affairs of men.

God appears in almost every part of their national history,—not only on signal occasions, when interposing in a miraculous manner for their deliverance from Egyptian oppression and danger, and for their final establishment in the land of promise, but in the ordinary course of their experience in that country; and while they lived and acted as people have done always and everywhere, forming their plans, prosecuting their labours, and pursuing with energy and perseverance the most promising means of success in every department, God is represented as working with them and for them in all their undertakings.

He gave them laws and institutions adapted to the special duty they were selected to promote; so that, while other people have to wait the slow progress of time, ere they attain the perfection of their social and political system, the Israelites rose at once to the dignity of a free, independent, regularly constituted, but peculiar people; for they had God for their King and Leader, and their historians write as if His presence were constantly felt among them. In time of war, He goes with them to the battle, arrays the hosts for the contest, stimulates the onset, devises stratagems, defends or demolishes the walls, delivers the enemy into their hands, sometimes overthrowing them without the stroke of a sword, and secures the relinquished property or conquered territories for His people. In time of peace, He makes them enjoy the highest measure of prosperity attendant on that righteousness which exalteth a nation. He builds the house, keeps the city, gives them the early and the latter rain, sows the seed into the soil, blesses the springing thereof, and crowns the year with His goodness. On the other hand, when they did evil, and broke their allegiance to Him, "the anger of the Lord was hot against Israel," and He sold them into the hands of foreign conquerors. Nay, not only is He described as exercising this vigilant superintendence over the nation generally, but as extending His providential care in the minutest manner over the lives and interests of individuals. Not a personal movement did any one make, nor a domestic occurrence take place; not an honour did any one receive, nor an office was he appointed to fill; but it is traced directly to the divine fountain of all good. If Jacob prospered, Laban is made to say, "I have learned by experience that the Lord hath blessed me for thy sake;" if Joseph rose in favour with his master, it was "because Potiphar saw that the Lord was with him;" if Job recovered from his various and protracted afflictions, and was restored to personal health and domestic felicity, "it was the Lord who blessed his latter end more than his beginning;" if David triumphed in the unequal contest with the Philistine, "it was the Lord who inspired the stripling's heart with courage, and directed his arm against the foe;" if Solomon was endowed with extraordinary wisdom, it was "the Lord who gave him a wise and understanding heart;" if Elijah performed the laborious duty of a courier before the king in his hurried journey to Jezreel, it was because "the hand of the Lord was strong upon him;" and if Daniel and his three friends made extraordinary proficiency in their Chaldee studies, it was because "God gave them knowledge and skill." Nay, as the God of providence, His kingdom ruleth over all, and all the kings of the earth are subordinate to His will. He raiseth up one, and setteth down another; He laid the towering pride of Nebuchadnezzar in the dust, and enlisted Cyrus as the instrument of accomplishing His destined restoration of the Hebrew exiles. Further, He is represented as holding all the elements of nature in His hand, and wielding them now in mild and benign influences for the happiness of a people, at another time "turning the fruitful land into barrenness, for the wickedness of them that dwell therein." In short, the agency of God is kept in view and acknowledged in every occurrence,—in events the most trivial and minute, as well as the most important; and thus the whole of the sacred history furnishes a continuous commentary on the doxology of the apostle, who, animated with devout admiration of the divine perfections as displayed in the kingdoms both of nature and grace, exclaims, "Of Him, and through Him, and to Him are all things; to whom be glory for ever, Amen." Men may talk of the reign of law, and that certain events take place as the necessary results of natural causes; they may philosophically descant on the rise and fall of empires, ascribing them to accident, or to causes merely of a political nature. But although there is admittedly a subordinate operation of secondary causes, the sacred historians never forget to look beyond, and ascribe them to the direct influence of Him who is the Governor among the nations, and the great First Cause of all things. How peculiar their phraseology! how different from the style in use amongst mere men of the world! An ordinary historian, if describing the rise and progress of a nation, would have enlarged on the profound sagacity, the broad and liberal views of the statesmen who laid the foundations of their social or political institutions, or improved and adapted them to the character and condition of an advanced age. If narrating a victory, he would have extolled the military skill and tactics of the general who formed the plan of the engagement, and the gallant bearing or daring courage of the troops who fought under his banner. Or if, having to speak of the dangerous illness of a royal personage, and his happy recovery from the verge of the grave, he would have dwelt on the great and widespread satisfaction which the unexpected intelligence diffused throughout the kingdom; and while he paid a compliment, it may be, to the skill and assiduity of the medical attendants, never made an allusion to that high unseen Power that suggested thoughts to the physician's mind, and imparted a healing virtue to all the remedial treatment he prescribed. How different the style of the Bible history! It is so composed, that we never rise from the perusal of it full of admiration for man, but always full of admiration for God. Where ordinary historians would rear a memorial of eulogistic praise to man, the sacred writers raise a monument of glory to God; and when we think that the large collection of historical tracts which the Scriptures comprise is written throughout in this style of pious acknowledgment of God,—a style so widely different from the prevailing tone and uniform tendency of all human writings,—we are irresistibly led to the conclusion that the sacred history, though traced by the pen and expressed in the language of man, is of a higher origin than the product of any human mind.

II. *A second characteristic of the sacred history is its typical nature.* — A type properly denotes a rude draught, or an imperfect representation of an object, in order to a more accurate and complete delineation of it. "To constitute one thing the type of another," says Bishop Marsh, "as the term is generally understood in reference to Scripture, something more is wanted than mere resemblance. The former must not only resemble the latter, but must have been *designed* to resemble the latter. It must have been so designed in its institution. It must have been designed as something preparatory to the latter. The type as well as the antitype must have been preordained; and they must have been pre-ordained as constituent parts of the same general scheme of divine providence. It is this previous design and this pre-ordained connection which constitute the relation of type and antitype. Where these qualities fail, where the previous design and the pre-ordained connection are wanting, the relation between any two things, however similar in themselves, is not the relation of type to antitype. The existence, therefore, of that previous design and pre-ordained connection must be clearly established, before we can have authority for pronouncing one thing the type of another. But we can establish the existence of that previous design and pre-ordained connection, by arguing only from the resemblance of the things compared. For the qualities and circumstances attendant on one thing may have a close resemblance with the qualities and circumstances attendant on another thing, and yet the things themselves may be devoid of all connection. How, then, it may be asked, shall we obtain the proof required? By what means shall we determine, in any given instance, that what is alleged as a type was really designed as a type? Now the only possible means of knowing that two distant, though similar, historic facts were so connected in the general scheme of divine providence that the one was designed to prefigure the other, is the authority of that work in which the scheme of divine providence is unfolded. Destitute of that authority, we may confound a resemblance subsequently observed with a resemblance pre-ordained; we may mistake a comparison founded on a mere accidental parity of circumstances, for a comparison founded on a necessary and inherent connection. There is no other rule, therefore, by which we can distinguish a real from a pretended type, than that of Scripture itself. There are no other possible means by which we know that a previous design and a pre-ordained connection existed. Whatever persons or things, therefore, recorded in the Old Testament, were expressly declared by Christ or by His apostles to have been designed as prefigurations of persons or things relating to the New Testament, such persons or things so recorded in the former are types of the persons or things with which they are compared in the latter. But should we assert, that if a person or thing was designed to prefigure another person or thing, where no such prefiguration has been declared by divine authority, we make an assertion for which we neither have, nor can have, the slightest foundation. And even when comparisons are instituted in the New Testament between antecedent and subsequent persons or things, we must be careful to distinguish the examples where a comparison is instituted merely for the sake of illustration, from the examples where such a connection is declared as exists in the relation of a type to its antitype."[1] These are the true principles of typical interpretation;

[1] *Lectures on the Bible.*

and as many writers have allowed a lively fancy to discover resemblances which are only apparent or very doubtful, we shall not admit any into our argument but what are sanctioned by scriptural authority. Now the whole of the ancient dispensation was a shadow of good things to come; and the wisdom of God ordained that the people who were chosen for a time to be the depositaries of divine truth, should be so modelled as, in their name and by their institutions, to prefigure the permanent spiritual church of the future which was to be established in all parts of the world. The names of *Israel* and the *seed of Jacob* are designations still applied to the people of God in the Christian church; and in the constitution of their peculiar society as a theocracy, God ruling them, and dwelling as King in the midst of them, was adumbrated the spiritual kingdom of Christ. All the regulations that were made for the education and government of that people; the character they were to sustain as a "kingdom of priests and a holy nation;" the privileges conferred on them, the ordinances established amongst them, as well as the leading persons who held civil and ecclesiastical office amongst them, bore a typical reference, and pre-intimated something in the life, character, or work of Christ. Of the personal types in the Old Testament there were very many, both before the law and under the law; and as, for the sake of brevity, we must limit ourselves to the notice of a few, we select only two of the former, viz. Isaac and Melchizedek. The most memorable event in the life of Isaac was his being surrendered by his father at the command of God, who thereby put the faith of the patriarch to the severest trial; and what was the meaning of this extraordinary act appears manifest from the words of our Lord, "Abraham rejoiced (rather, vehemently desired, earnestly longed) to see my day;"[1] and it is generally believed that this scene was arranged by God for the purpose of showing the pious patriarch, by a symbolical action, the office which the promised Saviour was to perform. That the transaction was pre-eminently typical, appears from the close analogy between the whole details and corresponding circumstances in the history of the Redeemer. The pre-intimation of the birth of Isaac to his mother, his miraculous conception, his name fixed by the angel previous to his

[1] Luke x. 24.

birth, his commanded sacrifice, the selection of the Mount Moriah—not by chance or for convenience, but by divine appointment—his being the sole victim, his carrying the wood, his being three days doomed to die, and his resurrection (ἐν παραβολῇ) in a figure or similitude, all prefigured the leading events in the life of the Saviour. Melchizedek was another type before the law, and the point in the Saviour's character he typified was the union of the kingly and priestly offices. Melchizedek, according to the general opinion, was a Canaanitish prince, an eminently pious and religious man, whose genealogy was perhaps designedly veiled in mystery, that he might be in this, as in other things, a type of Christ. He is mentioned in the sacred history as a contemporary of Abraham, and also in the 110th Psalm as well as in the Epistle to the Hebrews, where the apostle, aiming to show the pre-eminence of Christ's priesthood over that of Aaron, avails himself of the somewhat remarkable coincidences which happened to subsist between what is here related of Melchizedek, who combined in his own person the dignity both of king and priest. This fact enabled him to illustrate more strikingly to the Jewish Christians to whom he was writing the union of the same offices in Christ, who sits a Priest upon His throne. Again, as far as appears from the sacred record, Melchizedek was a priest not by inheritance. Though, as a man, he doubtless had a father and mother, and was born and died like other men; yet, as nothing is said on these points by the historian, the apostle, holding him forth precisely in the light in which he is represented in the history, and in no other, says that he was without father, without mother, without descent, having neither beginning of days nor end of life, but, made like unto the Son of God, abideth a priest continually; that is, he derived his office from no predecessor, and delivered it to no successor, but stands before us in the sacred record single and alone, constituting himself an order of priesthood. In this respect he was made eminently "like unto the Son of God," who was also a priest, not after the manner of the sons of Aaron, by descent from their predecessors, but after the similitude of Melchizedek, that is, by an immediate divine institution. These are the grand points of resemblance between Melchizedek and Christ; and we think it by no means unlikely that Moses, penning his narrative under divine guidance, was moved to omit the various particulars respecting the birth and parentage of Melchizedek, and the commencement and close of his priesthood, and to introduce him so briefly and abruptly into the thread of his history, for the very purpose of affording to uninspired penmen in after ages the means of very pertinently and forcibly illustrating this sublime feature of Christ's official character. These two are isolated types, as were all the other personal types before the law—Adam, Enoch, Noah, Abraham, Jacob, and Joseph. The types under it were more numerous as well as diversified.—Indeed, as has already been remarked, in all the various ordinances which God made known to His people through the medium of Moses, we everywhere find a Saviour significantly pointed out under the different characters which he bore. Among these various typical representations of His office and ministry, the high-priesthood holds a conspicuous place. Of what order of being He was to be, the apostle to the Hebrews informs us, by saying that "He was to be taken from among men;" He must be a man, one of ourselves, a partaker of our nature, and in all respects like to us.

For man, having become a sinner, could not

approach God except through the mediation of a high priest who was to be taken from among men. Aaron and his posterity were appointed to that office, and that not of themselves, nor of the will of man; for says the apostle, "No man taketh this honour unto himself, but he that is called of God, as was Aaron." The leading characteristic of the priesthood was holiness. An order of men, the sons of Levi, was set apart for this express purpose, separated from every secular work to the service of the sanctuary; and the great mark of their character engraven on the mitre of Aaron, "Holiness to the Lord,"—the solemn ceremony of consecration,—the splendid habiliments of his sacred office,—the holy oil that was poured on his head, symbolical of the Holy Spirit, to qualify him for his great work,—the purpose for which he was ordained, viz. to offer a continual burnt-offering,—the offering of a bullock every day for a sin-offering, and a lamb every morning and evening, and the gifts or freewill-offerings of the people;—the whole of these, both gifts and sacrifices, were to be presented by the priest as a confession of sin, an acknowledgment of divine favour, and a supplication of divine mercy. In the days of Aaron and his sons, the mediation between God and man was carried on by means of sacrifices and offerings; and of such importance were they, that the whole book of Leviticus, except a few verses, is occupied in describing their form and nature. Besides the appointed sin-offerings for particular persons and on peculiar occasions, we find one stated sacrifice in which the whole nation was concerned. The entire service of that day was committed to the high priest, who was never to enter the inner part of the tabernacle, called the Holy of Holies, except on that day, dressed not in his rich pontifical costume, but in pure white linen. He had to bring a sin-offering and a burnt-offering for himself; and having offered the first, he was to go within the veil with some of the blood, and sprinkle it before the mercy-seat. The high priest, by his mediation between God and the people, when the functions of the sacerdotal office were faithfully discharged, obtained for them the blessings of mercy, pardon, and peace. The heavy judgments which God had declared against the transgressors of His law were prevented when the high priest had made the customary offerings, and by means of them God was reconciled to His offending people. In short, the substitution of an animal in place of the sinner,—the imposition of hands on the head of the victim,—the victim legally subjected to the curse,—atonement made by blood, the worship of the church consisting largely of sacrifice;—every one of these circumstances has its antitype in the atoning and intercessory work of Christ, as is amply explained by the apostle to the Hebrews. Other personal types under the law were Moses, a typical mediator, Joshua, Samson, David, Solomon, Elijah in his ascension, Jonah in his living entombment for three days and three nights, Zerubbabel and Jehoshua,—in the history of all of whom, did space permit, we might show typical resemblances of a striking nature. But passing these, it may be proper to give a sample of types from the institutions under the law; and the most remarkable is the tabernacle. That sacred edifice itself, together with its splendid successor, the temple, the appointed meeting-place between God and His people; the ark placed in it, with the testimony, *i.e.* the two tables of stone containing the ten commandments, and a copy of the rest of the law, or divine communications made through Moses to the people; the mercy-seat or propitiatory, a covering of pure gold, spread over the ark, in which the tables of the law were kept, covering it exactly, and thereby bearing a deeply interesting and important signification; the Shechinah, or symbol of the divine presence, resting on the mercy-seat, and indicated by a cloud, from the midst of which responses were audibly given when God was consulted on behalf of His people; the shew-bread, a symbol of the full and never-failing provision which is made in the church for the spiritual sustenance and refreshment of God's people; the candlestick, with its seven branches, denoting the perfect light or knowledge the church would afford; the golden censer; the brazen pillars, Jachin and Boaz;—these and various other articles and vessels, too numerous to be specified, constituted the prescribed furniture of the tabernacle; and it is impossible to account for the extraordinary care which God took in the erection of this tabernacle, especially for His condescending to such minute details, except on the assumption that this tabernacle was to be of a typical character, and eminently subservient to the religious instruction and benefit of mankind, by shadowing forth, in its leading features, the worship and grand characteristics of the Christian church. The Epistle to the Hebrews illustrates this typical character of the Old Testament.

Besides the tabernacle, there were many other typical institutions, such as the passover, the feasts of pentecost and of tabernacles, the feast of trumpets and the feast of expiation, the burnt-offering, the sin-offering, the day of atonement. But passing these, it may be proper to specify some memorable events in the history of Israel that were eminently typical, such as the deliverance from Egypt, the passage through the Red Sea, the manna, the brazen serpent, the pillar of cloud by day and of fire by night; the frequent temporary appearance of the LORD in a human form, prelusive of His future incarnation, and prefigured to Abraham by the smoking furnace and the burning lamp, by Jacob's ladder, the burning bush, the cloud of glory; and His miraculous birth foreshadowed by various instances of conception beyond the ordinary course of nature. No reader of the New Testament can doubt the typical character of these events: for in several parts of the epistles they are spoken of; and particularly in the tenth chapter of the First Epistle to the Corinthians, the apostle, having recorded the miraculous passage through the Red Sea, and alluded to some memorable transactions in the wilderness, says: "Now all these happened to them for ensamples,[1] and they are written for our admonition, upon whom the ends of the world are come." "Whatsoever things were written aforetime, were written for our learning."[2] The writer whose duty it was to record these things in the course of his narrative, had a work to perform to which a man even of the highest natural ability and consummate thoughtfulness must have been unequal. He could not, for instance, have anticipated the dogmatic use which the apostle made of Jacob and Esau, or the allegory on Sarah and Hagar. An omission, a defective description, or a derangement in placing the furniture of the sanctuary, would have vitiated his record as a reliable history. One of these things, which prefigured

---

[1] The terms which denote a type are in Scripture numerous and varied. Τύπος is the common word. It occurs once in its natural and proper sense in the speech of Thomas, εἰς τὸν τύπον τῶν ἥλων—in the *print* of the nails (John xx. 25); but it is frequently used in its secondary signification, which we give it (Rom. v. 14; 1 Cor. v. 16; Col. ii. 17). In Heb. viii. 5, x. 1, the word used is σκιά, shadow, and along with it occurs the phrase ὑποδείγματα, patterns or figures. The apostle employs the word παραβολή, a parabolic figure (Heb. ix. 9, xi. 19). Elsewhere the word employed is ἀλληγορούμενα, allegories (Gal. iv. 24), and σφραγῖδα, seals (Rom. iv. 11). As to the antitype, the word ἀντίτυπον is found in 1 Pet. iii. 21. In the passage of Colossians where σκιά, shadow, is used, the antitype is called the σῶμα, the body, as it is called in Heb. x. 1, εἰκών; also μελλόντων ἀγαθῶν, and τοῖς οὐρανοῖς (Heb. ix. 23).

[2] Rom. xv. 4.

events in the life of Christ, or connected with Christianity in the distant future, would have been regarded as evincing a divine pre-ordination; but when not one or two instances only, but a whole institution, with all its appendages, and a peculiar dispensation, with the leading events which happened during its continuance, bore this typical reference to the worship and the church of a new and remote economy, the historian who recorded this complex system of types so exactly that they all suited their antitypes, executed a work which required more than human wisdom.

III. *The third characteristic of sacred history is, that there runs through it the element of a divine promise to be fulfilled in the distant future.*—A favourite subject of study in our day is the state of the aboriginal inhabitants of the world. Some writers of a speculative turn are directing their researches into prehistoric times, and on the basis of some vague conjectures, suggested by collections of artificial flints and groups of antique relics, are endeavouring to form elaborate theories respecting the character and primitive state of man. The sacred history proceeds upon a totally different principle; and although it gives in the beginning but a few detached facts, it has a definite object in view, which it pursues with undeviating steadiness. That object is not to describe man in his physical any more than in his intellectual and social progress; for it tells us very little of Adam. The actual information it gives us respecting his state in paradise is small indeed—not more than a few obscure statements necessary towards an understanding of the subsequent change. We are informed that he was good at his creation, subject to God, happy in himself, and invested with dominion over the earth and the lower creatures. But we are told nothing beyond these simple facts. Even the fall is briefly and obscurely related, although the painful certainty is clearly brought out, that the first pair abused their privileges, became disobedient, and died. For rescuing them from that state of sin and misery into which they had fallen, there was forthwith announced a hope of deliverance, which, though expressed in vague and indefinite terms, was sufficient to save them from despair; and the announcement of that deliverance, which was to be effected by a human descendant, forms the real starting-point of the sacred history; for the great object of revelation is to record the progressive development of the means by which mankind were to be regenerated and saved. The Scriptures, in short, contain the history of redemption; and they adhere to this main design with a unity of purpose, never interrupted nor broken by all the variety of secondary and secular subjects which are introduced. The minds of men—at least of the believing and pious portion of them—in all succeeding generations were directed to this promise of a deliverer; and it became a subject of constantly increasing interest, from the progressive communications made to those to whom God was pleased to reveal His gracious will. Those revelations were not made all at once, in the mature form and to the full extent in which we now find them. He who knew the nature and capacities of man unfolded His purposes simply and gradually, as the recipients were able to bear them; and in that progressive method of making known the system of revealed religion, we recognise a clear, unmistakeable proof of its having emanated from the all-wise God. Thus one single object only was first announced; when that had been left for a sufficient length of time to fix itself in the mind of the privileged receiver, a new communication was made; and that, again, at a certain interval was followed up by the addition of other circumstances, each of which tended to give a clearer and fuller view of the original announcement, as well as contributed to sustain and invigorate the exercise of faith. The sacred historians, therefore, were not left, like ordinary writers of history,—a Hume or a Robertson, a Macaulay or a Burton,—to record all the events and transactions of the ancient world at their discretion. Their minds were led by the guidance of the Spirit to the deliberate selection of those facts which tended to a definite purpose—the important purpose of tracing the onward course of the promise. Thus, instead of giving a full and detailed history of the primeval family, the narrative is confined to the one episode of Cain and Abel; and this episode is introduced with a view to explain that the promise was to run in the line of Seth. And the insertion of the genealogical register was to trace the direct descent from him. The blessing pronounced on Shem was recorded to point out the privileged destiny of his descendants; and it was in accordance with the same unity of design, that after a general account of the dispersion, showing the common descent of all mankind,—" for God hath made of one blood all nations to dwell on the face of the earth,"—the historian enters on the family history of Abraham. In the course of the narrative, he successively drops out of view all the patriarch's relatives who were not in the direct line of the promise. First, Lot is detached from the selected family; next Ishmael is lopped off as a rejected branch, and Isaac acknowledged as the heir; then Esau is deprived of his primogeniture, and Jacob receives the patriarchal legacy by benediction. Nay, not only is this peculiar plan adopted in recording the descending line of the Hebrew patriarchs; but a number of incidents are recorded, of a very trivial, some of a selfish and vindictive, others of a most offensive character, — giving unmistakeable evidence of what coarse materials the Divine Architect wrought out the sanctifying process. But the relation of those trivial incidents and revolting crimes was made, because it had in every instance a necessary or an important bearing on the future history of Israel in connection with the divine scheme of grace. "I see," says an excellent writer, "the promise all through Genesis. I confess myself wholly at a loss to explain the nature of that history on any other principle, or to unlock its mysteries by any other key. Couple it with this consideration, and I see the plan of Revelation proceeding with beautiful *uniformity*,—a unity of plan connecting (as it has been well said by Paley) the chicken roosting upon its perch with the spheres revolving in the firmament; and a unity of plan connecting in like manner the meanest incidents of a household with the most illustrious visions of a prophet. Abstracted from this consideration, I see in this book details of actions, some trifling, others odious, pursued at a length (when compared with the whole) singularly disproportionate; while things which the angels desire to look into are passed over and forgotten. But this principle once admitted, and all is consecrated,—all assumes a new aspect: trifles that seem at first not bigger than a man's hand occupy the heavens. And wherefore Sarah *laughed*, for instance, at the prospect of a son; and wherefore that *laugh* was rendered immortal in his name; and wherefore the sacred historian dwells on a matter so trivial, whilst the world and its vast concerns were lying at his feet, I can fully understand. For then I see the hand of God shaping everything to His own ends; and in an event thus casual, thus easy, thus unimportant, telling forth His mighty design of salvation to the world, and working it up into the web of His noble prospective counsels. I see that nothing is great or little before Him, who can bend to His purposes whatever He willeth, and convert the light-hearted and thoughtless mockery of an aged woman into an instrument of His glory, effectual as the tongue of the seer which He touched with living coals from the altar. Bearing this master-key in my hand, I can interpret the scenes of domestic mirth, of domestic stratagem, or of domestic wickedness, with which this history abounds."[1] Thus the sacred history, while it records the transactions of the past, points at the same time to the future; for it has a constant reference to Him who is "the end of the law," the substance of all its shadowy ceremonies. Moses, indeed, was specially privileged: for with him the Lord spake mouth to mouth, even apparently, and not in dark speeches; and he knew more of the mind of God than perhaps any of the writers of the Scriptures. Yet it is impossible to conceive that he could have written not only without error, but in the direct line of revelation, and with perfect truth and accuracy, concerning the character and work of the great Prophet whom God was to

[1] Blunt's *Scripture Coincidences*, p. 25.

raise up like unto him a thousand years after, had he not been enlightened, superintended, and directed by Him who gave him a divine commission at the burning bush. In the same way, did our limits allow, we might show that the later historical books are pervaded to a greater or less extent by the same element of the divine promise. Passing over the books of Joshua, Judges, and Ruth, in which, though it is not expressly mentioned, it is manifestly implied, we go to the books of Samuel, Kings, and Chronicles, which are histories of past events, but at the same time are prophetic histories, preparing the way for a more advanced view of the work of Christ—His kingly and priestly office. The histories of David and Solomon, which form the principal subjects of the two books of Samuel, form one continuous narrative. There is no interruption—no gap caused by the death of the former and the subsequent accession of the latter: for Solomon is appointed to the throne while his father is still living; David, the man of war, is conjoined with the Prince of Peace. And this twofold character of Christ is represented in David, the mighty king, who went forth conquering and to conquer, reigning till all his enemies are laid submissive at his feet; and in Solomon, the builder of the temple—the founder and the head of the spiritual temple, the church. In the books of Kings, a similar reference is strikingly contained in the continuous history of the two great prophets Elijah and Elisha,—the former merging at once into his successor by the transmission of his prophetic mantle, and the infusion of his spirit,—so that the consecutive ministries of those two prophets, so closely united in their sacred office, pointed to the unbroken continuance of Christ working after His ascension by His word and Spirit in the church. Lastly, in the historical books of Chronicles we see the influence of the prophetic element. They consist to a large extent of genealogies, than which few things are less interesting. But even the spirit of the genealogical register, as well as that of prophecy, is the testimony of Jesus. It was predicted that the great deliverer should be "the seed of the woman." The promise was, after the lapse of centuries, restricted to the posterity of Abraham, afterwards to the tribe of Judah, and at last to the family of David. Had not God ordained that genealogical records should be kept in all the Jewish tribes, and that unremitting vigilance and care should be taken to keep faithful registers, there could have been no means of ascertaining that Jesus was a scion of the royal house of David, and connected with the tribe of Judah. It was equally necessary that the genealogy of Abraham should be traced up to Adam, in order that clear, unchallengeable evidence might be possessed to prove that the Saviour was descended "from the mother of all living;" and thus of the same nature, "of one blood," with those whom He came to redeem. The enemies of Jesus often vilified Him for being a Nazarene, the inhabitant of a contemptible village, but they never 'attempted to deny that He was of David's royal line.

Thus the Scripture history is unique, unlike all other histories. It differs from them in character, inasmuch as it contains a narrative of God's procedure in the early ages of the world, and constantly acknowledges the reality of His moral government,—not as Colenso charges Moses with doing, like Minos, Lycurgus, and Numa, bringing Jehovah dramatically on the scene of human affairs, but tracing with pious feeling every event in the experience both of nations and individuals to the agency of Him whose providence ordains whatsoever comes to pass. It differs in character from all ordinary histories still further, that it describes a preparatory dispensation, which was perfect in its adaptation to an early age of the church, but the leading personages, events, and institutions of which were arranged so as to pre-intimate or foreshadow the most important phases of another and permanent economy that was to succeed it. And it differs from all other histories in its object, inasmuch as, while they refer exclusively to the past or the present, the sacred history has an element pointing to the future, which, like a thread of gold, runs through the whole of it, bearing upon events not to be realized till its close. No one who duly considers this remarkable structure of the Scripture history, can believe that its writers would have been able, by their own unaided powers, to preserve its leading characteristics consistently and fully through all the successive stages of the old dispensation. Moreover, the sacred history is peculiar not only in its character and object, but also in its form and contents. It might have been naturally expected, that in a professed communication from God, as the Scripture is, nothing would be found but the purest and loftiest sentiments, conveyed in a dignified and expressive style becoming the majesty of its Divine

Author; and that its main design—the development of a scheme of grace and salvation—would be kept prominently and uninterruptedly in view from the beginning to the end. But neither of these anticipations is realized by the actual character of the record. Instead of serving only as a channel for the transmission of sublime truths, the contemplation of which would keep the reader in direct and constant communion with heaven, the early portion of it is occupied largely with an account of worldly affairs relating to man: instead of assuming an unwonted elevation of style, it embodies its statements in plain and simple, sometimes in the most familiar and humble, forms of expression: instead of a continuous, regular, and complete exposition of the various subjects introduced, it consists of brief and fragmentary notices, abruptly broken, sometimes by the interpolation of rolls of names, of trivial incidents and domestic details, which are apparently unmeaning and useless; at other times, by the insertion of lengthened biographies of individuals, who seem to have had little or no claim to a place in such a record: and instead of carrying out the great object of revelation in a clear, undeviating manner, it not only enters into a description of the state, manners, and politics of the Jews, but diverges into foreign regions, giving reports of strange and exciting scenes, which tend to disturb and obscure the view of Scripture truth. Such features appear in a marked degree to distinguish the early books of the Old Testament; and considering whose word those books contain, we are led to conclude that those peculiarities were stamped upon them by the influence of divine inspiration. If the globular figure was determined upon by the all-wise Creator as the best adapted for the functions of the world, it could not be a matter of secondary importance in the eyes of the same infinite wisdom what should be the form of that sacred book which is the most valuable gift of His providence to man; and since the early portion of the Bible has been cast into the historic mould, we may be assured that this form was chosen as the most subservient to the purpose for which the Scripture was given. No method of communication that can be imagined —neither proclamation, nor promise, nor prophecy —could have been so efficient in influence, so conducive to cheer the hearts and sustain the faith of mankind in the predicted interposition of a gracious Deliverer, as practical evidences that the Mediator had already entered on His office, and was prosecuting His work for man's restoration to his original destiny. Those practical evidences are conveyed through the medium of history, and consist of recorded facts; they were given in the divine revelations made to the patriarchs, in the emancipation from Egypt, the subsequent establishment and national institutions of the chosen people in Palestine. But it was not in one country and at one period only the proof was given that the gracious interposition for man has been made. The sacred history shows, in the different scenes to which the narrative changes, progressive traces of the Mediator's agency in all ages and in various parts of the world,—in Egypt, and the countries bordering on Palestine, in Assyria, Babylon, Persia, Greece, and Rome,—not only by the most striking manifestations of power and wisdom on behalf of His people, but by pre-intimating the character of the great world-empires which rose in succession, and were designed to serve as pioneers in preparing the way for the introduction of that "kingdom that should not be moved." So deep and powerful was the impression produced by those practical manifestations, that throughout all the East an expectation prevailed of a King to be born who was destined to rule the world.

The other feature of the sacred history which remains to be noticed is, that whereas all other historians, from Herodotus down to those of the present day, have described people by a generalized view of their qualities, or by a philosophical exposition of the causes which contributed to their progress and prosperity or occasioned their decline and fall, the Scripture history proceeds upon a totally different principle. It selects one or two salient traits or outstanding acts, which, though insignificant of themselves, yet, when grouped together, serve as indications of character; and this is now acknowledged to be not only the true method of writing biography, but the best suited for the purpose of ascertaining the principles and motives of men. Thus we obtain a more vivid idea of the unsettled and uneasy state of the Israelites in the time of the judges, by notices of the many guerilla attacks made upon them from various quarters by the Arab borderers, than any historical sketch could convey. We learn more of the pious habits of the country inhabitants of Judea from the glimpses afforded us into the households of Manoah, Elkanah, and Jesse, and of their devoted adherence to the institutions of Moses from the honest independence of Naboth, than we could from any general view of society at those periods. And if we are apt to be surprised at the minute descriptions given of the conquests of David, as well as of the Oriental display and commercial undertakings of Solomon, and the apparently disproportionate space which the account of these have been allowed to occupy in the sacred history, a little reflection will enable us to discover the reason, viz. that these were the occasion and precursors of that gradual departure from the ancient constitutional order of things which led to the final overthrow of the nation.

But this feature of the sacred history—its dealing much in personal and domestic incidents—is deserving of attention in another point of view, as bearing directly on the great purpose of revelation, —that of training man to be a fellow-worker with God in his moral regeneration. It is in private life, and amid the discipline of daily occupations, that the spirit of religion is to be cherished, the habit of religion is to be strengthened, and the power of religion is to be established. In this view the Scripture history "is profitable for correction as well as instruction in righteousness," inasmuch as in its domestic details and biographical sketches it furnishes abundance of models for imitation as well as of beacons for warning; since every type of character, every variety of experience, every condition of life, is, in its essential features, represented there. Human nature is the same in every age and all the world over; and in the transactions recorded by the sacred historians, though connected with a form of society long ago extinct, every intelligent and reflecting reader may perceive, by the light which they reflect, the sure tendency of all the circumstances in which he is placed, and of every course he pursues in his individual probation. In short, the lessons taught by the Scripture history, as they are calculated, so they were evidently designed, to be *universally* useful; and seeing that providence has, through means of modern discoveries, not only thrown light upon many portions of it that long were obscure and apparently insignificant, but that researches are being made at present in Bible lands which promise to afford still more interesting and important illustrations of the sacred page, it would be rash and presumptuous to pronounce any part useless or unmeaning. What is passed over by one, may have interest for another; and thus all portions may be adapted for the benefit of the immensely diversified minds of mankind, when the word of God shall be circulated in all the world. All this about the Scripture history—the peculiarity of its structure and of its contents, so entirely different from those of all other histories, its adaptation for universal usefulness, and the yet unexplored depth of the mine in which its treasures of instruction are deposited—proves that the Scripture was not a mere human production,—that it was framed upon principles, and meant to subserve purposes, above and beyond the ordinary range of the human mind,—and consequently that it is inspired.

THE POETICAL BOOKS. — The Old Testament abounds with poetry. Many beautiful fragments of songs and poetical effusions are found interspersed throughout the Pentateuch, and in the books of Judges and Samuel. But the books which are properly poetical in character, language, and form, are Job, the Psalms, Proverbs, Ecclesiastes, and the Song of Solomon. These books exhibit the well-known features of Hebrew poetry, which is distinguished by this great peculiarity, that the poetical age of the Hebrews differed from that of all other nations, in being not mythical, but always historic; and with the solitary exception of David's

Elegy, all the poetical compositions we possess are consecrated to the service of religion. Poetry being so attractive a vehicle of truth, it is an evidence of divine wisdom that the Scriptures, which were designed for universal use, contain so many books cast into a poetical mould; He who knew what was in man, thus graciously communicating His will in a form calculated to gain the attention of multitudes, who feel didactic works in prose to be uninteresting and insipid. Since the art of poetry, then, was cultivated by writers under divine inspiration, and the Spirit of God chose it as a proper channel for conveying to the world a knowledge of divine truth, all who are capable of reflection will set a due value upon compositions which, besides being in the highest sense poetical, possess the still more important quality of being inspired. —This inspiration belongs to JOB.

We do not enter into the various questions that have been agitated in regard to this book: whether Job was a real or a fictitious person; whether the book is an account of actual conversations, or is merely an allegory; whether it was composed by Job or some other author. The probability is, that it was founded on fact—on the circumstance of an eminently great and good Arabian Emir having been overtaken by a succession of heavy afflictions, and visited by friends who came to condole with him in his calamitous condition. According to the usage of their country, after sitting for a time in the indulgence of silent grief, they engaged in social discourse, their conversation turning on points of great speculative difficulty in religion. The views advanced by the different speakers were afterwards embodied and expanded in a poetical composition, enriched with an exuberance of beautiful imagery, and great variety of illustration from natural scenery, as well as the vegetable and animal products of Idumea and Egypt. And as this work had become known to Moses during his forty years' sojourn in Northern Arabia, he, having under divine guidance put it into its present form, introduced it as a sacred writing to the Israelites, to whom, during their prolonged privations in the wilderness, the patience and restoration of Job were calculated to afford a seasonable and instructive example. With the exception of a prosaic prologue and epilogue, which shed the interest of a living history upon the piece, it consists of a series of poetical dialogues on the mysterious features of the divine government as displayed in the calamity of Job. But passing all other views of the poem, the only point with which we are concerned here is the question of its inspiration; and that it is possessed of an inspired character, is established by the authority of our Lord, who quotes it.[1] Further, it is attested by Paul, who introduces an extract from it with the formula, "It is written,"[2] and by similar references on the part of other apostles.[3] On such high attestations, the book must be regarded as possessed of divine authority — as an undoubted portion of inspired truth. But being the record of a religious debate in a poetical form, it must be viewed as a whole, not as disintegrated and in parts; for while it abounds throughout with noble and sublime descriptions, it is impossible to approve of many sentiments propounded by the various friends, and even by Job himself, who, under the influence of excited feeling, was misled so far as to curse the day of his birth. Especially, it is impossible to appeal in support of doctrinal truth to the views of those angry disputants, who not only contradict each other, but whom the divine oracle declared to have in many respects

---

[1] Matt. xxiv. 28, compared with Job xxxiv. 30.
[2] 1 Cor. iii. 11 with Job v. 13.
[3] Jas. iv. 10, 1 Pet. v. 6, with Job xxii. 29.

spoken erroneously. They gave forth their own sentiments, which were partial, prejudiced, and often wrong: for they were not inspired. But the author who embodied their sayings in this splendid poem, giving unity, expansion, and an artistic form to their conversational thoughts, *was* inspired. He had a moral purpose to promote, of great importance to the faith and comfort of mankind; and his book, as vouched for by the high authority of Christ and His apostles, is entitled to be ranked with the other Scriptures that were given by inspiration of God. But in order rightly to perceive the purport of it, the book must be read with discriminating intelligence. The successive dialogues in the drama, though each essential to a full view of the subject under discussion, and exhibiting different phases of it, are to be considered only as accessories to the denouement, preparing the way for the solution of the important problem given in the speech of Elihu, seconded and confirmed by the utterances of the divine speaker.[1] In those utterances the kernel of truth is contained; and all who, like Job's friends, wander in mazy labyrinths lost, perplexed by the apparent discordance of circumstances in human

[1] Ch. xxxviii.-xlii.

life and the course of the world with the principles of infinite rectitude and benignity, will find the grand invaluable lesson which this book was designed to teach is this, that instead of the afflictions which befall the righteous being the punishment of secret extraordinary sins, "whom the Lord loveth He chasteneth, and scourgeth every son whom He receiveth."

THE PSALMS, as the Hebrew name (Tehillim) indicates, was used as the title of a book comprising a large collection of hymns or songs for divine worship and praise. They were required for that elaborate system of vocal and instrumental music introduced into the public service of the sanctuary by David, who from his imaginative genius and devout feelings furnished the sentiments and words of the songs, as, with his exquisite knowledge and taste for music, and skill in the mechanical arts, he also formed the instruments which accompanied the psalmody. They are commonly designated "The Psalms of David," as he composed the greater part of them, and he is the only author mentioned in the New Testament.[1] His name appears in the titles of the psalms more

---
[1] Luke xx. 42.

frequently than that of any other; and many psalms which appear anonymous are proved, both by external and internal evidence, to have been his compositions—such as Ps. ii.[1] and xcv.[2] The mission of David as a lyric poet was to embody and invest with charms of verse sacred truths which had been previously revealed: in other words, it was not only to contemplate the grand and beautiful in nature with feelings of devout admiration and gratitude, but to draw forth from under the typical forms of legal services their latent meaning and spirit, adapting them to the various spiritual exigencies of individuals and the church. Accordingly, the doctrinal and spiritual truths which had long floated down the channel of the ancient church in the formality of a complicated ritual, received through him a living spirit and power, and being incorporated with the songs used in public worship, became the common and established faith of the ancient church. Through his instrumentality, religious worship acquired a spiritual character before unknown amongst the Hebrew people. Associated with him, as writers of the Psalms, were a noble band of leaders, "the sons of Korah," including Heman, Asaph, Jeduthun,

[1] Acts iv. 25.   [2] Heb. iv. 7.

and Ethan, who were endowed with talents for the kindred arts of poetry and music, and being moved by the Holy Spirit, consecrated their gifts to the production of compositions similar to those of their royal patron. Solomon also, and Moses, are to be ranked amongst the psalmists; and a few are considered on internal evidence, or on critical grounds, to date after the return from the captivity. But the whole collection, as we have them, was completed in the time of Malachi, upwards of four hundred years before Christ.[1] It is of no importance to our present purpose who wrote this or that particular psalm, except for establishing the fact by the early date, that this devotional book was honoured with the testimony of Christ and His apostles, which is given no less than seventy times in the New Testament. No book, indeed, in the sacred canon is so fully certified as this; and although the evidence already adduced in favour of its inspiration does not need any confirmation, it may be not irrelevant to add, that a strong additional evidence for its inspired character is afforded by its universal adaptation to the feelings and the circumstances of God's people in every age,—an adaptation which no hymns

[1] See Note C.

of mere human composition, however admired for poetic beauty, have ever equalled or approached. They are very various in their character and spirit. Some of them are purely devout effusions, dedicated to the praise of the Divine Being and His works, or to thanksgiving for blessings received. Some consist of private and personal prayers—for mercy to pardon or grace to help; while others are intercessory for the peace, prosperity, and extension of the church. Some contain the records of religious experience, describing the lights and shadows of spiritual life, with all its hopes and fears, its comforts and victories. Some psalms are historical, giving an epitomized narrative of the most memorable events in the Jewish church, with a view to stimulate the national sense of gratitude to their heavenly King and Head, as well as to foreshadow the far higher objects of a spiritual nature, which the Egyptian bondage, the exodus, the Red Sea, and the travels through the wilderness typified. Some are imprecatory against the enemies of God and the church; while others are obviously and exclusively prophetic, containing many interesting and most striking predictions of Christ and His church. The objection often brought against the inspiration of this book, that many of the psalms breathe a spirit of fell revenge, is deprived of all weight when it is considered against whom the imprecations are directed—certainly not against private and personal enemies. A malicious and vindictive spirit is not only condemned with severity in various parts of the Old as well as of the New Testament; but David himself was so far from being actuated by implacable feelings against his unrelenting persecutor, that he more than once saved the life of Saul, when it was in his power to have taken it. On the other hand, pious men have always desired and prayed that all obstacles to the diffusion of the truth, as well as to the peace and prosperity of the church, might be removed; and if these obstacles were presented in the persons of infidels or persecuting tyrants, that they might be overthrown, and the wickedness of the wicked brought to an end. The psalmist, who was filled with zeal for the divine glory, sympathized so strongly with these views, that he could say, "Do not I hate them, O Lord, that hate Thee? and am not I grieved with those that rise up against Thee? I hate them with perfect hatred; I count them mine enemies."[1] This view is essential to the right

[1] Ps. cxxxix. 21, 22.

appreciation of this book; and accordingly Bishop Horsley remarks, that "the misapplication of the Psalms wholly and exclusively to the literal David has done more mischief than the misapprehension of any other parts of the Scriptures, amongst those who profess the belief of the Christian religion."

David, besides his sacred lyrics, consecrated to the service of the sanctuary, was endowed with the prophetic gift; and although he was not called frequently or on an extensive scale to exercise the office of a prophet, he did compose psalms which contained very striking predictions of the Saviour, such as the second, the eighth, sixteenth, the twenty-second, and the hundred and tenth. At an advanced period of life he introduced another prediction in this remarkable manner: "David the son of Jesse said, and the man who was raised up on high, the anointed of the God of Israel, and the sweet psalmist of Israel, said, The Spirit of the Lord spake by me, and His word was in my tongue."[1] The word here rendered *said* is a very peculiar and solemn expression, intimating to *speak by divine inspiration;* and standing as it does associated with his designation as "the sweet

[1] 2 Sam. xxiii. 1, 2.

psalmist of Israel," the announcement that "the Spirit spake by him" would seem to imply a direct claim on his part to the guiding and elevating influences of inspiration in the composition of all those devotional songs which he had prepared for the service of the church. But the probability is, that this declaration referred not to his psalms, but to the last of his utterances as a divinely inspired prophet, in which, as a farewell testimony, he made a solemn profession of his faith in that great promise which had been made to him through Nathan, regarding the perpetuity of his dynasty in the person of the great Messiah. It is a remarkable prophecy, showing how clearly he perceived the typical character of his own kingdom, and the spiritual, ever-enduring kingdom of Christ. It is frequently referred to in the New Testament.[1] But any further remarks on the character of David as a prophet are postponed, in order to be comprehended under the general head of the prophetical writings.

THE BOOK OF PROVERBS is the first in the Bible to which the author's name is prefixed, and it has been, with scarcely an exception, the uniform

[1] Matt. xxii. 43; Acts ii. 29, 30, iv. 25, xiii. 33–37.

opinion of the church that that author was Solomon. As Eastern monarchs were in ancient times always attended by a secretary, whose duty it was to chronicle not only every interesting and important incident that occurred, but all the remarkable sayings he uttered in conversation, there can be little doubt that Solomon, who was so fond of oriental display, would have an officer of this description amongst his royal retinue; and it may well be supposed that the memoranda of sage remarks and oracular observations made on all subjects, human and divine, by a person of such extraordinary wisdom, and kept during his extended reign, would amount to an immense collection. Accordingly, it is recorded [1] that "he spoke three thousand proverbs;" and out of this vast number a selection was made and embodied in the present collection, apparently under the superintendence of Solomon himself. The latter portion, from the twenty-fifth chapter, was transcribed from an unpublished manuscript of Solomon's by order of Hezekiah, and added to the previously existing book, most probably forming part of those measures of religious reformation which that pious king adopted, by the encouragement and aid of the

[1] 1 Kings iv. 32.

prophets Isaiah, Hosea, and Micah, who are believed to be "the men of Hezekiah" referred to. As the Psalms are called the Psalms of David because he was the principal author, so this book is called the Proverbs of Solomon, although the two concluding chapters are ascribed to other authors. Their names are obviously symbolical, signifying, Agur = collector or teacher, Lemuel = devoted to God; and they delivered their *massa* or oracle to their pupils, not by their own wisdom, but by the Holy Spirit, as that term implies a claim to divine inspiration. The Hebrew word rendered proverb (Mashal) denotes a comparison, and this name "proverb" was probably given to it because the form or matter of the proverb involved a comparison. It was called also by the Hebrews a parable when expanded into details; and it was a favourite mode of expressing their thoughts, as it is to this day, not only amongst the nomadic tribes of Arabia, but amongst the Persians, the Chinese, and other people of the East, who delight in sententious sayings and proverbial philosophy. Sometimes, in order to aid the memory, they were thrown into a poetical form; and so are these Proverbs of Solomon, which, being arranged in couplets, triplets, and other modifications of versification, exhibit all the varieties of that parallelism which is a peculiar feature in Hebrew poetry. The book is interesting, not only from its poetical form, but for the invaluable treasures of practical wisdom it contains; and, as has been often remarked, having been in existence five centuries before "the seven wise men of Greece," and seven centuries prior to Socrates, Plato, and Aristotle, its early age precludes the idea of the wisdom with which it is replete being drawn from any of those famous sources of human philosophy. A slight comparison also will suffice to show that it is immeasurably superior in spirit as well as in execution to the apocryphal books of Wisdom and Ecclesiasticus; and we are led to the conclusion that he whom God was pleased to endow with the gift of extraordinary wisdom, was "moved by the Holy Spirit" to make a selection of his oracular sayings for the benefit of his fellow-men. It was recognised by the ancient church as a canonical book, and its inspiration is established by the highest testimonies, numerous quotations being made from it in the New Testament. And although, in the progressive development of divine truth, it is inferior to the pure and high-toned morality of the Sermon on the Mount, the book of Proverbs occupies an important rank amongst the books of Scripture.

Whether the book of Ecclesiastes was written by Solomon or by some later author, who adopted that royal voluptuary as the leading character or hero of his didactic poem, it does not fall within our province to inquire. The grand object of the piece is, by a general survey of earthly scenes, to contrast the vanity of human pursuits, when looked to as the chief end of life, with the blessedness of true wisdom or religion. This is its scope; and although there is considerable difficulty in interpreting some passages, which seem here to inculcate sensual epicurism,[1] and there to lean towards fatalism and scepticism,[2] yet these anomalies are only apparent, arising from the discursive nature of the poem; and the writer, guided by a better philosophy than that of the schools, shows that the chief good—the happiness which all men are pursuing, but which so few succeed in obtaining —is the attainment of heavenly wisdom: that is the grand end, and all other things are only the means towards its acquisition. Accordingly, after his poetical tour through all the diverse scenes of human life and occupation in an experimental

[1] Ch. iii. 12, 13, 22.   [2] Ch. vii. 16, ix. 2-10.

search after true happiness, he arrives at the grand "conclusion" of the "whole" inquiry,—that since worldly good does not yield solid satisfaction to a human soul, and there is a future judgment, which will rectify all the seeming disorders of the present state, "man's whole duty is to fear God and keep His commandments," by a faithful discharge of the duties, and a sober, thankful enjoyment of the blessings of life. The title of Ecclesiastes to be ranked amongst the sacred books cannot be doubted. It was received into the canon by Ezra and his prophetic colleagues, when a general collection was made under their inspired direction, after the return from the captivity. It is included in the Septuagint version, which was made before the Christian era; and although no passage is quoted, no allusion is made to it in any part of the Old or New Testament, it undoubtedly composed one of the books of divine authority which our Lord called τὰς γραφάς, the Scriptures.[1]

The Song has been previously noticed in Lecture I.

The Prophetical Books, which come next after

[1] Matt. xxii. 29.

the historical and poetical, form the third division of the Old Testament, and occupy an important place in the sacred volume. Viewed in their true and proper character, as containing the revelation of a connected series of events in the remote history of the world and the church, they present a collective body of evidence, which cannot be gainsaid, attesting the divine truth and inspiration of the Scriptures.

> "Heaven from all eyes has closed the book of fate,
> All but the passing page, the present state."

As to the great mass of occurrences which are destined to chequer their own personal history, men know nothing; and although individuals may be able in a few instances to trace the course of events, because experience or a far-seeing sagacity enables them to penetrate a little further than others, yet mankind are universally ignorant of what is to happen in time to come. They cannot see, if we may say so, above a yard or two before them; and they are as incapable of describing the transactions of to-morrow, as they are of writing the records of eternity itself. Were a person, then, to foretell with clear and unhesitating confidence, an event which would produce deep and lasting effects on the physical condition or the social and moral interests of a people, and his prediction to be verified in all respects, we should be disposed to regard that person as endowed with a faculty of foresight above the reach of ordinary men; and were a succession of persons to appear, predicting not one event only, but a multitude of events, which would overthrow certain specified nations existing at the time of the prediction, describing the exact order and manner in which those national vicissitudes would take place, and representing them all as merely preparatory to the advent of a universal king, and the establishment of a new form of society, which would extend all the world over,—and these oracular utterances were to be realized by the accomplishment of the principal of these events, so exactly in time, place, and character, as to give a sure and reliable pledge of the whole being fulfilled in due course,—the conclusion would be forced upon thoughtful minds, that the persons capable of diving so far into the dark and unknown depths of futurity, were gifted with a foreknowledge above the natural powers of humanity,—in other words, that they were inspired. Now this is precisely the case with the authors of the particular class of books we are now approaching. The predicting of future events was not, indeed, the primary or the stated duty of their office. The name for a prophet in the original is *Nabhi, a speaker;* and it is applied in the Old Testament Scriptures, sometimes to designate the patriarchs as men who were in close relations with God, and whose intercessory influence as His friends was of great avail in obtaining His favour;[1] at other times, to describe a person employed to communicate some revelation from God; and as such a one, in delivering his message, spoke of necessity under the influence of divine inspiration, he was called "man of God" by the sacred historians,[2] and "man of the Spirit" and "messenger of the Lord" by the prophets,[3] while the utterance made by him was called "the word of the Lord;"[4] and on different occasions it is used also as an appellative of men who were supernaturally moved to pour forth poetical and highly figurative effusions about God and divine things in a bold energetic manner,[5] and to prophesy things to come.[6] In addition to *Nabhi,* two

[1] Gen. xx. 7 ; Deut. xxxiv. 10 ; Ps. cv. 15.
[2] 1 Sam. ii. 27, ix. 6 ; 1 Kings xiii.
[3] Ezek. ii. 2 ; Hos. ix. 7 ; Hagg. i. 13.
[4] Num. xxiv. 3 ; 2 Sam. xxiii. 1 ; Ps. xxxvi. 1 ; Prov. xxx. 1 ; Jer. xxix. 31.
[5] Ex. xv. 20, 21 ; Num. xi. 29 ; 1 Sam. x. 5, 10-15 ; Luke i.
[6] Amos iii. 7, 8.

other words occur in the historical books,—*Roëh*, a seer, an ancient term, nearly though not wholly confined to Samuel;[1] and the other *Chozeh*, which is found in the later books. All three terms are used in one passage to distinguish different phases of the prophetical character.[2] It would be entirely out of place here to trace the origin and progress of this sacred office. Suffice it to observe, that while there were "prophets since the world began,"—Enoch, Noah, Abraham, Jacob, and Moses, —in the time of the judges the prophets began to come into prominence, as occupying the functions of religious teachers, which the priests were unwilling or unable to perform; and that under the auspices of Samuel, who founded or established seminaries for the education of young persons qualified to undertake the duties, a regular supply of prophets was provided, who were of the greatest use in contributing to preserve the interests of sound morality and genuine religion during the declining period of the monarchy, and some of whom exercised an influence of extraordinary power over the court as well as the nation. The prophets were the preachers of their day; and by the peculiarities of their dress and manner, as

[1] 2 Chron. xvi. 7, 10; Isa. xxx. 20.   [2] 1 Chron. xxix. 29.

well as by the impressive and solemn character
of their utterances, they produced effects on the
character of their age unequalled by the greatest
pulpit orators of modern times. Men of burning
zeal for the glory of God, and for the maintenance
of the cause of righteousness, they were accustomed, in the earnest discharge of their sacred
functions, to encounter opposition, and to brave
difficulties from which other men would have
shrunk; and it was mainly, or rather solely, through
their indomitable energy that the true religion
was preserved or revived in that land which God
had chosen as its sanctuary or asylum in ancient
times. But it is not so much in the character
of teachers of righteousness that we are to view
them, as in that of rebukers of unrighteousness,
who denounced God's judgment on the idolatries
and sins, whether of His own sinful people or of
the nations who unrighteously executed the just
judgments of Heaven upon them. They predicted
many future events; and the nearer of these, by
the fulfilment of their prophecies, accredited to
those who would listen to their proclamations, the
events that were more distant; while to us, the
then more remotely future, the prophecies relating
to Christ, which are now fulfilled in the gospel

history, or to the extension of the church in all parts of the world, which has taken place in modern times, confirm the credibility of the earlier. The four great prophets, Isaiah, Jeremiah, Ezekiel, and Daniel, stand by themselves in our version; while the twelve prophets at the head of whom stands Hosea, were called "the minor prophets," not from the less importance of their prophecies, compared with those of the preceding four, but from the smaller space and extent of their prophecies. The whole collection of their prophecies does not equal in bulk the prophecies of Isaiah alone: for God, who in His wisdom determined that no prophecy of the earlier prophets, such as Samuel, Elijah, Elisha, and others, should be committed to writing, willed also that a very small fragment of what the later prophets had spoken in His cause should be preserved. Their collected writings, which were comprised in one prophetic roll, have been reckoned, both in the Jewish and Christian church, as forming one book; and they themselves, like the apostles, were called "the twelve." Shortly after the close of the memorable services of Elijah and Elisha, the latter of whom flourished in the time of Joash, "there arose in the next reign, that of Jeroboam II., the first of that brilliant constellation of prophets, whose light gleamed over the fall of Israel and Judah, shone in their captivity, and set at last with the prediction of him who should precede the Sun of Righteousness. Then Hosea, Amos, Jonah, prophesied in the kingdom of Israel. Joel was probably called at the same time to prophesy in Judah, and Obadiah to deliver his prophecy as to Edom; Isaiah a few years later. Micah began his office in the following reign of Jotham, and prophesied, together with Isaiah, to and in the reign of Hezekiah; Jeremiah, Ezekiel, and Daniel, on the eve of and during the captivity in Babylon. The order, then, of 'the twelve' was probably altogether an order of time. We know that the four greater prophets are placed in that order, as also the three last of the twelve. Of the five first, Hosea, Amos, and Jonah were nearly contemporary; Joel was prior to Amos; and of the four remaining, Micah and Nahum were later than Jonah, whom they succeed in order."[1] Now, the most remarkable feature in the writings of those prophets is, that they comprise a continuous series of prophecies directed against the countries bor-

---

[1] Pusey, *Introduction to the Minor Prophets*; also Henderson's *Minor Prophets*.

dering on Judea, or connected with God's ancient people by political relations. There were isolated prophecies contained in the earlier books of Scripture of a specific character, referring to individuals and their posterity, and arising out of particular circumstances,—such as that which related to the sons of Noah;[1] that respecting the descendants of Abraham, their affliction in Egypt, their extorted deliverance from the power of tyrannical oppression, and their final establishment in the promised land at a specified period;[2] Ishmael, who was destined to be the ancestor of a powerful nation, whose secluded state and wild irregular character are still exemplified in the Arabs;[3] Esau, whose family "should be cut off," till there should be "none remaining of the house of Esau;"[4] Judah, that the sceptre would depart from him;[5] David, that he would be elevated to the throne of Israel,[6] —that a succession of heavy disasters would befall his royal house,[7] and yet that his dynasty would retain the royal authority;[8] Josiah;[9] Cyrus, and his edict for the restoration of the captive Jews;[10]

[1] Gen. ix. 25-27.
[2] Gen. xv. 13-16.
[3] Gen. xvi. 10-12, xvii. 20.
[4] Jer. xlix. 17.
[5] Gen. xlix. 10.
[6] 2 Sam. iii. 18.
[7] 2 Sam. xii. 11.
[8] 2 Chron. xxi. 7.
[9] 1 Kings xiii. 2.
[10] Isa. xliv. 28.

Nebuchadnezzar and his extraordinary affliction;[1] the birth of the Baptist;[2] Peter and his uncommon form of martyrdom;[3] and that which concerned the last of the apostles.[4] All these were prophecies delivered at a time and in circumstances when there was no indication in the course of things that the predicted issues would take place, and when the result could not be ascribed, on any ground of reason, to the penetration of great sagacity or a shrewd conjecture. There are prophecies respecting countries, places, and nations, which were doomed as a punishment for the sins and provocations of their inhabitants, some to long, others to perpetual desolation or destruction: such as Amalek, the remembrance of whom was to be utterly put out from under heaven;[5] Nineveh, whose destruction was to be complete;[6] Babylon, that it should be a desolation for ever, a possession for the bittern, and pools of water;[7] Tyre, a place for fishers to spread their nets upon;[8] Egypt, a bare kingdom—the basest of the kingdoms;[9] Jerusalem, that it should be trodden down of the Gentiles,[10] and the whole coast of Judea laid deso-

---

[1] Dan. iv. 19, 36. [2] Luke i. [3] John xxi. 19.
[4] John xxi. 22. [5] Ex. xvii. 14. [6] Nahum iii.
[7] Isa. xiii. xiv. [8] Ezek. xxvi. 4, 5.
[9] Ezek. xxix. 14, 15. [10] Luke xxi. 25.

late;[1] Idumea, and its famous capital Petra;[2] Ammon,[3] Moab,[4] Bashan and Gilead, that their pastures should fade and their oaks be destroyed.[5] Modern travellers have in great numbers visited those localities; and in the accounts they have published, the descriptions they have given of the gloomy desolation and widespread ruin that mark the scenes, they have used—in many cases unconsciously—the very terms in which the ancient prophets denounced the doom. Striking as is the correspondence between the denunciations of prophecy and the blasted appearance of those once busy and populous but anathematized places, none are more wonderful than the prophetic descriptions of the four universal empires which were to arise in succession, and the ten kingdoms into which the last was to be subdivided—comprehending the rise, progress, characteristic government, and overthrow of each of them in turn;—these are so graphic and minute, that they may be said to embrace the general history of the world for several centuries. Besides these prophecies which have long ago been accomplished, there are various

---

[1] Lev. xxvi. 31-33; Isa. vi. 10-12; Jer. ix. 11, xix. 15; Mic. v. 11-14.
[2] Jer. xlix. 7-22.   [3] Jer. xlix. 1-5.   [4] Isa. xvi. 14.
[5] Nahum i. 4; sa. xi. 12; Zech. xi. 2.

others which are in the course of being fulfilled in the present day, respecting the dispersion of the Jews, their grievous and protracted sufferings, their continued isolation from all other people, and their obstinate unbelief;[1] respecting the extension and universal establishment of Christianity;[2] the apostasy, tyranny, and idolatries of the Church of Rome; and respecting a period of millennial glory.[3] Such predictions are found in the prophetic books respecting the state and destiny of all the contemporary nations, which came into contact with the Jewish people while fulfilling God's purposes in Palestine, which seduced them by their idolatries, or oppressed them by their insatiable ambition for the acquisition of territory and power. They are not single and detached predictions, uttered by one individual or at distant intervals, and either expressed with the ambiguity of oracular responses, or arresting attention by marvellous glimpses into futurity. On the contrary, they were delivered by various messengers who were commissioned for the purpose; and they constituted part of a scheme of revelation, by which

---

[1] Lev. xxvi. 38, 39 ; Deut. xxix. 62, 67 ; Ezek. v. 10, 15 ; Hos. iii. 4.
[2] Ps. ii. 8 ; Isa. liv. ; Mal. i. 11.
[3] 1 Tim. iv. 1, 3 ; Rev. xiii. xvii.

God taught His ancient people to know that He was Governor among the nations. Joined together, they form a continuous chain of prophetic intimations, which, read in the light of their fulfilment, are virtually a record of ancient history; and by their minute graphic pictures of the characters of the people against whom they are directed, of the physical productions of their country, of their grovelling superstitions and vices, of the causes of their decline and fall, and the death-like silence and desolation which for the wickedness of their inhabitants should reign for ever in those spots which were once teeming with life and activity, they furnish striking proofs of the reality and retributions of a superintending Providence. They occupy a large, though not the principal, portion of this third division of the Old Testament. For, parallel with this line of predictions, there runs another line, longer, more connected, and more important in its bearings upon us, relating not to the vicissitudes of worldly kingdoms, but to the progressive development and universal establishment of the kingdom of God in Christ. "The spirit of prophecy is the testimony of Jesus;" and from the moment that the interposition of a Saviour became necessary, till the appointed period for His advent in the world, there was a series of prophetic announcements, at the times and in the circumstances which appeared to infinite wisdom the fittest to stimulate the faith and hopes of the church by additional revelations. Not to dwell on the vague promise that He was to be a partaker of human nature, peculiarly "the seed of the woman," the first definite announcement was that He should descend from them in the line of Abraham; then that He was to spring from the tribe of Judah, and afterwards from the lineage of David. His office was prophetically described—His union of priest and king—the virgin state of His mother —the lowliness of His parentage—the obscurity of His station—the time of His appearance— the place of His nativity—His entrance upon His public ministry—His miracles of power and beneficence—the attributes of His character as a man and as a King of Zion—the opposition made to Him—His expiatory sufferings—the fulfilment of minute circumstantial predictions at His death —the extension of His gospel—the prevalence of universal peace and righteousness under His reign;—all these, and various other features of His character and work, are announced by one or other of the prophets, who employ all the pomp of language, and enlist all the harmony of poetic numbers to portray in fitting strains the glories of Messiah. This is more or less the burden of all the larger prophetic books; and more especially of him who, from the number, variety, and clearness of his predictions, has been styled the Evangelical prophet. While, in common with the rest of his prophetic brethren, he occasionally touches upon subjects of contemporary interest; forewarns his countrymen of the home disasters or the foreign captivities which their vices and apostasy would entail; and describes in awful terms the vicissitudes that would lay some ancient kings and kingdoms in the dust, or denounces the curse that doomed the land of others to perpetual sterility and desolation,—the predominant topic that occupies the mind of Isaiah is the character and office of the great Redeemer. That forms the chief burden of his prophetic song; and never is the fulness of his genius and inspiration brought out into stronger activity; never does his harp send forth livelier or more elevated notes; never does his glowing fancy, in its range through nature, collect such a group of rich and splendid imagery, as when, transporting himself into the

K

visioned future, he contemplates the glories of the King of Zion. Several portions, indeed, of Isaiah's prophecies give an account of the Saviour's personal history, with reference more especially to the tragic events that were to mark its close, so plain, so circumstantial, and so discriminating, that, with a slight change from the future to the past tense, it might stand for one of the narratives written by the evangelical biographers.

So large a collection of prophecies, relating to such a variety of subjects, as that which is contained in the Scriptures, would form, it might be supposed, a basis for the ascription of a divine origin and character to the Book which could not be easily shaken or undermined. Notwithstanding, the attempt has been made by the school of modern Rationalists, who endeavour in several ways to eliminate the predictive element from the sacred volume.[1] In general, they fritter down prophecy into nothing more than the shrewd conjectures of sagacious men. But they apply this principle differently. Some, for instance, contend that insulated prophecies were introduced into the place where they stand after the events,[2] — a polite way of rejecting them as forgeries or fic-

---

[1] Note C. [2] Davidson, i. 198, 338, 428.

tions. Of this description are Jacob's prophetic delineation of the future fortunes of his sons;[1] Balaam's prophecy regarding Israel;[2] the anathema denounced on the rebuilder of Jericho;[3] Samuel's account of the style and exactions of the future king;[4] Isaiah's prophecies regarding Hezekiah and Sennacherib.[5] Allowing that some of these might have been spoken, it is insinuated that the speaker lived long enough to correct his prophecies by the light of later events, and thus imparted to those which referred to proximate occurrences a definiteness they did not exhibit when he gave them utterance; or that if the events were so remote as to put this solution of the difficulty out of the question, they allege that the prediction was actually given so near to the occurrence, that human sagacity could easily anticipate it, and thus what ignorant credulity exalted into a prediction, was nothing more than the foresight of observant and reflecting men. Of the former kind is Ezekiel's account of the grovelling superstitions practised in Jerusalem, which, though purporting to have been obtained in prophetic vision,

---

[1] Gen. xlix.
[2] Num. xxii.–xxiv.
[3] Josh. vi. 26; cf. 1 Kings xvi. 34.
[4] 1 Sam. viii. 11.
[5] Isa. x.–xiv.

was really derived from the reports of persons who brought him the intelligence direct from that capital; and of the latter kind—that is, the prophecies which were afterwards modified and adapted to the actual state of things—are Moses' predictions in Deuteronomy,[1] Isaiah's prophecy of Arabia and of Tyre,[2] and Jeremiah's prophecy of the seventy years' captivity.[3] There is no weight in such objections as these. For in regard to Jacob's dying prophecy, which is pronounced by those critics a *vaticinium post eventum*, it is a groundless assertion, since there is distinct evidence that important integral parts of this prophecy,—viz. the separation of Levi for the priesthood,[4] and the appointment of Joseph's two eldest sons to be heads of tribes,—were accomplished before the settlement in Canaan. In regard to Balaam's prophecy, it was delivered, as well as his death recorded;[5] and Moses' prophecies regarding the localization of the tribes, and the future rejection of the unbelieving Jews, were uttered and deposited in the ark, before the entrance into the promised land. The other prophecies mentioned

---

[1] Davidson, i. 383, iii. 15, 19, 98.
[2] Ch. xxi. xxiii.   [3] Ch. xxix. 10.
[4] Ex. xxxii. 29; Num. i. 49; Deut. x. 8, 9, xviii. 1.
[5] Num. xxxi. 8.

above are treated in a similar manner or assumed to be spurious, and on the ground of bold assumptions rejected. Other Rationalists resort to a different explanation of the prophecies, particularly those relating to the changes and disasters which befell the countries bordering on Palestine, ascribing them to political foresight, and considering them as parallelled by Seneca's supposed intimation of the discovery of America, Dante's anticipation of the Reformation, Burke's of the French Revolution, and others of the disruption from this country of the United States.[1] Such a view of the prophecies is scarcely deserving of notice; for it degrades the Scriptures to the level of an ordinary book, and represents those events as mere political changes which God denounced as His judgments upon the nations for their accumulated sins.[2] A third class of Rationalists

[1] Stanley's *Jewish Church*, p. 463, first series; Strachey's *Hebrew Politics*.

[2] The language of Scripture is directly antagonistic to this view: "Remember the former things of old : for I am God, and there is none else; I am God, and there is none like me; declaring the end from the beginning, and from ancient times the things that are not yet done." "Seek ye out of the book of the Lord, and read; no one of these shall fail, none shall want her mate : for my mouth it hath commanded, and His Spirit it hath gathered them" (Isa. xxxiv. 16, xlvi. 9, 10). "Though I make a full end of all nations whither I have scattered you, I will not make a full end of you" (Jer. xxx. 11).

labour to expunge the Messianic element out of the prophetic books, and apply all that is commonly interpreted as realized in Christ to Hezekiah; the fifty-third chapter of Isaiah they consider a personification of the suffering Jews of the captivity, or a historical sketch of the persecutions of Jeremiah.[1] Most triumphantly have all these infidel views been overcome, and the truth established. It is established not only on the soundest principles of criticism, but by the steady and hereditary attitude of the Jewish nation, who, though blinded by their engrossing idea of a temporal king, have uniformly viewed these prophecies as pointing to a Messiah; and so thoroughly did their faith in His appearance, as predicted, mould their character and aspirations, that, while all other people have looked back with admiring delight to some patriot king in the past history of their nation, the Jews alone *looked forward* to a golden age, when a perfect Ruler would rise up from amongst themselves to govern the nations.

Since the prophetic books then contain, beyond all controversy, direct, clear, and striking predictions of future events, the important fact to be

---

[1] Jer. xi. 19, 23, xviii. 18-23, xx. 10, xxiii. 33-40, xv. 10, xxxvii. 13-15, xxxviii. 4-20.

ascertained is, that they were publicly known in a written form at a date sufficiently distant from the event as to preclude the possibility of ascribing the prophecies to the penetration of natural sagacity. No difficulty can be felt on this point, when it is recollected, that it is to men of the prophetic order we owe the whole of Old Testament literature, and that previous to the reign of Josiah the prophets confined their moral and religious instructions to the oral discourses they addressed to their contemporaries. At that time, which has been called the Assyrian period, from the circumstance of the frequent allusion made by the prophets to the Assyrian invasions of Palestine, Joel, Hosea, Isaiah, Amos, Micah, Nahum, Jonah, flourished; and from the time of Josiah, which, from similar allusions to the captivity, has been called the Chaldean period, appeared Zephaniah, Huldah, Jeremiah, Habakkuk, Ezekiel, Obadiah, Daniel; and after the return from the captivity, Haggai, Zechariah, and Malachi. "It was the golden age of the prophets in the capacity of writers. Those of the Assyrian period were poets. Isaiah is without an equal; and as for Joel and Nahum, all effort to commend them to readers of taste would be useless. In the other prophets there are passages of great splendour; and in all of them there is such a lofty tone of piety and zeal for God and His honour, with such inflexible morality, as almost transports the reader into New Testament times."[1] The publication of their works was not their own voluntary doing, for they were enjoined by their heavenly Master to commit their messages and visions to writing; and as prediction was frequently followed by hortatory discourses, so the insertion of both in the record will account for the miscellaneous character of the prophetic books.[2] And all of them were publicly known and acknowledged by the Jewish nation as canonical works before and at the period when Malachi, the last of the prophetic class, lived, about 400 B.C. As a further evidence of these books being in general circulation, we may state that later prophets frequently allude to and quote from the works of their predecessors: cf. Nahum i. 15 with Isa. lii. 1, 7; iii. 7 with Isa. li. 19; iii. 4, 5, with Isa. xlvii. 5, 9; Hab. ii. 18, 19, with Isa. xliv. 19, 20. Jeremiah's prophecy is

---

[1] Moses Stuart on the Canon, p. 92.

[2] Isaiah was commanded to write his visions, viii. 1, 16-18; in one book, xxx. 8. Jer. xxx. 2, 17, 18, 23, 29, xxxvi. 2, 17, 18, xlv. 1, li. 60; Ezek. ii. 9, 10, iii. 1, 3, xxiv. 2, xliii. 11; Dan. xii. 4; Zech. v. 1; Hab. ii. 2.

interspersed with quotations from the latter part of Isaiah, particularly in ch. l., li., which consist almost wholly of extracts from that prophet. When the second book of Chronicles was written, the Prophecies was a well-known work (2 Chron. xxxii. 32), and Daniel learned from the study of Jeremiah that the appointed duration of their captivity had expired (cf. Dan. ix. 2 with Jer. xxv. 11, 12). Thus the date of the prophetic books collectively is sufficiently ascertained; and though we should admit that some of the prophecies respecting contemporary nations were really the anticipations of political sagacity, there are prophecies in abundance scattered throughout the Scriptures which cannot be accounted for on any natural principles, —prophecies uttered at a very remote period, and which, independently of all intermediate contingencies, were yet literally verified. Of such a character was the prophecy regarding Cyrus; and no laboured attempt to prove that this portion of the book was written by a younger Isaiah, who was personally acquainted with the Persian monarch, and knew his secret politics, can remove the marvellous mystery of this passage.[1] Of such a character is the prophecy of Moses concerning the

[1] Isa. xlv. 1.

desolations of Palestine, which are so widespread and so striking as to extort from the French infidel Volney an unconscious acknowledgment of its fulfilment: "From whence proceed such melancholy revolutions? For what cause is the fortune of those countries so strikingly changed? Why are so many cities destroyed? Why is not that ancient population reproduced and perpetuated? A mysterious God exercises His incomprehensible judgments; He has doubtless pronounced a secret malediction against the land." "Wherefore hath the Lord done thus unto this land? What meaneth the heat of His great anger?"[1] The fulfilment of these and many other remarkable prophecies, uttered at a time which entirely precludes the idea of human prevision, establishes not only the truth and authenticity, but the inspiration, of the Scriptures. In predicting events so remote, depending upon so many unforeseen contingencies, and so far beyond the reach of human knowledge, the Hebrew prophets must have been indebted for the miraculous power of penetrating the mysteries of the future to the guidance of Him who "knows the end from the beginning;" and every unprejudiced and reflecting mind will be convinced that

[1] Deut. xxix. 22-24.

the only conclusion to be come to is, "that prophecy came not in old time by the will of man, but holy men of God spake as they were moved by the Holy Ghost."[1]

[1] See Note D.

LECTURE III.

Promise of the Spirit's Aid to the Disciples when brought before Magistrates and Synagogues—Specific Promise of the Spirit to be with them in their Apostolic Mission; to bring all things to their Remembrance, and to lead them into all the Truth.—The Composition of the Gospels—Comprising a Record of the staple Topics of the Apostles' Ministry—Qualifications of the Evangelists—Gospels of Mark and Luke—Causes of the Variety in the Gospels—Each drawing from the Stores of his Personal Knowledge, and each writing for the Instruction of different Classes of People—The Contents of the Gospels afford a strong Argument for their Inspiration—Record of lengthened Discourses, Parables, and Prophecies, of numberless Miracles—Wonderful Harmony—Our Lord probably employed the Greek Language—Apparent Discrepancies—Incidents of a Supernatural Character—The Star—The Day of the Nativity—The Heavenly Voices—The Transfiguration—The Acts of the Apostles—Descent of the Spirit—Rapid Propagation of the Gospel—Book complete.—Epistles—Authors of them—Paul the Author of most of them—All the Writers supernaturally qualified — Supposed Disclaimer of Inspiration by Paul — General Deductions—Quotations from the Prophecies.

Our Lord had chosen from the general body of His followers a select band of disciples, in numbers corresponding to the twelve patriarchs of the Jewish church, whom He kept constantly near His person, with a view to their being trained to future usefulness in advancing His cause, and becoming the fathers of the Christian church. As soon as they appeared sufficiently prepared for the duty, He despatched them on a preparatory mission throughout Judea, to announce the approaching advent of the kingdom of God. On the eve of their departure, He apprised them fully of the difficulties and perils they would have to encounter. In particular, He gave them distinct premonition that they would be summoned before magistrates and synagogues on account of their connection with His cause, and counselled them on such emergencies not to be overwhelmed with anxiety, nor to make a formal preparation for their defence, but to rely on seasonable assistance from above (Matt. x. 19, 20; Mark xiii. 11; Luke xii. 11, 12, xxi. 14, 15). These four passages record counsels given by our Lord to His disciples, it would appear, on different occasions; but all of them contain an assurance of divine aid, suited to any exigencies that might arise in the course of the mission. And they prohibit, not what it is naturally impossible altogether to avoid,—the considerate forethought which every prudent and reflecting person takes before he speaks,—but only such a disquieting concern about what and how they should give their testimony, by which people brought into new and untried circumstances are often distressed and overwhelmed. Most men become excited, tremulous, and lose their self-control; nay, some, holding a high rank in literature, have been known, when summoned to compear as witnesses before a judicial court, to fall into errors and inconsistencies which covered them with shame, and seriously damaged the cause in which they were engaged.[1] As the apostles were men of humble condition, and had little, if any, beyond ordinary education before their call to the service of Christ, they would naturally be nervous and abashed when appearing at a public tribunal, especially in the character of accused persons, called publicly to testify for Christ; but in the prospect of such trying occasions, their Master fortified them with an assurance of divine aid, according as their exigencies might require. The promise made to them is similar to that held out to Moses when excusing himself from undertaking the mission to Pharaoh, on the ground that "he was not eloquent,

---

[1] Pope, when called to appear as a witness in a judicial court, spoke only a few sentences full of false grammar and incoherent statements. And it is well known that Cowper's mind was unhinged by the prospect of his being appointed to a public office in the House of Lords.

but slow of speech, and of a slow tongue." The Lord said unto him, "Who hath made man's mouth? Have not I, the Lord? Now therefore go, and I will be with thy mouth, and teach thee what thou shalt say" (Ex. iv. 11, 12). And so Jesus said to His apostles, "It shall be given you in the same hour what ye shall speak. For it is not you that speak, but the Spirit of your Father which speaketh in you." Or, as it is said in another place, "It is not ye that speak, but the Holy Ghost." "Settle it therefore in your hearts, not to meditate before what ye shall answer. For I will give you a mouth and wisdom, which all your adversaries shall not be able to gainsay nor resist." An instance of the fulfilment of this promise is furnished on the occasion of Peter and John appearing before the Sanhedrim, after their cure of the lame man at the Beautiful gate of the temple (Acts iv.). Though they were in the presence of a venerable court, of which they had all their lifetime heard the fame, and to which, in common with their countrymen, they had been taught to look up with mingled sentiments of awe and submission, they were neither daunted nor perplexed; and when commanded not to speak nor teach in the name of Jesus, firmly replied,

"Whether it be right in the sight of God to hearken unto you more than unto God, judge ye." The promise was fulfilled still further in the discourse of Stephen before the council (Acts vii.); of Paul before Felix, who trembled in the secret consciousness of guilt (Acts xviii. 12, xxiv. 10–25, xxvi. 1–29), and also of the same apostle before Agrippa. The circumstances anticipated in the four passages referred to were altogether extraordinary; and neither the counsel of Christ nor the promise of imparted aid is applicable to ordinary times and conditions of the church. Both of them were given in prospect of the first mission, which was confined to the lost sheep of the house of Israel. Both of them were exclusively personal to the apostles, and bore special reference to the difficulties and perils to which "the witnesses for Christ" would be exposed in their own country during the first period of the church's history. Another and a very different promise was needed as well as given, when the apostles were invested with the commission to go into all the world and teach (disciple) all nations.

In the interesting and solemn discourse which our Lord addressed to His disciples at the close of the last supper, He informed them, amongst other things, that they were destined to be His ambassadors in proclaiming His religion throughout the world,[1] and that they would be furnished with supernatural qualifications for this arduous duty. The apostolic office to which He was going to appoint them was designed to supply the want of His personal presence,—was, in fact, to be the continuation and the complement of His own ministry. And as Christ Himself had the Spirit resting upon Him without measure, He now promised to bestow the extraordinary gifts of the Spirit upon those who were to be His substitutes or representatives in the organization of the early church. "I will pray the Father," said He, "and He shall give you another Comforter, that He may abide with you for ever, even the Spirit of truth, whom the world cannot receive. He shall teach you all things, and bring all things to your remembrance, whatsoever I have said unto you. He will guide you into all truth. He will show you things to come. He shall glorify me; for He shall take of mine, and shall show it unto you."[2] This promise, given in such special circumstances, comprehends several particulars, which it is of the greatest importance carefully to consider. First,

[1] John xx. 21.   [2] John xiv. 16, 17, 26, xvi. 13, 14.

the presence and aid of the Spirit of truth. The apostles could not have so long breathed the atmosphere of the Saviour's society without catching the tone and sentiment of His holy circle. They had felt it to be pervaded by an air of sacredness, and they had caught a sympathetic glow of sanctity; for they were all, with the exception of Judas, good men, and advanced to some extent in religious knowledge and perception, as is evident from the confession made by Peter, in their common name, that they had penetrated the mystery of their Master's nature: "Thou art the Christ, the Son of the living God."[1] But they had not yet gotten a key to the spiritual character of His kingdom, though they were now about to obtain it. And surely the necessity of the Holy Spirit in conducting them to this attainment must be obvious to all who are acquainted with the gospel history. The disciples were to be "witnesses of Christ" in all the world, *i.e.* to bear a public testimony amongst both Jews and Gentiles concerning His doctrines, His miracles, and His doings. At that time, when their future destination was announced to them, they were totally incapable of discharging such an office. They had, indeed, attended

[1] Matt. xvi. 16.

their Master during the whole of His public life, and witnessed all that He had said and done. But many of the events which had marked the ministry of Christ, as well as many of His most important discoveries of Himself, were imperfectly or not at all understood by them, and appear to have been effaced from their minds as rapidly as the waves of the sea obliterate the footprints of the sand; so that, however earnest and desirous the apostles might be of doing honour to their Master, by bearing testimony to all the things He had spoken and done, they would, in their state of ignorance and unfitness, have been able to say little of Him after His departure, beyond the fact of their having seen and heard Him. They required, then, in the first instance, to be enlightened and guided into a knowledge of what was right and necessary to teach; and this was the first part of the promise: "He (the Spirit of truth) shall teach you all things." "He shall guide you into all truth." Not, of course, all truth in a literal sense, comprehending moral truth, historical truth, scientific truth, and political truth, for none of these constitute the truth referred to. However useful and interesting these may be in the several departments to which they belong, they dwindle into utter insignificance in comparison with that which, in regard to its divine origin and its paramount importance, is emphatically denominated "the truth." It was this truth, the truth as it is in Jesus, into which the Spirit was to guide the disciples. "He shall bring all things to your remembrance, whatsoever I have said unto you." The facts of which they were to be witnesses as relating to Christ, they already in part knew, for most of these had been matters of sense and personal experience. But very faint and obscure must have been the impression of what had occurred at a distant period; and of much which they had seen or heard during the early parts of His ministry, few or no traces would remain. The fact is, that the first disciples were plain, uneducated men, unaccustomed to continued efforts of intellectual attention, and much occupied with secular work, like the average description of hearers in our churches, who remember very little of the texts and sermons they have heard from ministers; and so we may reasonably conclude, that, from misunderstanding or misapplying the drift of their Master's daily teaching, through the influence of their Jewish prejudices, they would retain but a very vague and indistinct impression of all that they had heard since they joined His company. Circumstances, indeed, might tend to perpetuate the remembrance of some things. In a certain state of mental excitement, the memory is wonderfully active; so that facts and conversations are revived which had dropped out of mind; and every one is conscious from experience, that at unexpected moments, and in an unaccountable manner, things that had long fallen into oblivion are revived,—nay, a whole train of ideas, objects, and associations are often called suddenly up to mind, as it were by a conjuror's wand. As the minds of the disciples, then, would be intensely excited by the transactions relating to the death and resurrection of Christ, their vivid impression of these momentous events would touch other links of association, and recall former incidents of His ministry, which lay dormant in their minds. The general course of His history, with many of the outstanding circumstances of their connection with Him, would start up in vivid remembrance; and had they made a written record of these things as they rose in succession to their minds, they might, from a mere natural exercise of memory, have been able to give an honest account of the most prominent scenes in their Master's history. But such sudden mental excitement was not sufficient for the certain and full recollection of all that He had said and done in detail, especially for authentic reports of controversial discussions between Christ and opponents, as well as of long-connected discourses, and their spiritual import. For enabling the apostles to accomplish this, the Lord promised them the Spirit of truth, not only to aid them by a seasonable and distinct revival of old and forgotten truths, and of all things essential to the full publication of the gospel, but still further to make known to them things the announcement of which they could not bear as yet. Moreover, the Holy Spirit, with whose divine influences they were thus to be favoured, was to "abide with them for ever." This would constitute a marked distinction between them and the ancient prophets, on whom the Spirit fell only occasionally. Such permanent assistance was absolutely indispensable for the duties of their mission. For circumstances might call them to give a particular exposition of one portion of Christian truth here, and of another portion there; but as it was to be their duty to teach all things relating to the doctrine of Christ in all quarters of the world,—

as it was of vital importance that they should not fall into the smallest error, either through misapprehending or misstating the gospel, it was necessary that they should be rendered equal to every occasion by the constant inspiration of the Spirit of truth. In this memorable promise, then, made by the Divine Founder of the church, was comprehended all that was necessary to constitute complete inspiration (John xvii. 6-8, xx. 22, 23),—a full and perfect knowledge of the subjects which the Saviour had plainly and repeatedly communicated to His disciples during His personal ministry, as well as of many important things in which He had not as yet so thoroughly indoctrinated them (Luke xxiv. 49; Acts i. 8). This promise began to be fulfilled to them on the day of Pentecost; and from that time they gave unmistakeable evidence both of extraordinary gifts of religious knowledge, and of mental energy far above the common level of humanity. The process of preparation had long been slowly and progressively carried on under the immediate superintendence of Christ. But now the Spirit began His work of spiritual enlightenment; and just as the inflammable fluid, that is conducted in pipes under ground of a city, lies dark and hidden in those subterranean repositories, until the hand of man applies the torch,—when the dark shades of night are suddenly illuminated with a brightness that rivals the splendour of the day,— so the apostles, who up to the day of Pentecost were in the darkness and perplexity of ignorance [1] and national prejudice, were suddenly introduced into the full light and joy of spiritual knowledge. The truth that had lain unknown or dormant in their breasts was brought home to them with demonstration of the Spirit and with power. From that moment their dreams of ambition in that temporal kingdom Christ was expected to erect disappeared; for they now understood it in its spiritual nature and its spiritual blessings. Links of association were touched, which brought up the whole chain of the Saviour's life and ministrations to their memory; while incidents and parables, admonitions and promises made by Christ directly, as well as the whole character and design of the Old Testament, seen in a new light, were found to have a meaning and to carry a force which could never have been discovered without the aid of that Spirit who brought all

---

[1] They did not understand their Master at the Last Supper (John xix. 16–18).

things to their remembrance, and taught them the nature and relative connection of gospel truths. What an astonishing difference in the intellectual perception and reigning desires of the apostles took place during the short period that elapsed between the resurrection of Christ and the day of Pentecost! It could not be the *subjective* elevation of the minds of *all* the disciples at one and the same time; for that is not in accordance with the ordinary course of nature. It was a change *objectively* produced by the supernatural influence of the Divine Spirit; and being simultaneous, it must be concluded to have been produced in fulfilment of the Saviour's promise. It might be, that after they had been furnished with the key to the spiritual character of Christ's kingdom, their knowledge of the constituent principles of the gospel was gradual; for, like other men, the disciples differed in natural abilities and in degrees of natural acuteness, and some of them might " grow in grace and in the knowledge of their Lord and Saviour " more rapidly than others. The Sun of righteousness had shone into their hearts; but, like the light of the natural sun, it might advance only by a gradual course into the fulness of the perfect day. And the inspired records of the primitive church clearly show,[1] that even after the descent of the Holy Spirit, there were some things about the new dispensation which they were not yet able to bear. But whether they were made perfect in knowledge at once through the Spirit, or their progress, though rapid, was progressive, it is of no consequence to inquire: for of this great fact we are sure, that they were all completely equipped for their apostolic work before the first Gospel was published,—reckoned to have been eight years subsequent to the ascension of Christ,—and that they were miraculously preserved not only from error and intellectual obscurity, but from any diversity of views on the great doctrines of faith and duty which they were specially appointed to teach.

Now the promise of Christ, thus fulfilled by the endowment of the apostles with the gifts of the Spirit, doubtless included the power of writing as well as speaking with certain truth and infallible authority. Such a medium of instruction was evidently implied in their office as witnesses of Christ. For surely their divine commission, to "go into all the world, and teach the gospel to every creature," was not limited to their lifetime;

[1] Acts x. 9-47.

nor could it be meant that those truths should be made known to mankind only by their oral addresses. Nay, our Lord expressly said to them, "Lo, I am with you alway, even to the end of the world;" and unless they had all of them been endowed with an earthly immortality, His declaration must have signified that He would accompany their writings as well as their oral discourses with His Spirit and blessing. It cannot be supposed, that if, as teachers of religious knowledge, they were supernaturally aided in addressing groups of people on the great themes of the gospel, they would not enjoy the same divine assistance in their written instructions to the churches; or that all needful aid would be imparted to them in the use of their tongues, when occasion demanded, to deliver themselves from danger, but would be withheld from them in the exercise of their pens, though the unguarded or ignorant employment of these might imperil the spiritual safety of others. No such distinction is made or hinted at; and the fact is, that if a distinction had been intended, it was more important that the apostles should be qualified to write well than to speak well. An error committed in their oral preaching would be local only in its effects, or limited to a particular group of hearers; whereas an unsound statement, or an omission of some important truth, if conveyed in a written communication, might disseminate the seeds of error far and wide, and perpetuate its baneful influence in every church, in every country, and in every age till the end of time. As the commission of the apostles bore that they were to be the organs of religious instruction to the whole world, and they equally with other men were mortal, shortlived creatures, the necessity of their performing part of their allotted work through the medium of written compositions was imperative; and they must have entered upon this department of their duties with feelings of painful doubt and anxiety, if they had reason to anticipate that the preternatural aid they enjoyed in the delivery of their public discourses, would be withheld the moment they began to cast their instructions into a written form. But the promise of Christ already adverted to, that "the Spirit of truth would teach them all things, would bring all things to their remembrance, and abide with them for ever," implied no such limitation: it was given in the most general and comprehensive terms; and it offered a full security to the Christian church in all future time, that the apostles, whom the Lord delegated at His departure to "go into all the world, and disciple all nations," were furnished with intellectual, moral, and spiritual powers to communicate religious instruction to the world, whether by the tongue or the pen.

The New Testament was written entirely by men furnished with those extraordinary endowments of the Spirit, and consequently they were inspired writers. The Gospels occupy the first portion; and as it was needful to possess a faithful record of the sayings and doings of Christ, the church has received in these evangelical biographies memorials of His highly interesting and instructive life, which are worthy of her fullest confidence. A Plato or a Xenophon might be at liberty, in writing *memorabilia* of Socrates, to feign many things of their master, which a profound devotion to his memory, or a romantic admiration of his philosophy, might suggest as imparting a higher or more attractive interest to their subject; but the evangelists could not indulge in such fictitious embellishments, as they were under the influence of a controlling Guide, who did not permit them to err in the way either of improper omission on the one hand, or of fictitious additions on the other. And if there is any feature in the Gospel narratives more admirable than another, it is the union of unimpeachable fidelity, of transparent truthfulness, and of the most artless simplicity, in relating scenes and deeds of more than mortal grandeur, which ordinary historians would have employed the most elaborate terms in describing. No express command, indeed, was given to preserve memorials of the Saviour, nor was any injunction needed. Gratitude and devotion to the memory of a revered Instructor would naturally prompt many of His followers to draw up reminiscences of Christ; and it is well known, that in the first century multitudes of what have been called spurious Gospels sprang into existence, and courted the honour of being received into the number of the church's sacred books. Some of these might be amongst the biographies to which Luke especially alludes in the beginning of his history, and which, though truthful in the main, were written by ordinary teachers or obscure men in the church. But the most vigilant caution was exercised in admitting no books into the canon, except such as were the works of an apostle or inspired man; and it was through such a process of jealous, careful examination, the Gospels of

Matthew, Mark, Luke, and John were admitted by universal consent into the canon. Their contents had formed the burden of the apostolic testimony, the cycle of oral teaching by the "witnesses for Christ" in the assemblies of the first converts; and carrying with them the special power of the Holy Spirit, which rested on the apostles while speaking them, their embodiment in a permanent form was hailed as a precious privilege by the early church, and has always been recognised as part of that Scripture which is given by inspiration of God. One Gospel, written under the superintendence of that Spirit who brought all things to the historian's remembrance, might singly have been profitable for instruction and correction in righteousness. But divine wisdom has given to the church the benefit of four Gospels; and as it was a principle of the ancient law, that out of the mouth of two or three witnesses every word should be established, it is a boon for which we have the greatest reason to be thankful, that there are so many separate and independent memoirs of a life, the knowledge of which is so unspeakably precious, and the truth of which, to be received, must rest upon the immoveable foundation of apostolic authority. Mark and Luke, indeed, were not in the number of the original disciples to whom the promise of the Spirit was made. But neither the name of apostles, nor the supernatural influence of the Spirit, was exclusively confined to the twelve;[1] for many of the disciples in the first age were favoured with the extraordinary gift. Amongst the number, there are the strongest reasons for believing that Mark and Luke possessed the supernatural endowments of the Spirit; and that, being advantageously situated for access to the best information, as the personal friends and constant associates of apostles,—Mark of Peter, and Luke of Paul,—they wrote the evangelical narratives which bear their respective names under the immediate inspection and with the sanction of those apostles. Mark's is the briefest of the Gospels, written, as the early records of the church affirm, under the eye of the Apostle Peter, and with a special view to circulation in Italy and amongst the Romans generally. It contains numerous proofs of original and independent knowledge possessed by the writer. The very opening words proclaim the good confession of Peter upon which Christ builds His church, viz. His eternal Sonship. Various incidents are related and divine utterances recorded in this

[1] Acts xiv. 4, 14; Rom. xvi. 7; 2 Cor. viii. 23; 1 Thess. ii. 6.

Gospel which are not found in the others;[1] and as the author uses the present tense more frequently than the other evangelists, appearing to realize the transactions as actually before his eyes, reciting often the words of Christ in the original Aramæan dialect as if the very sound of that divine voice were still ringing in his ears, and noticing the very expression of the Saviour's aspect, as if the features of that blessed countenance were indelibly engraven on his memory, he impresses the reader with a belief that he has recorded the very words that he heard from the inspired lips of Peter, and thus confirms the saying that was common in the first centuries, that this Gospel, though called Mark's, as he was the historiographer, was really Peter's. With reference to Luke, though his name is not expressly mentioned, he has been universally believed to be the author of the third Gospel. There is a strong confirmation of this belief furnished by the words of Paul, "We have sent with him (Titus) the brother whose praise is IN THE GOSPEL through all the churches."[2] From a careful inquiry who was the associate of Paul here intended, there is a probability, amounting almost to a certainty, that it was Luke; and then the

[1] Ch. xiv. 37, xv. 43, xvi. 7. [2] 2 Cor. viii. 18.

emphatic words, IN THE GOSPEL, refer beyond doubt to his written narrative of our Lord's life. Luke is further mentioned by Paul as "the beloved physician;"[1] as one of his fellow-labourers;[2] and shortly before his martyrdom, as his sole companion ("only Luke is with me"[3]); and, as some think, is also pointed to by "the true yoke-fellow."[4] Now, feeling as he did an intense interest in everything relating to Christ, Luke was desirous to impart a reliable account of Him to the church. Instead of being satisfied, like many who had written ephemeral memoirs of Jesus, from information taken up at second-hand, from incidental conversations or floating traditions, he had made it his business, his principal and long-continued study, to collect materials for an evangelical history; and if a historian who, with a competent share of natural and moral qualifications, has enjoyed access to every available source of information, does possess a strong claim to the confidence of the public, Luke is well entitled to the highest credibility as a biographer of Jesus, inasmuch as he recorded what had been delivered to him by "eye-witnesses and ministers of the word." But his claims to our confidence rest on stronger grounds than even his

[1] Col. iv. 4. [2] Philem. 24. [3] 2 Tim. iv. 11. [4] Phil. iv. 3.

constant and familiar intimacy with those who had been from the beginning " eye-witnesses and ministers of the word." He had received his intelligence not only by tradition, in common with the " many " who had previously undertaken to write, but from the inspired lips of Paul confirming that tradition, and securing him from any error or mistake in the record of it. It appears from Acts xvi. 10 that he joined the company of that apostle at Troas, on the eve of his sailing for Europe, and from that time he was seldom if ever separated from his society. Now, from their frequent and daily conversations about the subject which was of paramount interest to both of them, Luke could not fail to imbibe the sentiments and profit by the heaven-derived knowledge of the apostle; and that the Pauline influence is clearly traceable in the composition of his Gospel, may be shown by appealing to two passages only, where the coincidence is so striking between them and parallel statements in the Epistle to the Corinthians, that no doubt can exist as to the source whence the evangelist drew his information.[1] Luke, then, could say with the greatest propriety and force of mean-

[1] Cf. Luke xxii. 19, 20, with 1 Cor. xi. 23, 26; also Luke xxiv. 34 with 1 Cor. xv. 4, 5.

ing that he "had a perfect understanding of all things;" and hence, possessing such full and unerring information on all things relating to the life and ministry of the Saviour, it seemed good to him, it was right and proper, it was a high and imperative duty in him, to communicate this knowledge to the church; for a talent so important and useful was not given to be hid or buried in the ground. From these considerations, then, it is clearly deducible that Mark and Luke were evangelists, probably in the number of the seventy disciples; that, at all events after the ascension of Christ, they both moved habitually in apostolic circles; and that, as the information they embodied in their respective narratives was, according to the general testimony of the early Christian church, submitted to the revision and published with the sanction of Peter and Paul, their Gospels are to be regarded as stamped with inspired authority as much as those of Matthew and John.

The advantage of having so many collateral Gospels is obvious; for, as they are not complete but fragmentary records, containing such portions of history only as fell within the notice of the writers, or was obtained from documents in possession of the early church,—suppose one evangelist to have omitted a particular incident, or passed it over with a slight notice, another would not. In fact, the very source of the dramatic interest in the New Testament scenes must be looked for in the total want of collusion amongst the evangelists. There is no evidence which can lead to the conclusion that Mark and Luke had consulted the preceding Gospel of Matthew. Each, drawing from the stores of his personal knowledge, writes in his own characteristic style, and laying hold of outstanding memories that were entwined round the roots of his inner nature, required as little to consult a fellow-witness, as a man needs, in rehearsing the leading circumstances in the life and death scenes of a parent or a child, to seek collateral vouchers for his facts. Hence it was, that, left to themselves, and unmodified by each other, the evangelists attained so much variety in the midst of inevitable sameness. One writer was impressed by one circumstance, another by a different event; and thus the preservation of the individual character of the four, while traversing the beaten track of the evangelical history, contributed, through the presiding influence of the Holy Spirit, to ensure the accuracy and completeness of the Gospel record. There was another cause which led to the variety which is discernible in the character and structure of the Gospels, viz. the circumstance of each of the evangelists writing for the instruction of different classes of people, and consequently being influenced in the selection of materials introduced into his history with reference to that leading design. Thus Matthew, who composed his Gospel for the benefit of the Jewish converts in Palestine, designed to exhibit Christ as the long-expected Messiah; and accordingly the tenor of his inspired narrative is principally, though not exclusively, directed towards the establishment of that important truth. It is with this view the genealogy of Jesus is traced from Abraham and David, and his close connection with a Jewish family is shown at length. It is with the same view that traits in the character as well as incidents in the history of Christ are frequently pointed out as direct fulfilments of prophecy; and amongst the closing scenes of His life, his entrance into Jerusalem in the character of the King of Zion, seated upon an ass, and His rejection by the rulers and people in that capacity, together with many detached references to the Messianic kingdom, are brought into prominence as all contributing to establish the claim of Jesus to the character and honours of "Him that was to come." The second Gospel was written by Mark for the Roman converts; and the leading design of it being to exhibit Christ the Son of God in the form of a servant, a prophet on earth, the choice of incidents and discourses that form the staple of the narrative was made with a view to sustain that special representation of His character. Luke compiled his Gospel for the benefit of the churches in Greece and Asia Minor, which he had visited in company with Paul; and in subserviency to his grand design to exhibit the magnitude and extent of divine grace in the scheme of salvation consummated by Christ, who appeared an incarnate Saviour, he delineates the true humanity of the Saviour, by giving not only an account of His birth, infancy, and quiet residence with His parents at Nazareth, but tracing His descent as "the seed of the woman" from Adam the first man, and by recording many instances of His having engaged in prayer, particularly on the eve of great crises in His life, His baptism, His choice of the twelve apostles, His transfiguration and suffering. A special feature of this Gospel is the method which Luke proposed to observe in the composition of his history: "It seemed good to me to write to thee *in order*."[1]

[1] Luke i. 3.

Certainly not in exact and consecutive order of time; for there are several parts of this Gospel in which the evangelist breaks in upon the chronological succession, and groups together a number of minor details, merely from their occurrence in a certain place or district that had been mentioned. The "order" in which he intended to write, was not a succession of time, but of events which he connects chiefly according to their moral bearing, of which his narrative of the temptation may be adduced as an early example, obliging him to omit the stern repulse, "Get thee behind me, Satan." In short, Luke's object was to arrange events in such an order as would mark great and progressive stages in the life and ministry of Christ. Accordingly, it is commonly remarked that he has divided his history into five large and distinct sections, which are easily traceable: the first embracing a narrative of the birth of Christ, ushered in by a record of the circumstances which preceded, attended, and immediately followed that auspicious event; the second relates the incidents which marked the period of His infancy and youth; the third is dedicated to a brief account of the preaching of John, preparatory to an account of the baptism and genealogy of Jesus; the fourth contains a full and varied narrative of the public ministry of Christ; and the fifth comprises the details of His last journey to Jerusalem, and all the exciting incidents connected with His trial, crucifixion, resurrection, and ascension. From this vidimus, it is evident that an orderly method characterizes the Gospel of Luke, which is entirely wanting in the more simple and artless narratives of the two preceding evangelists; and it was the more necessary for the author to observe a well-digested plan, as he wrote his Gospel for the use of the enlightened and cultivated people of Greece and Asia Minor, who were accustomed to the artistic style and method of the classic historians. The difference of the fourth Gospel from all its predecessors is this: that while the other evangelists, each with different views, wrote a history of the Saviour's life, John set himself to compile a history of His *person* and *office*, with an unexpressed but unmistakeable reference to some dangerous errors that were prevalent in the church. Accordingly, the knowledge of this design will account for various striking peculiarities which distinguish his Gospel, as well as for the omission of not a few events of greatest interest and importance in the personal history of the *man* Christ Jesus. Thus, for instance, he commences his Gospel with a sublime view of the Saviour in His pre-existent state before the creation, or the commencement of any providential dispensations in the world; then he represents the Word as stooping from the majesty of His uncreated nature to tabernacle with man on the earth; and omitting all mention of His birth, parentage, or youth, introduces Him on the stage of time as actually engaged in His prophetic office. He discards genealogies, as not belonging to that official character; throws the Jews out of view, as rejected at the late date of his narrative; takes no notice either of the agony in Gethsemane, or the cry of desertion on the cross,—all these, as belonging to the nature and weakness of humanity, are passed over in this Gospel; while, on the other hand, he gives prominence to other things omitted by the preceding evangelists—things which tend to illustrate the Saviour's glory, and develope the latent grandeur of His official character. Not to dwell on the marvellous episode of the restoration of Lazarus, the most stupendous of all the miracles of Christ, John has recorded other incidents demonstrating the superhuman power and unparallelled graces of the Saviour in greater number and to a higher degree in the close, perhaps, than at an earlier period of his life; and in the exclamation of Christ when the traitor left the paschal table, "Now is the Son of man glorified, and God is glorified in Him,"—in the calm majesty of demeanour, which awed and overwhelmed His captors in the garden,—in His miraculous restoration of Malchus' ear,—in the piercing glance by which He upbraided Peter for his apostasy,—in His unmurmuring submission to all the indignities connected with His mock trial and condemnation,—in His filial attention to His mother, even when He hung upon the cross,—in the virtues which then irradiated the setting of the Sun of Righteousness,—and in the circumstantial details given of His resurrection life, culminating in the ascension,—he who had evidently the most spiritual apprehension of his Master's character, has brought out the moral glory of Christ more fully than the earlier historians. Not that any component attribute of the Saviour's character was overlooked or entirely omitted by any of them. But one view of the divine subject was made more prominent by one evangelist, another by another; and every parable, every miracle, and every incident recorded by them all, gave a more attractive aspect to the infinite glory. Thus the variations and omissions found in the Gospels, and on which rationalistic criticism has so much insisted as objections fatal to the inspiration of the evangelical narratives, serve, when viewed in the light of the design contemplated in their composition, to furnish proofs that the authors were guided by the Spirit of truth; and the many different aspects in which they were led to exhibit the character and glory of Christ, contribute to establish the beauty, excellence, and perfection of the divine word.

The contents of these books, viewed collectively, furnish strong internal evidence of the inspiration of the writers. It is true that most of the events relating to Christ, which the evangelists have recorded, had fallen under their own observation. "That which was from the beginning, which they had heard, which they had seen with their eyes, which they had looked upon, and their hands had handled of the Word of life, that declared they" in their Gospels. But in relating the vast variety of scenes and occurrences which the eventful ministry of Jesus embraced,—His journeys by land and His voyages by sea, His interviews with the different sects and parties of His country, His dignified reproofs and crushing replies to the scribes and Pharisees, His implacable enemies, and the series of instructive conversations held with His disciples,—the most retentive memory would have been wanting in some and have erred in other things, had it not been for the promised aid of the Spirit. With reference only to His reported discourses, let any one try to recall a public discourse on miscellaneous topics heard some years before from the lips of a person of note, and commit to writing his recollection of the sentiments and language employed by the speaker,—he will find that, after the utmost efforts, he will not be able to reproduce more than a few short and detached fragments of the address, which had strongly riveted his attention and interest at the time of delivery. It is true that, in a state of society where there are no means of diffusing and transmitting knowledge beyond oral instruction, no books, no periodicals, no written documents, the human mind has always exhibited a strong capacity to apprehend and preserve the precise words of admired or respected teachers. The memory is wonderfully tenacious; and not only striking sayings and doings are handed down by popular tradition from generation to generation, but treasures of legendary tales and national poetry are thus fondly kept and repeated with little variation from father to son. In this way, it is probable that the

Iliad of Homer was at first preserved by the rehearsal of the strolling bards of ancient Greece, as we know that Italian story-tellers are to this day in the practice of reciting long passages of their country's songs. The minstrelsy of the Scottish border was taken down in writing by Sir Walter Scott from the lips of the Liddesdale peasantry; and the rhapsodical lays of Ossian were known to have been floating in the memories of the Scottish Highlanders long before Macpherson introduced them in a collected form to the knowledge of the literary world. Renan says, that "the Vedas, the ancient poetry of Arabia, have been preserved by memory for ages, and yet those compositions present a precise and delicate exactitude of form." The same writer asserts that the Talmud, which was floated down the stream of time for centuries in the popular traditions, is still possessed of a reliably historical character; and he is consequently led to concede the same quality of historical verity to the evangelical biographies. But it can require no great amount of thought and consideration, to see that there is a vast difference between the mental efforts of preserving in memory collections of light and attractive ballads, with the adventitious aid of versification and rhyme, and of remembering incidents, conversations, and discourses connected with different times and places, especially when the meaning or object of these was imperfectly or not at all understood. Amongst the contemporaries of our Lord, who had heard His addresses or seen His miracles, multitudes would retain a vivid impression of them, and describe both to eager listeners wherever they went. But as memory might fail or become less exact in course of time, imagination would be enlisted to supply the missing links: and hence it was natural for the followers of Christ, in their desire to possess permanent and reliable memorials of Him whom they revered as their Saviour and their Lord, to look for such narratives to those who "from the beginning had been eye-witnesses and ministers of the Word." Now, when it is considered that long didactic discourses, spoken variously by Christ on the shores of the lake, on the slope of the mountain, and in the cities of Palestine, are reported at length in close verbal connection, such as the sermon on the mount,[1] addressed at an early period of His ministry to a promiscuous crowd, unfolding principles and breathing a strain of sentiment no less elevated than original; His address to the

[1] Matt. v.-vii.

disciples in prospect of their first mission;[1] His numerous discussions about the Sabbath; His earnest and impressive dissuasive against giving offence to any of the faithful,[2] evidently preserved verbatim and with its rhythmical cadences; His representation of spiritual blessings under the highly metaphorical form of the bread and water of life, and of His own flesh and blood, imperfectly understood at the time by the hearers; the exhortation at the communion-table, and the impressive prayer before leaving, which was not embodied by John in his Gospel till half a century afterwards, yet is so full, so coherent, so worthy of the speaker, and so suited to the solemnity of the occasion,—it is impossible to resist the alternative conclusion, either that the evangelists composed speeches, and, like the classical historians, put them into the mouth of their Master,—an hypothesis which no genuine Christian can for a moment entertain,—or that their memories were supernaturally quickened and invigorated by the Spirit of truth, who brought all things to their remembrance. There is the record of various prophecies uttered by the Saviour, which it was necessary to record in their minute and circumstantial details,—that,

[1] Matt. x.   [2] Mark x.

for instance, concerning His own death and resurrection, the temporary desertion of all His disciples, the fall and eventual martyrdom of Peter,—the destruction of Jerusalem, so minute and circumstantial in details,—the dispersion of the Jews, and the propagation of His gospel throughout the Roman empire previous to the termination of the Jewish polity,—all of them spoken at a time and in circumstances when there was no apparent ground to anticipate those predicted events; and the faithful record of each prophecy, with an exact account of the occasion when it was delivered, compared with the accomplishment, must be regarded as a clear proof of the inspired character of the recorders. There is also the relation of numerous parables,—spoken in the country, in the city, and at the sea-side;—some of them bearing on rural or pastoral life, some relating to the social manners of opulent citizens, some taken from the sea; and others, particularly those uttered towards the close of His ministry, descriptive of the treatment He Himself received from the rulers of His country, and prophetic of their doom; and when it is considered that, as the moral of a parable always depended on the minutest points in the framework being exactly fitted in,—and every one of the parables recorded in the Gospel histories is admirable for its beauty, aptness, and symmetry of parts,—the reader must be persuaded that the evangelists have recorded these illustrative stories faithfully as *our Lord told them*, and not written "cunningly devised fables" of their own invention. Nor is this all. Our Lord *did* as well as *said* many remarkable things during His personal ministry; and it cannot be supposed, to use the words of Alford, "that the light poured by the Holy Spirit upon the *sayings* of the Lord would be confined to them, and not extend itself over the other parts of the narrative of His life on earth. Can we believe that those miracles, which, though not uttered in words, were yet *acted parables*, would not be, under the same gracious assistance, brought back to the minds of the apostles, so that they should be placed on record for the teaching of the church?" The remark is important, and founded on a just view of the life and ministry of Christ, of which miracles formed an essential part. These miraculous displays of almighty power were not isolated facts, nor accidental occurrences, that were embraced by Him, when some happy opportunity presented itself of performing them. Though apparently fortuitous and rising out of particular circumstances, they were all foreseen by His omniscient mind and met by His unerring wisdom, as transactions which not only afforded a general proof of His divine character, but were fitted in every particular case to illustrate the grand blessings of His gospel. In other words, they not only furnished a collective body of evidence sufficient to convince candid and reflecting observers like Nicodemus, that He who performed them was a teacher come from God, but to serve as *emblems* of the spiritual benefits His religion would confer upon mankind. They were precisely the kind of miracles which it had been predicted the Messiah, when He came, would perform.[1] Hence it was essentially necessary for the honour of our Lord, both as "the Prophet who was to come" and as the Saviour of the world, that a full and accurate report of those wonderful works should be preserved for the benefit of the church. They were performed in an almost infinite variety of ways;—by a touch, a word, or the secret emanation of healing virtue from His person; on patients sometimes near, at other times at a distance from, the spot where the Saviour was; on the bodies of the sick, the paralytic, and the dead, no less than on disordered minds, afflicted

[1] Cf. Matt. xi. 4, 5, with Isa. xxxv. 5, 6.

with malignant and mysterious forms of disease, which no known type of lunacy can parallel. Moreover, some of them, which were designed to carry an important significance, were repeated;[1] and at each repetition, several circumstances were varied in a manner that unmistakeably indicates a moral design—the inculcation of an interesting and instructive lesson to the believer.[2] Minute accuracy, therefore, in recording this diversity of circumstances was essential, otherwise the full object of the miracle could not have been understood; and as the disciples, when they saw those miracles performed, were not aware of their emblematical character,—did not perceive that the divine power so mercifully exerted in relieving man from physical evils was *symbolical* of the Saviour's ability to free him from the far more deeply seated spiritual evils that have afflicted humanity ever since the fall,—it is clear that the evangelists could not have been even correct historians of these wondrous works, had they not been superintended by " the Spirit of truth, who not only brought all things to their remembrance, but taught them all things, and guided them into all truth."

---

[1] Matt. xiv. 13 ; Mark vi. 39 ; Luke ix. 16.
[2] John vi. 5-14 ; Luke v. 4-6 ; John xxi. 11.

In the relation of those discourses, parables, and miracles, there is a beautiful harmony pervading the three first Gospels,—a harmony all the more wonderful, when it is considered that the evangelists seem to have written independently of each other. And as this harmony extends in many passages to the employment of the same phraseology, there is no way of accounting for this similarity of expression, under the presiding influence of the Holy Spirit, so probable as by adopting the theory advocated by Hug and Roberts, that in all the principal scenes of His ministry our Lord spoke in Greek, which was almost universally spoken and understood both in and out of Palestine.[1] Still, with all this harmony, there are some minor discrepancies, arising partly from the want of completeness and chronological arrangement in the evangelical narratives, and partly from the circumstance of our Lord having apparently repeated some of His most important sayings at different times, and in connection with different events. These discrepancies have been paraded by hostile critics as fatal to the inspired character of the evangelists, and therefore it may be expedient to advert to a few of them, in order to show

[1] See Note D.

how they admit of a satisfactory reconciliation. For instance, in Matt. xxiii., mention is made of Zacharias. Who this Zacharias was, is a point on which interpreters are not agreed. Zacharias, or Zechariah, the prophet who wrote the book bearing his name, states himself to be the son of Barachiah; but of the manner of his death we have not any account in the Old Testament history. But there was another Zacharias, who is said in 2 Chron. xxiv. to have been slain in the manner described by the command of Joash. This Zacharias, however, is spoken of as the son of Jehoiada. Some suppose that his father Jehoiada bore also the name of Barachias; and in point of fact there did exist in the days of Jerome, in the fourth century, a Hebrew copy of Matthew's Gospel, in which the name Jehoiada stands instead of Barachias. On the whole, it is probable that he is the person intended. . Matthew (viii. 28–34), relating our Lord's voyage to the country of the Gadarenes, says, "There met Him two demoniacs;" whereas Mark and Luke make mention only of one. Something peculiar in the circumstances or in the maniacal fierceness of one of those persons may have rendered him more prominent, and led the two latter evangelists to specify him more particularly. The three first evangelists relate a miraculous cure of the blind, performed by our Lord in His passage through Jericho to Jerusalem. Matthew mentions two blind men without naming them; while Mark and Luke mention only one, whose name Bartimeus they give most probably on account of his being a noted beggar. His usual station might be at the entrance of the town, on the northern side; and hence Luke, describing our Lord's journey from Galilee, says, "As He came nigh unto Jericho." Then, hearing that Jesus of Nazareth was passing by, and not being able to reach Him through the dense crowd, he was hastily led to the opposite gate of the town, where he was joined by a companion in misery in making a common application for mercy; and hence Matthew and Mark say, that "as Jesus went out of Jericho, two blind men came to Him."[1] Then Jesus, as Matthew relates, had compassion on them both, and touching their eyes, healed them. Luke, by anticipation, as is common with all historians, "relates the whole transaction, when he first introduces it, rather than by cutting it into two parts, to preserve a more painful accuracy, yet lose the effect which

[1] Matt. xx. 29-34; Mark x. 46 to end; Luke xviii. 36-43.

the whole narrative related at a breath produces."[1] Matthew represents Pilate as proposing Barabbas, while according to Luke the proposal emanated from the people. Mark clears up the difficulty, by stating that while the people hinted at the usual custom, Pilate yielded to their wishes in this particular case. The inscription on the cross is given variously. But the main fact was, "The King of the Jews," and that is recorded by all the evangelists. In his account of the resurrection,[2] Mark describes *one* angel at the sepulchre *sitting*, where Luke specifies *two standing*, and being *suddenly* present before the women. The discrepancy in this case may be traced to the narratives referring to a different *time* in the account of the heavenly apparition. Such is a specimen of the discrepancies that occur in the evangelical narratives; and were we fully acquainted with all the circumstances, we should most probably find that other discrepancies are in like manner apparent rather than real, affecting neither the great and glorious portrait of our Lord, nor the inspired character of His biographers.

There are incidents of a different kind, of a supernatural character, the introduction of which

---

[1] Bengel.   [2] Mark xvi. 5; Luke xxiv. 4.

into the Gospel narrative is considered by some in the present day to invalidate the writers' claims to inspiration. Amongst these are the star that appeared in the east, and that stood over Bethlehem; the song of the nativity, and the other attendant circumstances of the Saviour's birth and infancy; together with the voice from heaven, which on three occasions attested His dignity, and the transfiguration scene. These, it is alleged, cannot be considered admissible within the region of sober history. No doubt it was a common device in ancient times, and amongst idolatrous people, to represent the birth of eminent persons as marked by various prodigies, and distinguished by the descent of deities, which were supposed to prognosticate the future greatness of the child of destiny. How different is the sacred narrative of the birth of Christ! The incidents which it details are completely consistent with the most enlightened ideas of the perfections of the Almighty, and the relation of them is stamped with the most evident characters of truth. They took place in a manner too public for the introduction of an imposture, and in an age too enlightened to admit of the circulation of any fabricated tale of wonders. Moreover, they are in perfect unison with the more than mortal dignity of Him whose advent they attested and proclaimed. Nay, further, so much are those early incidents that marked the birth of Christ of a piece with the extraordinary course of His life and ministry, that they reciprocally prove and establish each other. The miraculous incidents, like the heralds of an earthly monarch, serve to usher in with due honour the arrival of Him who exhibited such unmistakeable signs of incarnate Divinity; while, on the other hand, the unequalled purity and devotion of His character, and the sublimely comprehensive benevolence of His aims, were worthy of being celebrated by heavenly choristers in a song so superlatively grand, and well suited as a birthday ode to inaugurate a new dispensation of Providence. There are who rank this song of the nativity amongst the poetical myths found in the early traditions of all people, and thus not coming within the legitimate province of history. But this song is infinitely superior to the highest efforts of human genius; it was utterly beyond the conception of a Jewish mind; especially, it was a song to the invention of which neither the shepherds, nor Joseph, nor Mary, were equal; and as it cannot be supposed a forgery by a man of truth and piety as Luke was, the narrative of which it forms a part must be accepted as related by the evangelical historian. The voice from heaven has been classed with "the airy tongues that syllable men's names," and scouted as a popular form of superstition to which the Jews were exceedingly prone. But of the reality of this voice no believer in the Scriptures can doubt; and it was uttered on three occasions, each forming new stages in the course of our Lord's ministry sufficiently momentous to justify so extraordinary an attestation. The first was at His baptism; and the voice from heaven, containing a direct allusion to the Messianic prophecy, "Behold my Servant, whom I uphold; mine elect, in whom my soul delighteth,"[1] was designed to signalize Christ's entrance on His public ministry, and seems to have been heard only by John.[2] The second was at His transfiguration,—a symbolical scene, enacted for the benefit of His disciples at the commencement of His last suffering stage. The words, "Hear ye Him," were added on the disappearance of Moses and Elias, who had descended from heaven, as it were, to resign their legislative and prophetic commissions at His feet; and they were so audible, that Peter, in language of

[1] Isa. xlii. 1.   [2] John i. 32-34.

peculiar strength and grandeur, appeals to them as affording an incontestable evidence of the divine origin and authority of the gospel.[1] The third occasion when the voice from heaven was heard, was after Christ's last entrance into Jerusalem, and when His spirit was deeply agitated in the immediate prospect of His sufferings. The voice, referring to its former declaration, both at His baptism and His transfiguration, announced, in a strain even more exalted and extensive than before, that "glorification of His name" which was yet to take place.[2] Then, as to the transfiguration scene, which some have the hardihood to allege is a fiction of the evangelists, it was so utterly beyond their power to imagine the splendid drama, that the actual spectators were at first bewildered and afraid by what they saw and heard, although its sublime disclosures produced a most animating and indelible impression on their minds of the truth of Christianity. The Apostle Peter makes a special reference to this memorable incident in a passage of his second epistle, where he expresses an earnest desire not only that his instructions might be always remembered, but that the Christians of his own and every future age might know

[1] 2 Pet. i. 17, 18.   [2] John xii. 28.

the solid, immoveable foundation on which his faith in the gospel rested,—not on the traditional authority of the church,—not on the deductions of human philosophy,—not on the mere opinions of any man however eminent, or any body of men however learned or wise, but on the testimony of witnesses regarding what their eyes had seen, their ears had heard, their hands had handled of the Word of life,—a testimony in bearing which they had already encountered persecution and sufferings in various forms, their adherence to the truth of which had already been tested by the death of some, and would ere long be tested by the martyrdom of more. In this passage Peter indicates his thorough unmoveable faith in the truth and certainty of that which he had preached, intending thus to hint, that they to whom he wrote might feel the same confidence, as resting on the basis of undoubted verity. In proof of this he alludes to the transfiguration,—a transaction which formed a remarkable exception to the usual state of humiliation in which the Saviour lived on earth ; and omitting to notice the attendance of two glorified saints, who had for ages been enjoying the felicities of the invisible world, and who then descended to the earth, arrayed in the splendid costume of their better country, seen in earnest colloquy with the Son of God, holding one of the most extraordinary interviews that ever took place on earth, he directs attention to a mightier phenomenon, viz. the honour and glory which was conferred upon the Saviour by the sensible tokens of the divine presence, — in the words of commendation that were borne to His character and office by Heaven itself. This wonderful, this unparallelled fact, the apostle declares that he and his brother disciples — James and John — all three heard distinctly with their ears, as they all three saw with their eyes the radiant robe of glory with which the person of Christ was invested; intimating by this declaration that there was as much certainty of the gospel, even in a human way, as could possibly be obtained of anything that is done in the world, since men cannot have a stronger assurance of anything than by the evidence of their senses, both their sight and their hearing. Accordingly, such was the very effect which this supernatural scene produced upon the minds of Peter and his brother disciples; for although, perhaps, they did not perceive all its import and its bearings till after the resurrection, we find them ever after appealing to the transfiguration as affording an incontestable evidence of Christ's divine majesty.[1] Peter adds, "We have also a more sure word of prophecy, whereunto ye do well that ye take heed;" and it is strangely maintained by Rationalist writers, that the apostle intends in these words to represent "the word of prophecy" as far more trustworthy than any transient, ambiguous sounds heard in the air. The very reverse is the case; for the apostle, in contemplating the irresistible proof of the divinity of the Saviour's mission which was afforded by the heavenly declaration, proceeds to state that thereby was supplied an additional confirmation of the truth of the Old Testament Scriptures, one of the prominent features of which was the chain of predictions contained in them respecting the Messiah and His kingdom. And now that the most important of these prophecies had received their fulfilment in the appearance, sufferings, and glorification of the Saviour, their certainty was confirmed; they were made, as it were, "more sure;" and their authority heightened in the minds of believers. In themselves, "the prophecies" could not be rendered "more sure;" they could receive no increase of certainty, being the words of Him of

[1] John i. 14; 2 Pet. i. 16, 17.

whom it is declared, "Hath He said it, and shall He not do it? Or hath He spoken, and shall He not make it good?" But subjectively, or as received by men, they were susceptible of higher degrees of assurance, in proportion as subsequent predictions threw light upon those which had been previously given, and especially as the events transpired to which they pointed.

THE ACTS OF THE APOSTLES follow the Gospels in the order of the New Testament books, as in the narrative of the recorded facts, although the composition and publication of the history preceded by a considerable period those of the fourth Gospel. External as well as internal evidence attests Luke's authorship. The dedication to Theophilus—the same person whose name appears in the introduction of the third Gospel—implies that the author meant to represent this new work as a continuation of the former historical record; while the similarity of the language as well as the style tends strongly to confirm this impression of its origin. And a lengthened chain of testimony proves[1] that the general voice of Christian antiquity ascribed it to

---

[1] Eusebius, *Eccl. Hist.* iii. 25, v. 1; Irenæus, *Advers. Hæres.* L. iii. c. 14, 15; Tertullian, *De jejunio*, c. 10; Clement, *Strom.* L. 5.

Luke. It was natural that one who felt so deep an interest in the *origines sacræ* of Christianity, and who had shown such patient and persevering diligence in tracing out the certainty and order of the minutest facts relating to the life and ministry of Jesus, should evince a corresponding desire to perform a similar service in recording the subsequent progress of the Saviour's cause; and enjoying, as we formerly showed that Luke did, access to the best and purest sources of information, there was no one in apostolic circles who was so well qualified by circumstances to chronicle the most interesting and memorable transactions which marked the first age of the church. With regard to the latter part of the book,—from ch. xvi. 10, where he begins to use the first person, and writes as a constant companion and fellow-traveller with Paul, —there is no doubt it is unreasonable to suppose the intervention of a new and different hand;[1] and as to the first portion of the history, his sojourn along with Paul's retinue in Jerusalem and Cesarea,[2] where he would mingle in the society of the Christian inhabitants most eminent for rank and intelligence, must have brought to his knowledge whatever facts are mentioned in this

---

[1] See Note E. [2] Acts xxi. 15, xxi. 8–10, xxvii. 1.

history which Paul himself could not communicate. The same reasons, then, that induced us to admit the credibility of Luke's Gospel, necessitate a similar reception to the Acts; and the general character of that history, as a record of supernatural facts, prepares us to anticipate a continuation of similar miracles in this evangelical sequel. The course of it is precisely what we should look for. In the close of the Gospel history, we find our Lord promising to His disciples that He would send the Holy Spirit to supply the want of His bodily presence; and we naturally expect that a book which is professedly a sequel of the evangelical history, will furnish some evidence of the fulfilment of that important promise. Accordingly, the first part of the Acts is occupied with a record of the descent of the Spirit, and of the mighty change which was consequently effected on the character and views of the disciples, who were thenceforth qualified at once, and in a degree which they could never have attained by ordinary means, for the functions and the exigencies of their apostolic mission. They were to be witnesses of Christ to the world — to bear a public testimony to Jews and Gentiles concerning His doctrines, His miracles, and His death. But at that time they were totally incapable of discharging such an office, and "they were to tarry in Jerusalem until they received the promise of the Father." Without entering on the reasons which rendered it expedient that this promise should be fulfilled in Jerusalem, the fact is, that on the day of Pentecost, when the disciples were assembled, this miraculous event took place, by the visible descent of the Spirit upon each of them; and the effect was, that "they were endued with power from on high." Knowledge is power; and the mere fact of the apostles being spiritually enlightened in the knowledge of the truth, made them "endued with power:" for from that moment we see them united in a holy confederacy that could not be broken, displaying a spirituality of views, a devotedness to truth, a sanctity of purpose, a unity of sentiment, which can be accounted for in no other way than by tracing it to the impulse and energy of the Spirit's teaching. From being totally in the dark as to the ultimate designs of their Master, how suddenly was a light from heaven shed on their ignorant and prejudiced minds! From being timid and wavering followers of Christ, how animated were they with a spirit of bold and resolute confidence, that carried them dauntless into the presence of kings and rulers! From being easily discouraged and prone to despondency, how were they, even amid perils or in prisons, lighted up with a perennial joy! From being selfish and narrow-minded Jews, who looked with proud, supercilious contempt on all other people, how were their bosoms filled with a spirit of expansive benevolence, that reached to the farthest limits of the world, and laboured for the salvation of all mankind!

But besides the enlightening influences of the Spirit, the disciples on this occasion received also extraordinary endowments, consisting in the gift of tongues and the power of working miracles. These were the seals of apostleship; and the disciples took every fitting opportunity of declaring that they derived those extraordinary powers from Christ.[1] They were vouchers of their high commission, credentials of their might, as well as of their ability to perform the extraordinary services they had to render in the proclamation and extension of the truth as it is in Jesus. The narrative is simple, natural, and, like the Gospel history, entirely free from the use of exaggerated terms, even in the recital of the most striking events or the most stupendous miracles. It is most interest-

[1] Acts iii. 6, iv. 10, etc.

ing and most valuable as a record of the organization of the Christian church, and of the principles on which that new and spiritual society was founded; for it enables us to see the first germs of what was afterwards developed in the several epistles which were addressed to the Christian churches of the primitive age. It is in one point of view an incomplete history; for while it opens with a general account of the apostolic proceedings, and carries on in the same style till that great crisis when the apostles became convinced that the distinction between Jew and Gentile was henceforth to cease, it begins from that point to narrow its course, and, instead of chronicling the movements of each of the apostles, confines itself to a record of the travels and labours of Paul. But in another point of view it is a complete history: for as Christ declared that, previous to His coming at the destruction of Jerusalem, "the gospel must first be preached among all nations;" so, by tracking the voyages of Paul, it shows us its introduction into all the most populous and influential parts of the Roman Empire, till it was at length established in Rome itself, the capital of the world. The objections brought against it are not such as seriously to affect the truth and authenticity of the history. The gift of tongues, that is, the power of speaking foreign languages in a manner intelligible to the natives of those countries, is certainly described as a reality;[1] and whether it was bestowed only for the pentecostal occasion, or was intended for continued use in propagating the gospel, it was a miracle that cannot be explained on natural principles. But it is not more incredible on that account, than the instantaneous bestowment of the faculty of speech on persons who had been born deaf and dumb. The historic difficulties in the speech of Stephen, as well as in the accounts of Paul's conversion, have been often removed; but we must refer the reader to the Biblical commentaries, within whose province an explanation of them properly falls. And a knowledge of the discourse of Peter in the upper room, of the counsel of Gamaliel to the Sanhedrim when that court was alone, of the letter of Claudius Lysias to Felix, and of the private conference between Agrippa and Felix about Paul, could have been obtained by Luke through the numerous Christians who were members of the supreme council in Jerusalem or officials of the provincial court at Cesarea. Having seen good reason for admitting the inspiration of the Gospel

[1] Ch. ii. 7-11.

by Luke, we feel constrained by a logical necessity to acknowledge the inspired character of this history also, which is the proper sequel of it; and we believe that the Spirit, who saw in the evangelist the qualifications of a competent recorder, "moved the holy man" to compile this history, which occupies an essential place in the canon of the New Testament.

THE AUTHORS OF THE VARIOUS EPISTLES contained in the New Testament are James, Peter, John, Jude, and Paul. When the authenticity as well as genuineness of their several compositions has been satisfactorily established, their inspiration and divine authority must be acknowledged as a matter of course, since the four first-named writers were amongst the select few to whom the Spirit was originally promised by the Saviour, and in whose possession the early church saw His supernatural gifts most liberally displayed. As the miraculous powers with which they were endowed showed that God was with them, and that they really were what they professed to be, His messengers to their fellow-men, the way was prepared for the welcome and respectful reception of whatever instruction they might deem it their duty to administer to the church. Accordingly, we find them claiming a submissive deference to the exhortation they gave, on account of its being invested with divine authority. Thus, Peter said to the Christians whom he addressed: "This second epistle, beloved, I now write to you, that ye may be mindful of the words which were spoken before by the holy prophets, and of the commandments of us the apostles of our Lord and Saviour." John, writing with a similar view, asserts: "We are of God: he that knoweth God, heareth us; he that is not of God, heareth not us. Hereby know we the Spirit of truth and the spirit of error." And the same apostle, at the commencement of his apocalyptic visions, says: "I was in the Spirit on the Lord's day, and heard behind me a great voice, as of a trumpet, saying, I am Alpha and Omega, the first and last: what thou seest, write in a book, and send it unto the seven churches which are in Asia." For men to express themselves in this manner, who were conscious of being under the direct and unerring guidance of God, was natural; and known as they universally were to have been appointed apostles of Christ, the certified appearance of their name and official designation in the inscription of any epistle addressed to the churches being considered a guarantee for its inspiration, ensured its reception into the sacred canon. Paul is the writer of the greater number of the epistles; and as he was not associated with the eleven when they were appointed to the apostleship, nor did he enjoy the benefits of the Saviour's earthly ministry, it is necessary to remark, that his appointment to the apostolic office emanated from as high authority, and was established by as indubitable evidence, as any of the others. He had all the signs of an apostle: for he had seen Christ Jesus; was endowed with the gift of tongues and the power of working miracles, and had received a commission directly from the Head of the church, with all the qualifications requisite for discharging the duties of the ministry among the Gentiles. At the time of his remarkable conversion, the Lord said to Ananias, who was dubious about the fact: "Go thy way: for he is a chosen vessel unto me, to bear my name before the Gentiles, and kings, and the children of Israel."[1] And no great time elapsed ere he was fully qualified for this mission. So far as preparation for the apostolic work was concerned, he had received neither encouragement nor aid from any of the earlier disciples. But though he had

[1] Acts ix. 15.

acquired Christian instruction in a manner very different from his brethren, the Divine Agent who imparted spiritual life and light to him was the same. What he wanted in opportunities of progressive training by human teaching, had been supplied by immediate revelation from Christ; and when, after a retirement of three years for Scripture study and communion with God, he issued from his Arabian solitude to enter upon his appointed mission, he was as fully equipped in a knowledge of spiritual things, and in ability to teach the saving truths of the gospel, as any of his brethren. He uniformly asserts that his religious knowledge was miraculously furnished: "I certify you, brethren, that the gospel which was preached of me is not of men. For I neither received it of man, neither was I taught it, but by the revelation of Jesus Christ."[1] "If ye have heard of the dispensation of the grace of God which is given to me to you-ward: how that by revelation He made known to me the mystery (as I wrote afore in few words)."[2] "For I delivered unto you first of all that which I also received, how that Christ died for our sins according to the Scriptures; and that He was buried, and that He rose again the third day ac-

[1] Gal. i. 11, 12-20.   [2] Eph. iii. 2, 3.

cording to the Scriptures."[1] While he thus traces all his knowledge of the nature and provisions of the gospel directly to divine instruction, he is equally explicit in placing his claims to teach it on the ground of his being invested with the apostolic commission: "Paul, a servant of Jesus Christ, called to be an apostle, separated unto the gospel of God."[2] "Paul, called to be an apostle through the will of God."[3] "We have received grace and apostleship—to all that be in Rome."[4] And towards the close of the epistle he asserts his divine right to admonish the Roman Christians: "I have written the more boldly unto you in some sort, as putting you in mind, because of the grace that is given of God, that I should be the minister of Jesus Christ to the Gentiles, ministering the gospel of God."[5] "My speech and my preaching was not with enticing words of man's wisdom; that your faith should not stand in the wisdom of men, but in the power of God."[6] "God hath revealed them unto us by His Spirit."[7] "Which things we speak, not in words which man's wisdom teacheth, but which the Holy Ghost teacheth."[8]

[1] 1 Cor. xv. 3, 4. [2] Rom. i. 1. [3] 1 Cor. i. 1.
[4] Rom. i. 5. [5] Rom. xv. 15. [6] 1 Cor. ii. 4.
[7] 1 Cor. ii. 10. [8] 1 Cor. ii. 15.

"But we have the mind of Christ."[1] "Let a man so account of us as ministers of Christ, and stewards of the mysteries of God."[2] "I received of the Lord that which also I delivered unto you."[3] "God hath set some in the church, first, apostles."[4] "Now then we are ambassadors for Christ, as though God did beseech you by us: we pray you in Christ's stead, be ye reconciled unto God."[5] "I write these things being absent, lest being present, I should use sharpness, according to the power which the Lord hath given me for edification."[6] "Paul, an apostle, not of men, neither by man, but by Jesus Christ, and God the Father, who raised Him from the dead."[7] "Paul, an apostle of Jesus Christ by the will of God."[8] Thus, in writing to the churches, he begins by asserting his apostolic office as conferring upon him a right to give them pastoral counsels and instruction; and while in the smaller and purely practical epistles, or in those addressed to churches where the course of things was smooth and tranquil, he was content to style himself "a servant of Jesus Christ," in the other epistles, which are dedicated,

---

[1] 1 Cor. ii. 16. [2] 1 Cor. iv. 1. [3] 1 Cor. xi. 23.
[4] 1 Cor. xii. 28. [5] 2 Cor. v. 20. [6] 2 Cor. xiii. 10.
[7] Gal. i. 1. [8] Eph. i. 1.

like those to the Romans and Ephesians, to an exposition of the peculiar doctrines of Christianity, or addressed, as that of the Corinthians was, to a church torn by dissension and disorder, he assumed the high tone of "an apostle,"—one who had received a special commission to speak in the name and announce the will of his divine Master,—whose appointment to the apostleship was not owing to his having passed through a course of educational training for his high office, as the prophets and other apostles did for theirs,—nor to his having been promoted to it by the collective suffrages of the Christian brethren,—but who had been called to it by the immediate will of God. And that will was made known not merely by his miraculous conversion, which was a matter of universal notoriety, but by the rare and exalted endowments of which he was possessed, and which afforded indisputable evidence that he had received the afflatus of divine inspiration. In his Epistle to the Colossians, where he also asserts his claim to be "an apostle," he designed further to show, that by virtue of his divine appointment he was invested with direct authority, not only to teach what ought to be believed in the way of doctrine and done in the way of duty, but what ought to be received and submitted to as the form and discipline of the church; that, in fact, he was a minister of Christ, armed with full power to exercise the keys of the kingdom of heaven, by virtue of that part of the promise to the apostles: "Whatsoever ye shall bind on earth, shall be bound in heaven; and whatsoever ye loose on earth, shall be loosed in heaven."[1]

In the Epistle to the Thessalonians, the first in order of time of the Pauline epistles, and in which the writer pours out his feelings in all the fulness of pastoral earnestness and love, Paul declares that he "thanks God without ceasing," not in selfish pride that his apostleship had been universally owned and honoured in that church, but for a higher and purer reason: "Because, when they received the word of God which they heard of him, they received it not as the word of man, but (as it is in truth) the word of God."[2] This is a statement of great significance as to the divine origin and authority of the gospel. Such high qualities as Paul had displayed were naturally calculated to win for their possessor a high name and ascendency over the Thessalonian people; and there can be no doubt that such a concentration of excellences as was

[1] See also 2 Cor. xiii. 10.   [2] 1 Thess. ii. 13.

exhibited in his conduct, had in the first instance prepossessed the minds of the Thessalonians in favour of the doctrines which he taught. What came from so good a man, they were prepared to receive with a favourable ear; what he urged upon them with disinterested earnestness, they were disposed to regard, on his declarations, as a discovery of great importance and value. But gratified as he might have been with this proof of their esteem and confidence, of what avail would it have been to them, if they had assigned to Paul the palm of superiority to all the philosophers, and if they had preferred his system of morals to all the rules which were so eloquently expounded in the schools of Greece? They would in that case have received it only as the word of a man, who was perhaps the wisest and holiest of men they had ever seen, but still as no more than the word of a man; and therefore Paul thanked God without ceasing, " that when they received the word which they had heard of him, they received it not as the word of man, but (as it is in truth) the word of God." This statement is brief, but it is very significant; and it intimates that the occasion of the apostle's thankfulness was on account not only of the fact, but the manner, of their receiving the gospel. It would have been but a slender ground of congratulation and joy, that the Thessalonians had entertained it on the mere *ipse dixit* of a stranger, however pious, intelligent, and disinterested he might have seemed to be. Their adherence to it would have been nothing more than simple and childish credulity, based on no solid or rational foundation, and resting only on the testimony of a single individual, irrespective of the intrinsic claims of the gospel; they would have been little able to satisfy their own minds, or to give to others a reason of the faith that was in them. The Thessalonians acted in a more enlightened and praiseworthy manner: they did not take the gospel simply on trust, sometimes doubting and disputing it, or receiving it only with a human faith, upon grounds of reason as the dictates of philosophy, or on account of the persuasive eloquence and great learning of the preacher; but they examined its claims. For the word "received,"[1] in the former part of the verse, signifies to entertain, to take into consideration, to put upon trial; and so, being, after earnest, dispassionate, and full inquiry into the nature of the gospel, convinced that it was "no cunningly devised fable," but all true and of divine

[1] παραλαβόντες.

origin, they "received it not as the word of man, but (as it is in truth) the word of God,"—with a divine faith, a ready subjection of their minds to its supreme authority, and with devout, reverend attention to it as a communication made directly from Heaven.

If the pious and benevolent heart of the apostle was filled with gratitude and delight by the enlightened and unanimous reception the church of the Thessalonians gave to the gospel as a divine message, we may be sure that he would be proportionally grieved and pained by its rejection or corruption in other quarters; and accordingly, we are not surprised at the strong terms of reproof he employed in writing to the church of the Galatians, which had embraced and openly supported perversions of the truth which entirely altered or destroyed its nature: " I marvel that ye are so soon removed from him that called you unto the grace of Christ into another gospel. But though we, or an angel from heaven, preach any other gospel unto you than that which we have preached unto you, let him be accursed."[1] Now this strong language does not imply the possibility of an angel proclaiming any new scheme of salvation,

[1] Gal. i. 8.

any more than of Paul's contradicting the doctrine he had formerly taught. The apostle resorts to such extreme suppositions only to exhibit in the most emphatic manner the immutable character of the truth which had been delivered to the church; truth which, coming from God, could not be altered by any authority, human or angelic, without exposing the presumptuous innovator to the curse denounced against those who add to, or take from, the divine revelations. Would the apostle have ventured to indulge in such vehement expressions of condemnation, if he had taught only his own private sentiments? Would a man of such profound humility and piety as Paul, who never thought of his own things, but uniformly of those of Christ Jesus, have allowed himself to be transported by such energy of feeling, as to pronounce even an angel accursed who should make the smallest change on the gospel which he preached, had he not been convinced, on the strongest and most irresistible evidence, that it was not the word of man, but the word of God? Would he have assumed so solemn a tone of remonstrance with the Galatians for their rejection of him who had "called them unto the grace of Christ for another gospel," if he had sustained no higher character than that of an ordinary human teacher of religion? He was "an ambassador of God," who had come "beseeching them in Christ's stead to be reconciled to God,"[1]—a minister plenipotentiary, duly accredited by the extraordinary gifts of the Spirit; and in that capacity he had to be true and faithful to the Prince who sent him: he was not at liberty to deviate from his instructions, or to shape them according to the fashion which his own taste or the fancy of his hearers might suggest; he was bound by the authority he owned, and the apostolic character he bore, to deliver the message entrusted to him, without adulterating it with any impure mixture, or enervating it by any human addition. In this respect, his teaching possessed a co-ordinate authority with that of Christ, as the Saviour had said, "He that receiveth *you*, receiveth *me*; and he that receiveth me, receiveth Him that sent me."[2] "He that heareth you, heareth me; and he that despiseth you, despiseth me; and he that despiseth me, despiseth Him that sent me."[3] Paul himself also declared to the Corinthians, respecting the things peculiar to Christianity, that "God had revealed them unto us (the apostles) by His Spirit. We have received the Spirit which is of God, that

[1] 2 Cor. v. 20.   [2] Matt. x. 40.   [3] Luke x. 16.

we might know the things which are freely given to us of God; which things we speak in the words which the Holy Ghost teacheth. We have the mind of Christ."[1] "We are to some a savour of life unto life, and to others a savour of death unto death." In these passages the apostle makes for himself and his associates a direct claim to divine inspiration. And in the Epistle to the Thessalonians, he says regarding those who contemptuously rejected the apostolic teaching: "He that despiseth, despiseth not man, but God, who hath also given unto us His Holy Spirit."[2] If despising the apostles' doctrine was tantamount to despising God, there could not be a stronger proof that their doctrine was divine. To show that his oral discourses were exactly in the same strain with his writings, he said to the Corinthians: "Moreover, brethren, I declare (by letter) the gospel which I preached unto you (by word of mouth), which *also ye received*, and wherein ye stand; by which also ye are saved, if ye keep in memory what I preached unto you."[3] "Hold fast the traditions which ye have been taught, whether by word or our epistle."[4] In these two passages the apostle puts his preach-

---

[1] 1 Cor. ii. 9–16.
[2] 1 Thess. iv. 8.
[3] 1 Cor. xv. 1, 2.
[4] 2 Thess. ii. 15.

ing and his writing on the same level; his epistles recapitulated the sentiments his discourses had expressed. What a source of unspeakable comfort it is, that we have still the guidance of this inspired apostle of Christ! We have not, indeed, the benefit of his living presence; but we have his instructions recorded in his epistles to the churches. There are some who affect to disparage the epistles of Paul,—to represent them as written by a pious and excellent, but still a frail and fallible man,— and who insist on assigning them a rank amongst the books of holy writ greatly inferior to that of the Gospels. Once adopt this style of sentiment; once withhold from Paul the character of inspiration; once regard him merely as an ordinary minister of the church, who had to ascertain the mind of the Spirit by the same natural means of study and research as those in the present day, and who, in imparting religious instruction, indulged in that rabbinical mode of allegorizing comment which was prevalent in later times; and we shall become unsettled in our views of the most important articles of Christian truth. Some parts will be rejected as mystical, others treated as abstract or doubtful speculations; and all will be brought to the tribunal of reason, as the sovereign umpire in all that we are to believe and do.¹ But let us carry along with us the lively conviction that Paul enjoyed the direct aid, the extraordinary gifts, of the Spirit, to preserve him from error and to guide him into all truth; and then we shall feel that, in placing ourselves at the feet of Paul, we are sitting under one who was "an apostle by the will of God." All that is contained in the epistles of Paul will come to us invested with equal authority, and entitled to equal submission, as what fell from the lips of the Lord Himself; and we shall be persuaded that, in believing him, our faith rests on a sure foundation, being built "not on the wisdom of man, but on the word of God."

Such is the light in which we are to regard the inspired authority of Paul; and accordingly his epistles are regarded by the vast majority of Christians not only as a most precious and important part of the Bible, but as the direct development and full extension of Christian doctrine. The epistles are, as it were, the cope-stone of revelation, so far as it makes known the will of God for our duty and salvation. Christ Himself, during His personal ministry, laid down the fundamental principles; but He employed Paul and the other

¹ See Note F.

apostles to show their application in the system of Christian truth, such as the doctrines of the death and resurrection of Christ. The fact of His death was attested, but not the end for which He died; and His resurrection was recorded in the Gospels, but it did not imply by logical necessity the resurrection of any one else; and therefore it was reserved for Paul to show that Christ died to take away the sins of the world, and that Christ was become "the first-fruits of them that slept;" that as surely as the first-fruits are a proof of the harvest, so is the resurrection of Christ a proof of that of all believers, who are the members of His spiritual body. Besides, the apostles had new truths to communicate; for the Saviour declared that He had many things to say to the disciples, but they could not bear these yet. These would be imparted by the Spirit of truth when the proper time for their promulgation had come, such as the overthrow of the Jewish polity, and the union of all men in Christ Jesus. Then there was the development of the peculiar doctrines of Christianity,—such as the atonement, justification by faith, the fatherhood of God, the intercession and the sympathy of Christ, a future state, judgment by Christ. Thus it appears that the epistles hold an important place in the sacred volume. As containing truths, the revelation of which could not be made known till the Saviour was "glorified," they are indispensable; they throw a flood of light on many of the sayings and doings of Christ; and as the authors of them wrote under inspiration, their epistles are entitled to be received with the same faith and submissiveness that are shown to the earlier books of Scripture.

It has been alleged, however, that this conclusion is not applicable universally to the epistles of Paul, and that there are passages in which he seems to doubt the fact of his own inspiration, or to disclaim all title to the possession of the heavenly power. So far is this allegation from being true, that the very passages which are adduced in support of it, furnish in reality proof to the contrary. Paul says, in reference to a subject of great delicacy, "I speak this by permission, and not of commandment;"[1] and again, "I have no commandment of the Lord, yet I give my judgment (in that particular case) as one that hath obtained mercy of the Lord to be faithful."[2] The matter to which the apostle refers formed no part of religious principle or practice; it pertained

[1] 1 Cor. vii. 6.   [2] Ver. 25.

neither to Christian doctrine nor Christian duty: it was a merely prudential recommendation, arising out of the peculiarly difficult position of the early church; and as the opinion of the apostle had been requested, he gave his friendly counsel as to the best course to be pursued. At the same time, he evinced a proper solicitude that his opinion should be viewed in its true light,—only as a friendly advice, not as an oracular response given with apostolic authority; and by the insertion of this caution, he left the inquirers at liberty to act in the circumstances as they felt disposed. But the statement of the apostle, that in this special affair he acted "by permission, and not by commandment," evidently implies that in other matters, viz. those of a purely Christian character, he *did* speak and write by commandment. An exception is acknowledged to prove the general rule. And accordingly, in the same chapter which contains the passages above referred to, when from a prudential counsel he proceeds to expound the principle of Christian law, the words, "I command, yet not I, but the Lord," put forth a claim, as strong as language can express it, to the character of one who, as minister or apostle of Christ, was employed to reveal His will to the church.

From a conjunct view of the various topics discussed in the preceding pages, and from a comparison of all the points embraced in the promise of divine aid to the apostles, with the bestowment of the extraordinary gifts of the Spirit which their subsequent history attests, we are warranted to draw various important conclusions, the principal of which, reserving others to be noticed in a subsequent lecture, are the following:—

1. That the apostles were completely enlightened in the knowledge of all the doctrines, duties, and promises of the Christian faith. No doubt or obscurity clouded their views of the truth as it is in Jesus after the day of Pentecost. Once had they been in darkness, thenceforth they were light in the Lord; and though that light had been progressive, they had, as apostles, learned the way of God perfectly.

2. Deduction is, that being under the infallible guidance of the Spirit of truth, they were qualified to be unerring instructors of the world in all that sinners are required to believe concerning God, as well as in all the duties required of men. Whether called to address the church in oral discourses, or to write for the Christian instruction of mankind in all future ages, they were preserved by the in-

fluence and direction of the Holy Ghost from error or misapprehension on the one hand, and from omission or defect on the other. That they are entitled to the most implicit credit in all their expositions of Christianity, must be inferred from that part of our Lord's promise which gave them a pledge that they "should be guided into all (the) truth;" and as "the Spirit of truth was to abide with them for ever," what stronger evidence could be furnished that they were infallible guides in the inculcation of religious sentiments and duties? To suppose that they could err in their public teaching, would imply, either that they had been imperfectly acquainted with the nature of the gospel, or that they had forgotten the views of it they had formerly obtained. But either supposition is plainly precluded by the promise of divine guidance and aid which was to be commensurate with the lives of all of them.

3. Observation is, that the admission of their inspiration is essential to their credibility as historians, or even honest, truthful men. They claim to be inspired; they assure us in every varied form of expression, that the promise was fulfilled in their experience, that they spoke by inspiration. There is therefore no medium; we must admit

that they were inspired, or conclude that they were impostors. But on this latter hypothesis, it is impossible to account for the phenomena that mark the history of the apostles, particularly the complete and continued unanimity of their *doctrinal* teaching, which is clearly traceable to the controlling influence of the Spirit of truth. How soon did a variety of opposing sects spring up in the primitive church, many of the early converts retaining an irrepressible attachment to the law of Moses, and ranging themselves under the leadership of the Judaizing teachers, who endeavoured to blend the institutions of the Jewish with the ordinances of the Christian church, or, through personal predilections for particular preachers, as the Corinthians, dividing into rival partisans of Paul and Apollos! How soon did the confederate reformers in the sixteenth century come into collision upon points of doctrine and discipline that separated Luther from Calvin and Zuingle! How soon did religious discord break out between Whitfield and Wesley, and the great religious revival of the last century was marred in its progress by the doctrinal differences of those eminent men! But no discrepancy of doctrinal sentiment ever disturbed the college of the apostles; and considering the infirmities, the passions, and the prejudices of men, in connection with the many discordant elements which existed in the primitive church,. it is evident that the unbroken reign of doctrinal harmony amongst the first teachers of Christianity was due to the enlightening and guiding influence of the Spirit of truth. Nor is this all. There was not only a perfect unanimity amongst the apostles themselves in their doctrinal teaching, but there is a similar unity of doctrine between them and the prophets of the Old Testament with reference to Christ. Paul describes the church as "built upon the foundation of the apostles and prophets, Jesus Christ Himself being the chief corner-stone."[1] The apostles are here put upon an equality in official dignity with the prophets; and both were guided by the influences of the same Spirit, who through their agency made the doctrine of the ancient church harmonize with the new. If Isaiah foretold of one who should be wounded for our transgressions and bruised for our iniquities; if David foretold of one who should not be left in the grave, nor see corruption, the apostles travelled through all the world, testifying that in Jesus these predictions were verified, He having borne

[1] Eph. ii. 20.

our sins in His own body, having "died the just for the unjust," having burst the fetters of death, for it was not possible He could be holden of it, and being set down at the right hand of God, till all enemies should be put under His feet. Thus John, Paul, and Peter confirmed the testimony of David, Isaiah, and Daniel; and Jesus is shown to be the chief corner-stone, in whose person and character the Scriptures of the Old and New Testament are united in one harmonious structure of truth. This wonderful harmony of doctrine could never have been attained, had not the same Divine Spirit that inspired the prophets of the Jewish also given its inspiration to the apostles of the Christian church.

It is objected that the apostles make often very loose and far-fetched applications of the ancient prophecies to features and events in the life of Christ. And it must be admitted that they do apply many passages out of the Psalms and other books of the Old Testament, which, if we had not been assured on their high authority, we should have hardly imagined to have any reference to Him. Nor is it probable that they enumerated all the predictions of the Messiah which are to be found in the prophetic writings, but only a very small part of them, while they often assure us that all the sacred writings principally centre in Him. As an instance of a loose accommodation of prophecy, reference is made to a passage in Isaiah: "The land of Zebulun and Nephthalim, by the way of the sea, beyond Jordan, Galilee of the Gentiles; the people which sat in darkness saw a great light, and to them which sat in the region and shadow of death light is sprung up."[1] The passage had an immediate reference to the temporal prosperity of the cities in the northern part of Judea, and held out to them the prospect of deliverance from the galling yoke of Syrian bondage, when the return of more happy and prosperous times would, after their protracted exile, be no less exhilarating and joyous than the cheering beams of the sun after a dark and stormy night. But as many actions and incidents in the lives of eminent persons under the Mosaic economy are held forth as types of Christ, and as we are led by apostolic example to consider many prophecies of the Old Testament, which both in the intention of the speaker as well as in the sense of the hearers had a reference to Jewish affairs, as receiving their full accomplishment in the events

[1] Isa. ix. 1, compared with Matt. iv. 12-16.

of the gospel; so the evangelist Matthew instructs us to regard this prophecy, which in the first instance pointed only to the emancipation of Zebulun and Naphtali from the tyranny and oppression of Benhadad and his successors, as then only completely fulfilled, when Jesus, the great spiritual deliverer of His people, appeared on their territory as the Sun of Righteousness, dispelling by His glorious beams a worse than Egyptian darkness. He had fixed His headquarters at Capernaum, which, being the metropolis of Galilee, and situated in the immediate vicinity of the Lake of Tiberias, was peculiarly suited to His design of preaching in the surrounding districts the gospel of the kingdom. While, in selecting Capernaum as His headquarters, our Lord followed the dictates of His own wisdom, He was fulfilling at the same time the remarkable prediction of Isaiah, the full accomplishment of which was realized by His ministry who was "the light of the world." Another instance of a similar application of ancient prophecy is furnished by the words: "When Israel was a child, then I loved him, and called my son out of Egypt."[1] Nothing is more evident than that this passage is historical, referring to an

[1] Hos. xi. 1.

early period in the past condition of the Hebrew nation, and that it was not the intention of the prophet to give it a prospective reference to any future event. But Israel was a type of Christ; and for the sake of Him who was to be the most eminent seed of Israel, the nation was called "my son," and the deliverance from Egypt was effected. The exodus in the one dispensation was typical of the safe restoration in the other; and hence the words of Hosea were rightly viewed by Matthew as receiving their full accomplishment in the safe return of the infant Jesus to the land of Judea. A different mode of applying an Old Testament prophecy occurs in reference to the passage in 2 Sam. vii. 11-17: "I will set up thy seed after thee, which shall proceed out of thy bowels, and I will establish his kingdom. He shall build an house for my name, and I will establish the throne of his kingdom for ever. I will be his father, and he shall be my son." This is the oath which God by His holiness sware to David, the covenant which He made with him respecting the perpetuity of his royal seed and kingdom.[1] This promise had a twofold aspect: the one pointing to David's fleshly seed and temporal kingdom, the other to the Mes-

[1] Ps. lxxxix. 3, 4, 35, 36.

siah and the kingdom of God. In respect to the former it was conditional, for it contains a threatening against such of his royal descendants as should commit iniquity.[1] The spiritual and eternal part of the promise respected the Messiah only, who was to come of the seed of David according to the flesh, but who was to be raised from the dead to sit for ever on His heavenly throne. In respect to Him it was absolute, and had its full accomplishment. That David himself *understood* its ulterior application to the Messiah, may *be inferred* from his words;[2] but it is declared certain by the Apostle Peter, who said, "The patriarch David, being a prophet, and *knowing* that God would raise up Christ to sit upon his throne."[3] And the author of the Epistle to the Hebrews quotes the words of God to David: "I will be his father, and he will be my son."[4] Doubtless the prophecy as well as the promise had a primary and subordinate reference to Solomon. But it was germinant, and had its full accomplishment in Christ. A third way of applying Old Testament prophecies followed in the New may be exemplified by Matt. ii. 23: "He came and dwelt in a city called

[1] 2 Chron. vii. 7, 18. [2] 2 Sam. xxiii. 5.
[3] Acts ii. 29, 30. [4] Heb. i. 5.

Nazareth, that it might be fulfilled which was spoken by the prophets, He shall be called a Nazarene." The evangelist uses the plural number, " the prophets,"—not any particular prophet. The general testimony of ancient prophecy was that the Messiah should be despised and rejected of men. The opprobrium which was attached to His chosen place of residence was extended to Him, the inhabitant; for a Nazarene was a proverb, a byword. The predictions were thus fulfilled. And the evangelist, in stating the fact, contents himself with a summary of their common import. He gives not the words of any prophet, but the general sense of all of them.

It is further alleged, that in making quotations from the books of the prophets, the writers of the New Testament implicitly follow the Septuagint, which is often obscure, erroneous, and widely divergent from the Hebrew in the prophetic books generally, and in Isaiah especially. For instance, the prophetic words, "Mine ears hast Thou opened,"[1] are rendered in the Septuagint, as quoted in the New Testament, " A body hast Thou prepared for me."[2] In other cases, the prophets' words are rendered correctly, though not literally, as Isaiah

[1] Ps. xl. 6.   [2] Heb. x. 5.

says of Christ, "Surely He hath borne our griefs and carried our sorrows,"[1] which are quoted from the Septuagint thus: "He hath taken our infirmities and carried our diseases."[2] And the words of the same prophet, "He was brought as a lamb to the slaughter, and as a sheep before her shearers is dumb, so He openeth not His mouth. He was taken from prison and from judgment; and who shall declare His generation?"[3] are rendered from the Septuagint, "As a sheep He is led to the slaughter; and dumb as a lamb before his shearer, so openeth He not His mouth. In His abasement the judgment (exercise of justice) was taken from Him; but who shall narrate His generation? for His life is taken from the earth."[4] The Septuagint was the translation in common use in the apostolic age, and therefore most familiar to the Jews of that time; so that it was as natural for the apostles to avail themselves of that version as it is for us to make use of our authorized version, which is no more inspired than that of the LXX., and susceptible, it is now admitted, as well as the Greek translation, of emendation and improvement in rendering the sense of the original. But it is

---

[1] Isa. liii. 4.   [2] Matt. viii. 17.
[3] Isa. liii. 7, 8.   [4] Acts. viii. 30–33.

not a correct statement to make, that all the quotations from the Old Testament contained in the New are made from the Septuagint. It has been ascertained by accurate examination, that there are eighty-eight verbal quotations in the New Testament from the Septuagint; sixty from other quotations, with variations; thirty-seven where the sense only is given, but not the words; sixteen differing from it, and approximating more nearly to the Hebrew original; and twenty-four which, differing from the present Hebrew text and the Septuagint, have yet been proved by the researches of learned men to be supported by the testimony of the oldest versions and manuscripts, but in which the sacred penmen have given not a quotation, but a paraphrase, to render the sense of the Old Testament more plain and obvious. Well-directed and extensive researches on this point tend only the more clearly and strongly to establish the spiritual intelligence of the writers of the New Testament; and thereby to satisfy every humble and sincere Christian, that he has a solid foundation on which to rest, when he implicitly accepts the New Testament interpretations of the Old. Since the process of revelation culminated in the ministry of Christ, and the appointment of His apostles to continue His ministry by acting as the divinely qualified instructors of the church in all matters pertaining to faith and duty, we must look to them not only as teachers of new and unknown truths, but as expositors of the Old Testament, from whose interpretations there is no appeal. Carrying the seal of their commission in the possession of the extraordinary gifts of the Spirit, the apostles, when acting in their official capacity, must be considered as expressing "the mind of Christ,"—inspired men, who, both in applying the words of ancient prophecy and exhibiting the spiritual aspect of facts in the life of Christ, communicated the word of God; and therefore it is the duty of all earnest followers of the Saviour to study their writings, to learn what "the Spirit saith unto the churches."

LECTURE IV.

Collateral Proofs of the Inspiration of the Scriptures. 1. External : Unity, Unsystematic Arrangement, Universal Application, Impartiality, and Reserve of the Scriptures on Matters not profitable. 2. Internal : True Idea of God given only in the Scriptures—Sublime Descriptions of the Divine Character—Anthropomorphisms—Prelusive Manifestations of God—Repentance ascribed to God—Cruelty ascribed to God—Mediation of Christ—Moral Character of Christ—Idea of Sin and Holiness—Proofs of the Inspired Character of the Sacred Books.

I. THE UNITY OF SCRIPTURE.—The Jewish Scriptures, or the Old Testament, is the most marvellous monument of ancient literature in the world : for that sacred book contains, in its simple and primitive annals, an account of the origin of society, government, and the arts; is enriched with many poetical effusions, which no efforts of uninspired genius have ever surpassed; abounds with traits of men and manners different altogether from anything observable in our western hemisphere; and, in short, comprehends a treasure of the most varied and valuable matter, far greater than can be found anywhere else in the same compass. But although the Scriptures do contain these and many other things of equal or superior interest, it is not on this account it is to be regarded as the best and most precious book in the world. Its grand peculiarity and distinguishing excellence is, that it is addressed to mankind as fallen creatures, to discover to them their state of sin and misery, and at the same time to point out the only efficient remedy for that condition. All the other matter it contains is subordinate to this main design,— has been introduced merely from being connected in some way or other with its progress and extension in the world, or being calculated to illustrate and enforce its provisions. The unity of its design is one of the most prominent features of the book; and this unity is all the more remarkable, considering the detached manner of its composition, the lengthened period during which it was in progress, and the many authors enlisted in its preparation. Individually they made their contributions, whether in plain history or animated song, whether in visioned pictures of a glorious future, or in didactic discourses about faith and duty,—each performing his part without foreseeing the great result he was helping to accomplish, or comprehending the gracious scheme which he was instrumental in advancing; and yet how marvellous, and unprecedented in the history of human workmanship, the composite structure they severally assisted in rearing, appears in its finished state, complete in every part, redundant or defective in none. In other words, the Scriptures, as we possess the sacred volume, was not the product of one writer in a single age: it consists of a large collection of miscellaneous books or tracts, written by forty different authors, who, so far from being of a priestly profession, or even moving in the same social circle, belonged to the most opposite extremes of society; and so far from having concerted one common plan of action, were separated, some of them, from one another by the distance of many centuries: kings and priests, shepherds and herdsmen, warriors and fishermen, a tentmaker, a physican; persons in high life and a humble condition,—enjoying various advantages of education, bred under different forms of government, possessing each his peculiar cast of mind, taste, and natural temper, who wrote amid great diversity of circumstances, of prosperity and adversity, of freedom and captivity, and of the outer influences which would affect intellectual exertion in the treatment of a subject, or the sentiments and views they might entertain and express;

and yet there runs through the whole book, from beginning to end, one grand principle or leading design—the development of a scheme of grace for the recovery and salvation of men. Thus were the several books of the Scriptures composed by men differing from one another in point of time, place, talents, learning, and many other advantages and outward circumstances of social position. And is it possible that those forty authors could have produced a book so completely consistent with all the truth which reason teaches concerning the being and perfections of God, and so powerfully commending itself to the understandings, the consciences, and the hearts of the wise and good in all ages ? The thing is incredible—an impossible achievement. The same uninspired author is not always consistent with himself. Men of probity and erudition, who have lived in distant periods and places, have often differed most materially on the same subject, nay, flatly contradicted and opposed each other; and some have even unconsciously contradicted their former sentiments. But here is a book, the latest penman of which lived fifteen hundred years after the first,—a book composed on a great variety of occasions, by persons differing exceedingly in natural abilities, in education, in dispositions, and indulging from taste and habit in the utmost diversity of style; persons trained under different influences, and owing to their separation both in place and time, having no means nor opportunity of acting in concert. And yet this book which they wrote is perfectly consistent with natural theology and with itself; giving the same views of God, of Christ, of salvation,—of man in his primitive, fallen, restored, and glorified state, —the same view of the things of time and eternity. Its universal harmony, its unbroken consistency, is one of the wonders of the world. And how is so singular a phenomenon to be accounted for? Only on this principle, that the penmen of this book were under the influence and guidance of the unerring Spirit.

II. THE UNSYSTEMATIC ARRANGEMENT OF THE SCRIPTURES.—The Bible is not a large book; it is very small compared with many other books, as well as with the great number, variety, and importance of the matter it contains. But had it been arranged in the most methodical manner, and been one connected chain of ratiocination from beginning to end, what would have followed? The whole must have been read, and closely studied, before the reader could have obtained any just and comprehensive knowledge of it as a whole, or of many of its parts, and derived much spiritual benefit to his soul. The premises and their soundness, the consecutive prosecution of the reasoning, the connection and bearings of all the parts, must have been perceived and assented to before any spiritual benefit could have been obtained. But where, in this case, is the Christian in many hundreds or thousands, to whom the Bible could have been of any use? Vast multitudes have not sufficient time thus to peruse the Bible, and far more have not the requisite ability to comprehend its plan, to understand its reasoning, and to feel the force of its demonstrative arguments. Had the Bible been written in this artistic form, it is easy to perceive that numbers of the saints now in heaven, and numbers on the way to its beatific mansions, were and are so deficient in mental capacity, in learning, and in the habit of study, that they never could have derived any real and permanent advantage from its perusal. In that case, like many books of human composition, written by men pre-eminent for talents and erudition, it would have been almost useless to the great majority of mankind, and, like those able and learned tomes, might have been confined to the libraries of the studious recluse, or appreciated only by people of education and intelligence. But in the desultory form imparted to it, the Bible is the book that is suited to all classes of men—to the king and to the subject, to the learned and to the unlearned, to the old and to the young. Here is enough to employ the talents of the most accomplished and acute; while the great truths, most necessary to be known, are revealed in so plain and familiar a manner, that the ignorant, the weak, even young children, may learn and derive advantage from the knowledge of them. There is strong meat for those that are of full age, and milk for babes.

Every part of the Bible, it is true, is not destitute of methodical arrangement; for the books of Job and Ecclesiastes, as well as the Epistles to the Romans and the Hebrews, are remarkable specimens of regular, continuous, and even elaborate composition. But the sacred volume, viewed in its general aspect, is not a book of artistic reasoning or of abstract doctrines, but a record of facts, a collection of maxims, illustrative of the divine procedure towards man. The love of God is exhibited in the marvellous fact that He gave His Son to be the propitiation for the sins of mankind;

the love of the Son in the fact that He humbled Himself, and became obedient unto death, even the death of the cross; the doctrine of divine providence in the narrative of the divine government of Israel; and the necessity, the pleasures, and advantages of piety, in the examples, songs, and prayers of ancient worthies of the church. These things are scattered, like Orient pearls at random strung, over the whole extent of the sacred volume; they are placed without order or any artificial arrangement—here a little, and there a little. Like the objects of the material world, which are found everywhere in great profusion, and cognizable by the senses of all, so the truths of Scripture are level to the apprehension and instruction of every one; and a uniform experience has proved, that from such short and plain statements of great principles, the majority of mankind derive all their knowledge and impressions of religion. They open the Bible, and read a psalm, a chapter, a parable, a short notice of some patriarch, prophet, or apostle, a part of the history of Christ, or some sententious passage embodying the sum and substance of the law or the gospel; and from these divine summaries they derive more light, more conviction, and more instruction in righteousness, than they could do from whole volumes of demonstrative reasoning, however clearly and logically conducted, however skilfully and artistically arranged.

III. THE UNIVERSAL APPLICATION OF THE SCRIPTURES.—It gives us a just and full delineation of all men in all ages. Some lived about six thousand years ago, and vast multitudes of them in all intervening ages, as well as in the present. They have inhabited all zones and regions, have been placed in circumstances the most diversified, and been occupied in the most varied pursuits; some have been savages, others civilised, rich and poor, learned and unlearned; some have been favoured with all the means of improvement and grace;— others have been destitute of any intellectual or moral guidance, except what the light of depraved reason, all but extinguished, supplied. What sage, what philosopher, has ever appeared, who has written a book that exhibits men, all men, just as they have been and are? None has appeared, and we may add with confidence, that such a writer, let his advantages be what they may, will never appear. But here is a book, written not by one, but by a considerable number of men, who lived in very different periods, at least the great majority of them, and therefore had no consultation together, who were neither travellers nor philosophers, living in a small contracted country, separated by national institutions, and hemmed in by mountain barriers from the world beyond; yet this book is a mirror in which not the inhabitants of Judea or of the Oriental world only, but all the generations, nay, all the individuals of the human race, in the essential attributes of their nature, may see themselves exhibited faithfully and fully to the very life. None but He who is the God of truth, and who knows what is in man, could have been the author of this book, given as it was at sundry times and in divers portions.

IV. THE IMPARTIALITY OF THE SCRIPTURES.—In all ages, so strong have been the tendencies of human nature to hero-worship, that to resist and overcome these has been the continual striving of God with man; and one of the distinguishing characteristics of His revealed word is the many and various safeguards it presents to our relapse into that leading sin of Paganism. In the Bible, indeed, we have the records of men of faith from the earliest time; the records of the best and noblest of the race that have ever lived in the world. We are furnished with full-length portraits of their characters and lives; we see their examples, we learn their reward, that we may be led to imitate their faith and holiness; but all attempts to transfer to them the honours of worship of any kind, or in any degree, would have been repressed in all good times of the Jewish church, both by the terrors of the divine displeasure, and the penalties of the civil law. The good men of the Old Testament church are too natural in their goodness, and too like ourselves, to be deified. We have the record of Abraham's lies as well as of faith; of Jacob's deceit as well as his piety; of the quarrel of the twelve patriarchs, and its consequences; of David's adultery, as well as his deep and fervent devotion; of Solomon's wisdom, as well as his weakness: all meet for instruction and admonition, but not for idolatry. The account of the patriarchal families and of the chosen nation seems a record of incessant backslidings and their punishment; yet so would that of any nation or family, were its story told with the same singular fidelity and circumstantial minuteness. In the New Testament we meet with a higher development of all

R

the moral and spiritual elements of character; yet still no approach to, nor encouragement of, hero-worship. The denial of Peter, and his later duplicity, the unbelief of Thomas, the vindictive spirit of James and John, the cowardice and desertion of all the apostles, the sharp contention of Paul and Barnabas, are recorded as faithfully as the treachery of Judas, or the enmity of the chief priests and scribes. Better, holier, and more disinterested they are represented than other men; yet still, men of like failings with us, to be admired and imitated only in so far as they were the faithful imitators of Him whom they proclaimed the light and the life of the world. No human history can be compared with that of the sacred volume in respect of impartiality; and whether we consider its faithful chronicles of scenes of barbarism and wickedness, calculated to reflect the blackest infamy on the national name of Israel, or the failings and errors even of apostles, as of John the apocalyptic seer, who was in danger of falling into idolatry by worshipping an angel, and who received a check from that heavenly messenger, it is an undoubted fact, that there is no book in the world that displays so honest and impartial a love of truth, in recording the errors and sins, as well as the virtues and excellences, even of good men.

V. THE RESERVE OF THE SCRIPTURES ON MATTERS NOT PROFITABLE.—The Bible is a wonderful book, and the evidence of its divine origin and character appears as much perhaps in what it withholds as in what it reveals. Look to the foolish and absurd legends which impostors have communicated, as in the Koran of Mahomet, or the fabulous traditions of Rome relating to the intercourse of its saints and heroes with God, and the marvellous scenes to which they were admitted in the upper world; and to every sober, enlightened, and reflecting mind, their narratives appear to bear the stamp and impress of fiction on the face of them. But how different the Bible, in which all the scripture or writing that is given by inspiration of God, is such only as is profitable for doctrine, for reproof, for correction, and instruction in righteousness! Thus, during the abode of Moses on the mount, what wonders he must have witnessed, what scenes of more than earthly glory and grandeur must have been disclosed to his view! And yet none of all these does he retail on his return to the people. Though, by telling his tales of wonder, he might have made himself an object of unequalled admiration, and drawn towards himself an interest of no common intensity, he spoke of nothing that tended merely to gratify an idle curiosity, or foster a spirit of vain and useless speculation; and the grand subject which he introduced, and on which he dwelt at large, on his descent from the mount, was to announce the will of God respecting the erection of a place of public worship.

When Moses reascended the mount, he was accompanied by a select band of attendants, whom he had been instructed to bring with him on that occasion. The persons selected for this distinguished privilege consisted of the most prominent and influential parties in the Hebrew camp,— parties most conspicuous for official rank and station, whose testimony to the glorious scenes unveiled to their view within the curtain of the enveloping cloud, would encourage the people to repose their faith in the delegated character and mission of Moses. It was in conformity to divine instructions these persons were selected to accompany Moses in his second ascent to the mount, in order that they might be witnesses of the divine glory, as well as of those intimate communications with God to which the leader was admitted; and their report of those supernatural scenes might confirm the people's faith in the divine legation with which he was invested. There was the greatest propriety and wisdom in the arrangement of this course : for although the conspicuous part which Moses had been honoured to act, in effecting the emancipation of his countrymen from the house of bondage, and in conducting them on their subsequent journeys through the wilderness, afforded unmistakeable evidence that he enjoyed the benefit of divine counsel and divine aid, this was a very different thing from his being invested with a delegated power to enact laws for their government; and as he was thenceforth to exercise that power, to assume the character and office of a lawgiver, and all his enactments were to be accompanied with sanctions of peculiar solemnity, it was necessary to convince them that all that he did and enjoined in his legislative capacity was stamped with the seal of divine authority. Nothing was better calculated to inspire the minds of the people with confidence in the delegated power and authority of Moses, than the scene on the mount, attested by the report of many competent witnesses, who would bear testimony that the law which Moses gave them was no political scheme of human device, but was indeed derived from the mind and communicated by the authority of God. In the passage that gives an account of their ascent[1] to the mount, we have an account of one of the most remarkable scenes that are recorded in the whole compass of the sacred history; and yet it is difficult whether most to admire the brevity of the record, or the simplicity of the language employed in narrating the sublime spectacle they were privileged to witness. There is no attempt at elaborate description; no tendency to amplify, either by the selection of striking circumstances, or even by the insertion of epithets such as an excited imagination is apt to indulge in; no expression of the feelings, whether of admiration or of awe, that pervaded the select group: and whether this omission is to be accounted for by the character of this book of Exodus, which is the brief and succinct journal of an annalist; whether it arose from the attention of Moses being more occupied in the composition of the history, with the object for which those attendants had been associated with him, than with the incidents of their limited experience; or whether the spec-

[1] Ex. xxiv.

tacle they witnessed was hastily passed over, as little or nothing compared to the far sublimer and fuller discoveries of the divine majesty and glory with which Moses was himself afterwards favoured,—the marked reserve he has maintained with regard to the details of a scene so far beyond the ordinary range of human experience, and on which a fictitious writer would have felt an irresistible temptation to enlarge,—this marked reserve speaks volumes as to his character as an inspired historian. The narrative bears on the face of it the stamp and impress of truth; and yet we may fairly presume, that though a very brief record of the scene has been transmitted to us, an ample detail of circumstances would be given by the delegates on their descent, which would be long and widely circulated amongst their countrymen, till it was gradually incorporated amongst the popular views of the Godhead entertained by the Jewish people. It was preserved by tradition, and seems even to have fed the imagination of the inspired bards of Israel. For the sublime and glorious spectacle to which the favoured attendants of Moses were now admitted, was doubtless the germ of many of the most magnificent descriptions, the symbolical imagery of the prophets—in those visioned theophanies which are recorded in their mystic pages. It is, however, a very brief record that has been given us of the remarkable scene to which the attendants of Moses were admitted. It is said, "they saw the God of Israel." Now it is a first, a fundamental principle of the true religion, that "no man hath seen God at any time." Moreover, as it is expressly declared, that at the promulgation of the moral law the people saw no manner of similitude, it is evident that the expression, "they saw the God of Israel," can mean nothing more than that they beheld the sign or emblem of His presence. They were favoured with a glimpse of His glory,— that form of it which is commonly spoken of in Scripture under the name of the Shechinah, exhibited on that occasion perhaps in a clearer and more vivid degree of effulgence than ever had been formerly witnessed. The Septuagint version renders it, "they saw the place where the God of Israel stood." Whatever it was they saw, it was evidently a something of which no image or picture could be made, and yet marked by such attendant symbols as impressed the minds of all the beholders with the strongest conviction that God was there of a truth; and it will be remembered, that all the divine manifestations to the ancient church were made by Him who is styled the Angel of the Covenant, and declared by Paul to be Christ. It is observable, however, that in the record of what the attendants of Moses saw, nothing of the sublime spectacle is described but that which was *under his feet*. Whether it was that their eyes, dazzled by excess of light, could not stedfastly look at the effulgent glory, or from a feeling of profound reverence, no attempt was made to report any part of the extraordinary scene, except the part on which the glory seemed to rest.

A similar reserve is maintained by Isaiah in describing the symbols of his famous vision. The elevated throne; the ample train or glory which filled the temple, like the long-flowing robes of oriental monarchs on grand occasions extending over the floor of the spacious chamber; the attendant seraphim, from a sense of unworthiness to behold the divine majesty, veiling their faces, and, to mark their reverential respect, covering their feet, or the lower part of their body, according to a practice in the East when persons go into the presence of royalty; their readiness to execute the behests of their Divine Master, and their delegated occupation in praising Him;—all these are circumstantially described; but no attempt is made to depict the glory of the Lord Himself. From the awful sublimity of such a theme the prophet shrank in conscious humility. And this Person, whose glory was so transcendently great, is declared, on the express authority of the Apostle John, to have been Christ: "These things said Esaias, when he saw His glory, and spake of Him,"[1] the Divine Word, "the brightness of the Father's glory, and the express image of His person."[2] This was but a visioned representation of the divine glory; for the prophet was in a state of ecstatic inspiration, and had the things signified by the symbols of the vision vividly impressed on his mind. But the apostles, long after, were favoured with a sensible manifestation of the supernatural glory of the Saviour on the Mount of Transfiguration. No one who reads the narrative of that wonderful transaction, can fail to perceive how admirably all the parts of the panoramic scene were calculated to heighten the glory of Christ, and to shadow forth the true purpose of His advent and ministry; and although the earthly spectators did not at once

[1] John xii. 41.   [2] Heb. i. 2.

arrive at a full apprehension of those sublime mysteries, yet when their minds were opened, and the Holy Spirit had led them into all the truth, we find them ever after appealing to the scene on the mount as affording an incontestable evidence of the character and glory of Christ. But in how simple and moderate terms is it related in the Gospels, and alluded to in the Epistle of Peter! Had an uninspired writer of talent and eloquence been called to describe such a scene, how would he have enlisted all his powers of imagination to heighten every circumstance, and have exhausted his vocabulary for superlatives to depict the surpassing magnificence of our Lord, when arrayed in His robes of celestial glory! The sacred penmen resort to no such artifices; but describe this most awe-inspiring spectacle in few and unaffected words, by saying: " He was transfigured before them; His face did shine as the sun, and His raiment was white as the light." The brevity and simplicity of this statement is to a reflecting mind far more significant and effective than the most elaborate description: for as the sun is the brightest object in nature, and no human eye can stedfastly endure the glare of His radiant disc, it is impossible for words to convey a higher idea of splendour, than that the face of the Saviour shone like that resplendent orb; and as light is the pure essence of whiteness, the other statement is as little capable of being strengthened by any addition, " His raiment was white as the light."

Another instance of reserve in the relation of spiritual and divine things is furnished by the Apostle Paul, who was favoured with "visions" of the divine glory, and "revelations" of the heavenly world, to a degree beyond what mortal man ever enjoyed. He was "caught up into the third," or the highest heaven, where he heard such words as man could not speak if he might, and as it would be unlawful to speak if he could; the divine purpose being, that the discoveries which God has made of Himself in that glorious world, should not be more fully made in the present state than they have been. There the works of God are exhibited on a grander scale, the government of God subsists in a more perfect form; and creatures vastly superior to man in capacities, in intelligence, and in moral qualities, inhabit the blessed region. The apostle was favoured with a transient revelation of its economy; and yet, so far from attempting to draw a highly-coloured picture, or even to dilate on the unknown wonders disclosed to his enraptured view, he sums it all up in the modest assertion, "It is not expedient for me, doubtless, to glory."

The last instance of this kind of reserve I shall mention is taken from the Apocalypse, connected with the sublime scene of which the rainbow forms so conspicuous a feature, and forming the first of those many-pictured visions that passed before the eyes of the apostolic seer in the caves of Patmos. In contemplating the group of images which this description contains, the mind of a reader is naturally directed in the first instance to the principal personage in the picture; and every one must be struck with the admirable, the prudent, and pious reserve of John, who has said not a word about Him who sat on the throne. Upon the furniture and appendages of the throne, especially upon the symbolical "rainbow that was round about it," the sacred writer has largely dwelt, for these are legitimate and practicable subjects of contemplation; but he has entirely refrained from the least approach to a description of Him who sat upon it—thus acting as the most exalted of creatures must ever be constrained to do, filled with silent adoration and overwhelming awe of that Being who dwells in light inaccessible and full of glory.

Such is the habitual reserve, the studied caution, which the sacred writers observe in all their allusions to spiritual and divine things. They act like men who are impressed with solemn awe, as feeling that they stood on holy ground; and this demeanour, which is common to all of them, produces a strong conviction that they spoke and wrote in the name and by the authority of God.

The same reserve is shown in other classes of subjects—such as their entire omission of all matters that are not subservient to the great ends of revelation, or are not profitable for correction and instruction in righteousness. We select an instance of this from the earliest annals of the world. Brief as is the account which the sacred historian has given of the various processes of creation, as well as of the original state and altered destiny of man, it might have been expected that he would have been more copious and minute in his details when he entered on the history of the human race, as they have ever since existed in the world. And perhaps there are few readers of the Bible, who, from the sympathies of a common nature, have not at times been conscious of a strong desire to possess a biography of the first pair. We might have wished to know something of their condition and habits,—to see Adam employed in the operations of the field, and Eve busy with her simple cares as a wife and mother. We might have wished to obtain a glimpse into their family circle; to be furnished with sketches of its different members, and anecdotes of the infant children; to learn how they divided their day, what was the internal economy of their household,—in what manner the first parents of mankind educated their offspring, and what was the general tenor of their lives. Above all, we might have wished to possess some information as to their sentiments and feelings on a subject the most important to the well-being and happiness of intelligent, moral, and fallen creatures; to learn whether they cherished a spirit of repentance and faith, to know their devotional habits, to have a record of the time and place of their engaging in social worship, as well as of the stated ritual that constituted their primitive form of religion. But the inspired wisdom that guided the pen of Moses, led him to pass over in silence all the incidents of their personal and family history; and the only fragment of their primitive annals that has been preserved is a painful episode, which exhibits an awful proof of the sinful nature which our first parents had transmitted to their posterity.

We select another instance of this kind of reserve from the commencement of the New Testament history; and it refers to the early period of that life which possesses an intense and never-failing interest for every Christian mind. Perhaps there is no reader of the Gospels but has felt the desire rise in his bosom to know some details of the childhood and youth of Jesus,—to possess some specimens of His opening faculties and progressive education; instances of His precocious intellect, His devotional habits, His earnestness and assiduity in searching the Scriptures, and the eminent example He gave of juvenile piety; how He worked as a mechanic, whether He associated with the villagers, or kept aloof from most of them as people of a rough, bad, and uncongenial character; what were His favourite haunts in His hours of leisure, what roads He frequented in the neighbourhood of that highland hamlet; whether He courted privacy, and loved, like Isaac, to meditate in the fields; whether any and what indications were ever given of the latent wisdom and undeveloped powers He possessed. But on all these matters an absolute silence is observed. The first thirty years of His life are involved in impenetrable obscurity. But if they have been passed over by His biographers in silence, it was certainly not from want of means and opportunities to obtain ample information. The minute circumstances recorded by Matthew and Luke at the opening of their respective Gospels show that both of them were on a footing of close, familiar intimacy with Joseph and Mary, and consequently had direct access to the best and purest sources of intelligence. When we remember that Mary, with regard to all that was said and done by her extraordinary Son, is recorded to have "kept these things in her heart," we cannot doubt that that earnest observer must have treasured up many anecdotes of interest relating to his early life; and we can as little doubt that these must have been often retailed to the evangelists, as to other friends of the family. But they have not transmitted those anecdotes, because the preservation of them would have served no purpose but to minister to the gratification of curiosity; and with the exception of some brief remarks on His subjection to His earthly parents, and His increase of favour with God and man, they have confined their evangelical narratives to the period of His public ministry. We might remark also, that there is no description given in any of the evangelical biographies of the features of our Lord, His size,

s

form, and demeanour,—a reserve evidently dictated by the same divine wisdom which concealed the burial-place of Moses.

We select a third instance of this kind of reserve from the close of the Saviour's ministry. A reflecting reader, who has pondered the records of His resurrection, must have often been conscious of many questions arising in his mind connected with that miraculous event, some of them perhaps trivial, others merely curious and speculative. They are such as the following: Whither did He go first on leaving the tomb? Whence did He obtain the clothes that He wore? Where did He lodge, when not with the disciples? Whence did He come, when He joined the two pious travellers of Emmaus, and whither did He go on leaving them? How did He with a real material body enter suddenly into the midst of their private assembly, and vanish with equal suddenness from the upper room? As He rose the first-fruits from the dead, and it was with the identical body in which He had suffered, did it undergo a change in His ascent, to fit it for that world which flesh and blood cannot inhabit? and how far did it differ from that spiritual body with which, according to Paul, the saints shall be invested in the future world? On all such matters the sacred writers maintain a prudent reserve, and in this respect furnish a striking proof that the Scripture, all of which is given by inspiration of God, contains nothing but what is profitable for correction and instruction in righteousness.

II. INTERNAL PROOFS OF INSPIRATION.

The revelations made in the Scripture concerning the character and will of God afford decisive proofs of the inspiration of the Scriptures.

I. TRUE IDEA OF THE DIVINE BEING.—Of God, and of His character, we can derive no certain knowledge from created sources. No angel has descended from his high abode, and mingled with mortals to communicate the tidings. No disembodied spirit has returned to reveal the secrets of the other world. And if none has come down the bearer of such intelligence, as certainly none of the wisest and most inquisitive of men has ever been able to soar aloft with adventurous wing to the knowledge of the Divine Majesty, and bring back from his mission of exploration the much wished-for, all-important information. We may, indeed, erect on the platform of this world a ladder to climb up by its lofty steps, and so obtain some glimpses of God as He manifests Himself in other and more elevated regions. Men did so in ancient times; but amid the speculations of many thousand years on the being and character of God, made by the greatest and wisest minds that ever adorned our fallen humanity, mankind never advanced a step beyond vague and dubious conjecture: every successive age was obliged to content itself with the knowledge of the preceding one, just as the creatures which are guided by instinct, and one race of which never outstrips or rises higher than another. Some light, indeed, was reflected from His works and the course of His providential dealings; but still, as through both of these men could see only through a glass darkly, the most enlightened and accomplished in the study both of nature and providence could be described as doing little else than seeking, if haply they might find God. With all the aids furnished by both departments of His works, they were still, like the blind, groping their way in uncertainty and darkness. And in weighing the opinions formed, the conclusions arrived at, by those who were not favoured and blessed with the guiding illumination of Heaven, it is impossible not to perceive how egregiously and fatally they erred in some views, in what painful doubt and uncertainty they were involved as to other points of the divine character, which it is most desirable and important to ascertain. Instead of a perfect Being, they conceived only of an imperfect one,—a creation of their own fancy,—labouring under material defects, contaminated by debasing passions, addicted to grovelling enjoyments, or degraded by the love and practice of odious vices. Others who are further advanced in knowledge, but possessing only the light of natural reason, are sadly perplexed by the apparently jarring views of God suggested by the phenomena of the material world and the course of providence. The regular succession of the seasons, the revolution of day and night, the usually tranquil and settled order of nature, and the profuse bounty that provides for the necessities as well as the enjoyment of man, and the innumerable tribes of living creatures which inhabit the earth along with him, inspire the idea of an amiable and beneficent Being; while, on the other hand, the aspect of the heavens, black and lowering,—the outburst of the tempest, that uproots the trees of the forest, overthrows houses, commits widespread havoc on land, and destroys navies at sea,—the roar of the thunder, the flash of the lightning, the ravages of the pestilence that walketh in darkness,—appal with the terrors of almighty power. Similar perplexity is produced by the varying course of providence: for the peace and happiness that attend the practice of sobriety and virtue, the prosperity that rewards the industrious, and the connection which experience shows to subsist between a patient continuance in well-doing and the secure enjoyment of life, tend to create a belief that the world is under the superintendence of a wise and good Being. But the moral disorders and strange anomalies that are ever and anon witnessed,—the triumphs of the wicked, the persecution of the best and most excellent persons solely for their devotedness to the cause of pure religion, and the unsuccessful struggles of honest families against the combined evils of poverty and disease,—are apt to force the conclusion, that if there is a God who loves good and hates evil, He is an arbitrary and capricious tyrant. Now it is in the Scriptures alone that the character of God appears invested with attributes suited to the majesty of the Supreme Being. It is there alone His eternity and immutability, His unity and spirituality, His awful majesty and moral perfections, are made known in a manner calculated to secure the esteem as well as the confidence of intelligent and rational creatures. It would be easy to multiply quotations to an indefinite extent, showing the vast superiority of the inspired volume to all other sources of knowledge regarding the God with whom we have to do. We must confine ourselves to a few only:—" Before the mountains were brought forth, or ever Thou hadst formed the earth and the world, even from everlasting to everlasting, Thou art God." " Of old hast Thou laid the foundation of the earth, and the heavens are the work of Thy hands. They shall perish, but Thou shalt endure; yea, all of them shall wax old like a garment: as a vesture shalt Thou change them, and they shall be changed ; but Thou art the same, and Thy years shall have no end." How strikingly is the eternal and independent existence of God represented in the fact, that He was before any part of the visible creation was called into being; and that although the material universe should perish or wear away like an old piece of clothing, He would continue, unshorn of His glory, undiminished in His happiness, and unaffected in His nature! On the memorable occasion of Moses requesting to see the glory of the Lord, it is said, in one of the most solemn and mysterious passages of the Bible, that the Lord, in compliance with the desire of His pious servant, descended in a cloud, and stood with him there, and proclaimed Himself the "Lord, the Lord God, merciful and gracious, long-suffering, and abundant in goodness and truth." Can anything surpass or equal the sublimity of this? A mere human philosopher would have selected some gorgeous description from the appearances of material nature, with which as a suitable train to array the Majesty of Heaven in descending upon the mount; but the simplicity of the scriptural narrative, unfolding not the full effulgence of His divine glory, which the weakness of humanity in its present state could not have endured, but enlarging only on the leading attributes of His *moral* character, at once commends itself to the minds of all as superior to aught that man could have said. In the sublime song of Moses contained in the 32d chapter of Deuteronomy, the following description is given of the Divine Being: "He is the rock, His work is perfect; for all His ways are judgment: a God of truth, and without iniquity; just and right is He." How infinitely does this exalt God above the empty and false objects to whom the votaries of heathen superstition give their blind and devoted reverence! In the song of thanksgiving offered by Hannah at the birth of Samuel, these exalted sentiments occur: "There is none holy as the Lord; for there is none beside Thee, neither is there any rock like our God. The Lord is a God of knowledge, and by Him actions are weighed." When Elijah had fled to Horeb after the slaughter of the priests of Baal, his impetuous temper having led him to dissatisfaction and despair, because all idolaters were not immediately extirpated in the kingdom of Israel, an important and most seasonable lesson was given him. The symbols of the divine power and majesty were exhibited to him in a whirlwind, an earthquake, and a fire; yet God was not in all these terrific phenomena. There was, however, a soft murmur or whispering sound that followed, symbolizing gentleness, patience, and mercy; and God spake in that voice. The design of this remarkable scene was to show the prophet that it was not according to the character of God to destroy or to coerce, but by the rational weapons of argument and preaching the word to persuade the idolatrous people to abandon a false and to embrace the true religion. The Psalmist has described the divine omnipresence by the following metaphorical illustration: "Whither shall I go from Thy Spirit? or whither shall I flee from Thy presence? If I ascend up into heaven, Thou art there; if I make my bed in hell (the place of the dead), behold, Thou art there. If I take the wings of the morning, and dwell in the uttermost parts of the sea, even there shall Thy hand lead me, and Thy right hand shall hold me."[1] This is a beautiful poetical amplification, to express in a vivid manner the common truth that evidences of divine agency are found everywhere. Jeremiah uttered a prayer in the following terms of sublime and enlightened devotion: "Lord God! behold, Thou hast made the heaven and the earth by Thy great power and stretched-out arm, and there is nothing too hard for Thee; Thou showest loving-kindness unto thousands, and recompensest the iniquity of the fathers into the bosom of their children after them: The Great, the Mighty God, the Lord of hosts, is His name; great in counsel, and mighty in work: for Thine eyes are open upon all the ways of the sons of men; to give every one according to his ways, and according to the fruit of his doings." Micah breaks forth into the following animated apostrophe: "Who is a God like unto

[1] Ps. cxxxix. 7–10.

Thee, that pardonest iniquity, and passest by the transgression of the remnant of Thy heritage? Thou retainest not Thine anger for ever, because Thou delightest in mercy." And to mention only one passage more: the New Testament gives this brief and simple, but rational and sublime character of God. He is "a Spirit, who requires that those who worship Him, should worship in spirit and in truth,"—a passage which intimates clearly and beautifully, that no material walls limit His presence, no favoured spot holds an exclusive right to enjoy it; but that wherever man may go, even to wilds where the feet of the adventurous traveller have never trode, nor the voice of human suppliant has ever been heard, there the sincere worshipper may receive showers of blessing from above.

It has been alleged, however, that the early Scriptures abound with passages of a very different tenor—passages which give a very different view of the Divine Being from that which is exhibited in the New Testament. Instead of representing the Divine Being in a manner worthy the Majesty of Heaven, and in harmony with His spiritual nature, they degrade Him by the ascription of acts and feelings identical with those of man. The allegation admits of an easy and satisfactory explanation.

The face, eyes, ears, hands, back parts, are obviously figurative expressions in the anthropomorphic style, as it is impossible to conceive of a spirit but through the medium of the senses, and there is no other way of describing what He does. The soul of man being created after the image of God, it is a spirit; and yet, in the full knowledge and belief that it is of a spiritual nature, we are accustomed to speak of seeing with the eye of the mind, of handling a subject, of taking a firm grasp of it, and of metaphorically applying various other expressions borrowed from the senses, to describe mental operations, which these aptly represent. Now, conceiving, as men generally do, that the human soul is the same in substance as the Divine Spirit, it is natural for them to describe the acts of God in the same figurative way as they represent the movements of their own minds, and endeavour to impress their imaginations with the vivid idea of His character by ascribing to Him hands, nostrils, ears, eyes, with every active function of the body and every emotion of the mind, just because it is the only way in which He can be brought into contact with the feelings of man, his hopes, his fears, his affections, his imaginative, and even his corporeal associations. What good reason, then, or what sound authority, is there for objecting to a mode of speaking in such constant and familiar use, and for casting it away, notwithstanding the example which has been set by sacred historians and prophets, who used it in writing of the Godhead, for the dry and unsubstantial representations of it into which modern theology, borrowing from philosophy, has fallen? Atheistic philosophers and poets may talk of God as a mighty power everywhere diffused through nature, a universal motion, an unknown existence, a mysterious essence, and think it great reverence to express such indefinite notions of Him. But the same writers who tell us that no similitude of the Divine Being was beheld on the mount, are wont to represent Him to the conceptions of a rude people, as seeing, hearing, smelling, coming down, and lifting up; and conscious experience teaches us, that the human mind cannot realize the idea of God from the abstract language of philosophy so strongly and so fully as when we speak of Him as the living God, the God that judgeth, whose eyes behold and whose eyelids try the children of men.

It is further said, that the actions attributed to Him are at variance with the higher revelation He has given of Himself in the gospel; and the recorded instances of His direct interference in the domestic affairs of the patriarchs, and the trivial interests of the Israelitish people, are opposed to the established course of providence in the world. Now we know that the meanest creature in which the principle of life is implanted has its allotted destiny, and is cared for by the Divine Being. And as man is of more value than many sparrows, the inference is, that every human being is an object of special care on the part of Him who rules the universe, and who, though acting in the remotest regions of space, is at the same instant in this world, taking cognizance of every person, his history, his movements, and his doings, as if he were the sole inhabitant in it. Besides, if we believe that God entered into a special covenant with the Jewish people, we must also believe that this dispensation was carried on consistently with the moral government of the world at large; and that if He had important objects to be promoted through the instrumentality of that nation, it was to be expected that He would take an interest in the personal and domestic concerns of those who were employed as the chief agents in accomplishing His will. Hence His frequent interpositions in the lives of the patriarchs, in the history of Moses, at the birth of Samson, and in the case of Elijah. Moreover, the divine appearances to Abraham and the patriarchs formed part of the religious education by which they were trained to the knowledge and service of the true God. By these frequent and familiar manifestations to Abraham, the personality of God was seen in opposition to pantheism, His unity as opposed to polytheism, and His infinite perfections in contrast with the gross conceptions of idolatry. As it is reasonable to think that in all these manifestations there would be the same tones of voice, and the same unequivocal tokens of the divine presence, there is little room for doubting that the patriarchs possessed the amplest means of satisfying themselves that it was God who addressed them. In the long series of miracles, conversations, and appearances, the patriarchs must have acquired a distinct and accurate knowledge of the Divine Spokesman or Revealer, as a man has of a friend, or a servant of a master, when he hears his voice or beholds his features. And these manifestations, which are so frequently recorded in the early annals of the ancient church, are not, as has been alleged, inconsistent with the statement made in a later portion of the Scripture, that "no man hath seen God at any time;"[1] for they were made by "the Angel of the Covenant," "the image of the invisible God," who, as Mediator, has carried on all the negotiations between heaven and earth since the fall. The identity of character and consistency of revelation maintained by this manifested Deity during many successive centuries, are themselves sufficient to prove the truth of the narratives which relate them; for they could not be the invention of the human mind. Nor can those who believe the wonderful fact, that "in the fulness of time" He became man, and tabernacled in the world, deem it incredible, that, by appearing from time to time to persons connected with the early church in the form of humanity, assumed at will on particular occasions, He gave prelusive intimations of His future incarnation. So clearly has the character of God been made known by Him who was the brightness of the Father's glory, and who, being in the bosom of the Father, came down from heaven to earth to declare Him unto us, that modern infidels have borrowed indirectly, and without acknowledgment, all their ideas of the Supreme Being from the mind of Christ; and that the humble peasant, who has no book in his possession

---

[1] John i. 18.

but the Bible, the very child who is learning the Catechism, has a far better knowledge of what man is to believe concerning God, than the greatest of ancient philosophers, who laboured by refined and metaphysical speculations to frame an abstract conception of the divine character.

Another objection that is brought against the scriptural idea of God is, that He is represented as *repenting*.[1] Repentance, in the literal meaning of the term, is impossible in the divine mind; and when ascribed to God, can be so only in a metaphorical, not a literal sense. In consequence of the imperfection of human language, and the purely spiritual nature of Jehovah, all descriptions of His character must, in order to be intelligible to us, be conveyed in phraseology borrowed from the operations of our own minds. In this way we feebly approximate to right ideas of His perfections. When repentance is attributed to God, it implies not a change of design, but a change in His mode of dealing with men, such as would indicate on their part a change of purpose. He allows the inward purposes of His mind, which in Himself are eternally one, for man's sake to be separated according to the order of time, that thus man may be able to

---

[1] Gen. vi. 7; Jer. xlii. 10, etc.

T

understand them. In fact, the great end and aim of the Scriptures is to reveal God to man, to give a description of His character, a history of His modes of proceeding, and an account of His laws. Now, if God were liable to repent or change, there could be no secure reliance on this revelation. In that case, the books of Scripture might be true at one time, and not at another,—true at the time they were written, and not true now. Since that time the character of God might have altered; He might have changed His mode of procedure, and framed a new code of laws. This is what actually happens amongst men: for there are few, if any persons, whose habits or manners or principles do not vary more or less at different periods of life; nor is there any Government that does not more or less alter its legislation, to adapt it to the circumstances of a more advanced age. In such cases, new descriptions of character and new codes of law become absolutely necessary. But God is always the same; and therefore the Scriptures are always a sure and unvarying expression of His will. The New Testament has now been written nearly eighteen hundred years, and some parts of the Old Testament three thousand. Yet the Bible is as faithful an account of its Divine Author at this moment as at the first; and it will remain so, if the world should last even millions of years to come.

But the greatest objection which has been urged is the aspect in which the Old Testament represents the character of God,—the aspect of a gloomy and vindictive Being, jealous of His honour, and ready to resent with condign punishment the giving of His glory to another. In accordance with this view of His character is the account of His proceedings, and His treatment of those who committed a breach of His laws. The whole character of His legislation, it is alleged, is draconic. But it must be remembered that, in dealing with the Jewish people, God had to maintain the discipline of a stern and inflexible sovereign; while, at the same time, He showed on many occasions that He was full of patience and forbearance, ready to forgive the errors and sins of His people, waiting for their repentance, and remitting their punishment. The whole character of His procedure is summed up in these striking words: "As I live, saith the Lord, I have no pleasure in the death of the sinner, but rather that He turn from his wicked ways and live. Turn ye, turn ye, from your evil ways; for why will ye die, O house of Israel?"

It is an interesting and instructive fact, that

these descriptions of the being and character of God were given to the Jewish people from the commencement of their national existence. At a time when religion was deeply corrupted in all other parts of the world,—when neither the astronomy of Chaldea, nor all the wisdom of the Egyptians, nor the refined taste and high civilisation of the Greeks and Romans, could preserve them from the grossest forms of idolatry and superstition,—this description of the true God was given exclusively in the land of Judea;—these views of His character were taught, not to select audiences in the schools of the prophets or the colleges of the priests, but to all classes of the common people in that country. Was not this a proof that the Jews were under the direct and special instruction of Heaven? and that the prophets who gave them religious instruction, so far superior to what a Socrates or Plato, a Cicero or Seneca, ever attained in the most enlightened times of Greece and Rome, were God-taught men?

Views of the divine character such as the preceding, so far transcending all that the unassisted mind of man could reach, evidently show that the book in which they are contained was given by inspiration of God. Who could have imagined such lofty ideas, or described such a perfect character, but those whose minds were illuminated, enlarged, and infallibly directed from above? And when we find that none but those ambassadors of God, whose writings are contained in the Old and New Testaments, have been able to give any exhibition of His character that is suitable to, or consistent with, the divine nature, we are to judge of what men can do from what they have actually done; and to conclude, that none could have represented the majesty and perfections of God in all their glory, but those to whom He Himself was pleased to impart the knowledge. This knowledge is contained in the Scriptures; and since all that we can observe and all that we can conceive of that exalted Being conspire to prove the truth of the representations which the sacred volume has afforded of Him, we are led by the clearest dictates of enlightened reason to believe that the Scripture was given by inspiration of God.

II. We have an additional confirmation in the official character and work of Him who, in modern phrase, is the hero of the book, whose peculiar ministry and qualifications for discharging it form the principal and engrossing subject of the Scriptures.

Every one who enters upon the office of mediator must possess the qualities and belong to a station that will secure for him the confidence of both the parties whom he undertakes to reconcile. In ordinary cases, among the nations of the earth, it is not difficult to meet with individuals who are competent, from their knowledge, their experience, and their high standing, for such an enterprise; but it may happen,—in point of fact, it has often happened in all the European embassies that were sent to China, for instance,—that the ambassador, though suitable to one of the parties, was not suitable for the other: though enjoying the full confidence of the Government at home, he was ignorant of the state, unacquainted with the prejudices, and could not accommodate himself to the circumstances, of that singular people. In consequence of this unsuitability, all the efforts at mediation made by the Governments of the West were fruitless, and failed. If we may borrow an illustration of things divine from things human, the Scripture appears to be given by inspiration of God, by its revealing and describing such a Mediator as was needed to reconcile fallen man to his offended Maker. In making known a Saviour who undertook the onerous task of mediating between God and His rebellious creatures, it seems essential that He should possess all the qualifications for the successful discharge of His arduous undertaking,—that He should possess a resemblance or identity with the nature of man, at the same time that He is of sufficient dignity to satisfy the infinite claims of God. Our own judgment, which revolts at the idea of one being our surety who had no knowledge of our state, no experience of our spiritual wants, tells us, that if any should interpose in our behalf, he should unite in his own person a twofold character,—an equality with God, and a fulness of sympathy, an identity of interest, with man. Now the Saviour whom the Scriptures make known is exactly such a one as meets all the necessities of the case. He was God and man in two distinct natures, and by this wonderful constitution of His person was peculiarly qualified for His great and unprecedented commission. Possessed of true divinity as well as of true humanity, He combined all those attributes of character that enabled Him to offer a basis of reconciliation which is at once well suited both to the dignity of the Supreme Government, and to the necessities of the wretched offenders,—a basis of reconciliation worthy of God to accept, and of man to confide in. Such a character was so utterly unknown within the whole range of human experience,—nay, it was so utterly beyond the loftiest conceptions of the human mind, —it was, in fact, such a divine original as affords plain and indisputable evidence that the Scripture which describes it was given by inspiration of God.

III. Further, the Scripture which represents the person of Christ as uniting such an unparallelled combination of properties as constituted Him a fit and acceptable Mediator between heaven and earth, has also described Him in another view that is equally striking, and that possesses no less claims to originality. I refer to His moral character, which, in the delineation of it drawn by His evangelical biographers, including the prophets,—for they also have portrayed it,—is represented in all the attributes of perfection; and this picture is not a rough draught, or a mere outline, consisting of general descriptions or loose indiscriminate eulogy, but is made up of a plain unvarnished history, illustrated by a series of incidents, and actions, and discourses, so various in the time, manner, and circumstances of their occurrence, that the character is fully elucidated and brought out; nay, the constitutional features can be distinctly traced; and the whole, when blended together, forms such an assemblage of moral qualities as mark Him out beyond all controversy the most extraordinary, the most exalted, the most perfect character the world ever saw. Such a character as He exhibited had never been so much as dreamed of before. At various times, indeed, men exercised their ingenuity in attempting to draw a character of ideal perfection. But the efforts were uniformly fruitless and vain; and the most successful of all such imaginary models of excellence are so far from realizing our ideas of moral perfection, that they are generally marked by a proud and selfish spirit, or deformed by vices and defects that are dishonourable to humanity. None of the wisest and the best of pagan philosophers ever made the most distant approach to the idea of such a character as that of Christ. Nay, the wisest and the best in former ages of the church, in all their pious aspirations after purity and goodness, were not much further ahead of them in conceiving such a model of moral perfection. And we may confidently hazard the assertion, that were all the saints of the Old Testament age before the appearance of Christ to have their separate excellences combined, and thrown, as it were, into a moral kaleidoscope, they could not furnish sufficient materials out of which a portrait of Christ might be formed. He not only rises to an immeasurable superiority above them all, but stands prominently forward to our view as altogether original. He went about in the unwearied office of doing good to the bodies and the souls of men, delivering the purest and most excellent counsels with the greatest familiarity and freedom from parade; and His daily conduct was a living commentary on the truth and excellence of His precepts. His wisdom as a teacher, though tried in the most unexpected manner and on the most difficult emergencies, was not only never at fault, but was ever bursting forth with new, unexpected, and increasing lustre on the admiration of men. And then, in His private character, He united such a combination of moral excellences,—such a piety to God, and a benevolence to men,—such an unbroken and exemplary attention to every personal, social, and relative duty; He exhibited such majesty united with so much simplicity, such greatness of soul together with so much condescension and grace, so much fortitude with so much gentleness,—such an assemblage, in short, of all the qualities that command admiration and draw forth esteem,—that in the whole range of history there has never appeared a rival to contest or an equal to divide with Him the homage of universal regard. He is the purest and loftiest of human souls, the Man who stands morally at the head of the species; the incarnation of all the virtues that exalt and sanctify humanity. How or from what source did His biographers derive the conception of such a character? Not from any previous model which they might have studied, and on which they might have improved: not from the imaginative stores of their own minds; for the most learned men, the most inventive geniuses even of that rare kind which first "exhausted worlds, and then imagined new," had never been able to form the slightest idea of it, or to make the most distant approach to it. And yet this character, delineated in the narratives of the humble fishermen of Galilee, has commanded the admiration of the greatest and the wisest of every subsequent age. Even the bitterest enemies of the gospel have joined in this tribute; and Rousseau, one of the leading champions of modern infidelity, has recorded it as his deliberate verdict, that if the humble evangelists had invented such a character as a fiction of their own, they would themselves be greater than the hero of their story.

But the Christ they portrayed was not a creation of the fancy. He was a real historical personage, who "tabernacled" in Judea eighteen hundred years ago. And that a number of different independent writers, including the prophets as well as the evangelists, who lived in different ages, whose minds were unpolished by learning or science, and who were strongly imbued with all the narrow prejudices of their country, should have united in contributing their several parts in presenting to the world the same portrait of the same unparalleled character, may be surely pronounced an impossibility, upon any other hypothesis than that they all were guided and influenced by the inspiration of God.

IV. The idea of sin given in the Scriptures affords additional evidence of their inspiration. Previous to the introduction of Christianity, the Greeks and Romans had not the conception of sin; and although *peccatum* in Latin, and *ámartia* in Greek, are both used as equivalent to sin in our language, yet these words, as used by classic writers, were far from embodying the idea which they afterwards expressed, when adopted into the service of Christians. The heathen mind was a total stranger to the sentiment; nor had it any channel through which it could find admission, till their views and feelings were revolutionized through the transforming influence of Christianity. They were familiar with the idea of guilt,—as a wound, a pain, a sense of moral uneasiness in the breast of an individual. But the idea of sin as a taint, an element of moral corruption, infecting the whole human race, and transmitted as a hereditary evil from the first man to all his posterity, was one to which the natural mind was utterly unequal. In like manner, holiness is an idea of which the mind of man has no natural conception. It knows well about virtue, as expressing those moral excellences which are held in common estimation by the world. But it never dreamed of such an exaltation of spiritual character as that which consists in all the intellectual powers and affections of humanity acting in perfect harmony under the sanctifying influence of true religion,—such a state of the soul as that which results from being created again after the image of God, in knowledge, righteousness, and true holiness. Ideas of this kind were altogether strange and unknown to the natural mind of man; and they prove that the book from which they were derived was given by inspiration of God.

In the case of all who have imbibed the true spirit of the Scriptures, and who are living under the habitual influence of its sanctifying power, the happy effects are seen in the embodiment of its beautiful and divine morality in their character and conduct. It is true that multitudes who profess to believe and walk according to the rules of the divine word come far short of this high standard of excellence; but still, however defective or contradictory the lives of its professed disciples may often be, the principles of the Bible remain in their own pure and exalted perfection; and, while all other systems, heathen and infidel, are utterly incapable of inspiring one generous or elevated sentiment, but, on the contrary, tend uniformly to vitiate the understanding and harden the heart, the inspired word, when understood and felt in all its heavenly influence, possesses the moral power of not only shedding a grace around the most splendid and most accomplished character, but of giving to the poorest and most uneducated, principles, motives, and rules for the government, together with sources of enjoyment for the solace and the happiness of life, which the wisdom of the world, with all its pretensions, can never impart.

LECTURE V.

Different Theories of Inspiration—Natural Inspiration or Genius —Religious Inspiration or extraordinary Piety—Inspiration of the Sacred Writers not subjective, but objective.—The Spirit of God: not His ordinary Influences, but extraordinary Gifts, miraculous Endowments manifested by the Performance of Great Works—Bezaleel, the Seventy Elders, Samson, Jephthah, Saul—and especially the Communication of Divine Truth.—Three Stages or Steps in the Process—The Revelation to the Messenger; his Apprehension of it, or the State of his Mind prepared for receiving it; and the Power of embodying it in Language.—First, the Revelation, "the Word of the Lord," came suddenly—Means of knowing the Word of the Lord—Not an Illusion of the Fancy—No private Interpretation.—Second, Different Modes of communicating the Divine Will—Condescending Familiarity to Adam—Face to Face in the instance of Moses—Afterwards by Dreams, Elihu, by Visions, and by Divine Illapses.—Third, Power of imparting the Truth revealed to Others—Necessity of this Power to stamp the Record with Divine Authority—Language emblematic, or modified by the Medium through which the Revelation was conveyed—Moved to speak and write— Hand of the Lord—Bodily Effects of the Communication, sometimes agitating—Prophets both active and passive— Instruments in communicating the Divine Will, but not unconscious Instruments—The Mechanical View of Inspiration adopted by Justin Martyr—This Dogma revived at Reformation — Coleridge's sarcastic Description of it as Spiritual Ventriloquism—Inconsistent with the Laws of our Mental Constitution—Divine Element — Human Element— Individuality—Diversity of Style—Action of each Distinct, while the Union leads to harmonious Co-operation—Incomprehensible—Writers of the New Testament—A Calm and Permanent Inspiration.

INSPIRATION, meaning the agency by which the Scriptures were produced, is a primary and fundamental fact in its literary history; and every reader who has duly pondered the views propounded in the preceding pages, must have seen in the leading characteristics of the sacred volume a basis broad and solid enough for the full establishment of that fact. Looking to the contents of the Bible,—to the structure and style of the sacred history,—to the lengthened chain of prophecies pointing to a distant future, many of which have been, and are in the course of being accomplished,—to its sublime doctrines,—and to its reigning character and aims, so different from the principles and spirit that pervade human productions, it is impossible for an intelligent and candid person to come to any other conclusion, than that in the composition of this book, there is discernible a superior wisdom, which superintended, directed, or controlled its penmen. How and by what means this influence was communicated could not fail to become a subject of earnest inquiry, prompted alike by intelligent curiosity, grateful piety, and a laudable desire to learn all the ascertainable facts connected with so remarkable an emanation of divine wisdom. The Scripture does not present to us, as an object of study, the nature or the manner of its inspiration. What it does propose to our faith is simply the divine inspiration of the word as delivered by the sacred writers; and after it has been admitted as a truth, that a spiritual agency was exerted on the penmen of Scripture, the *modus operandi* is unquestionably a matter of minor interest and importance. Nevertheless, men of speculative tendencies, who delight to investigate the causes and trace the course of things, were naturally led to consider the possibilities and probabilities of a divine influence being put forth in superintending and guiding the movements of the human mind in the production of the Bible. These being conceded, they were led further to inquire who were the privileged persons selected to communicate the mind of God to man; in what manner they were qualified by the inspiration of the Spirit for the office to which they were appointed; whether they were merely passive or active recipients of the divine afflatus, co-operating with all their energies in the discharge of their divine mission; what was the special fitness of the times and places when the intermittent spring of inspiration gave forth its purifying waters; for what immediate or remotely prospective ends the communications were made; and whether these communications received a colouring from the distinctive idiosyncrasies of the inspired messengers, or exhibited an unvarying uniformity of style and character. These questions, all of which cluster around the central idea of inspiration, though of secondary importance in religious practice, possess great interest in philosophy and speculation; and as numerous theories have been advanced and keenly advocated by eminent writers, it falls within the province of a work of this kind to examine whether and how far they are adequate to explain all the phenomena which appear in the Scripture. Whatever interest the question may possess in a metaphysical or psychological point of view, inspiration as a practical subject remains; nor can an intelligent belief in the reality of inspiration be affected by any hypothesis which theorists may form for determining the confines of the close mysterious influence that was exerted by the spiritual over the material, the divine over the human.

Rationalists, though professed believers, entertain in general a low idea of the character and authority of the scriptural record; and after eliminating the supernatural element entirely from the sacred volume, they are only carrying out their principle to its legitimate consequences, when they deny the reality of a miraculous influence in the production of the Bible. That denial, however, has been made in a variety of forms. Some maintain that the sacred writers communicated their religious teaching in myths, which, according to the tastes and habits of their age, were embodied in narratives invented as a literary framework for their public exhibition; others hold that the prophets and apostles, under a mental hallucination, mistook their own impressions and thoughts for realities, and recorded them as objective facts; while a third party, considerable both for numbers and influence in this country, as well as on the Continent and in America, virtually deny the inspiration of the sacred writers, while affecting to recognise them as men gifted with superior natural talents. They use the term inspired in the loose and secondary sense in which it is frequently applied; and in one point of view, there can be no objection to that application of the word: for, as "the inspiration of the Almighty giveth understanding," so every person of high intellectual endowments must be regarded as having received them from "the Father of lights, from whom cometh down every good and perfect gift." Accordingly, an eloquent Rationalist has said: "All genius is inspired. It is a scintillation of the Infinite, a beam of the great universal mind. Homer, Milton, and Shakspeare were inspired to sing; Socrates and Plato to teach men the philosophy of mind and morals; Newton and Laplace to investigate the laws of nature; Tell and Washington to vindicate the cause of liberty." And he considers that the prophets and apostles were in *like manner* inspired, by their showing themselves animated by a spark of the *mens divinior*, which is lighted up in the breasts of all nature's aristocracy. A little consideration, however, is all that is necessary to show that the sacred writers occupy a position peculiar to themselves, and which none who have risen to greatness in literature, science, or art, have equalled or can equal. The poet, even of that order to which is ascribed the power of creative genius, can only idealize the scenes of the natural world, and in his highest moods, when " his eye is in a fine frenzy rolling," and " his fancy from her pictured urn throws thoughts that breathe and words that burn," can do no more than take of the things of earth to form new and imaginary combinations of nature for himself; whereas the prophets were favoured with "visions of God," and sung of times when, all old things having passed away, there shall be "a new heaven and a new earth." The philosopher who, like Newton, described the laws of the planetary system, or, like Locke, marshalled the shadowy tribes of mind, discovered laws important in their bearing upon the enlightenment and welfare of mankind, but still laws which, though long hidden, were reachable by patient research and well-directed labour; whereas the sacred writers communicated a knowledge of heavenly and divine things which no human industry or penetration could have disclosed, and which never could have been known except through persons employed by God Himself in revealing these mysteries. The promoters of social progress, by the introduction of the steam-engine, the telescope, and the telegraph, have triumphed over the obstructions of time and space, and brought the most distant and opposite parts of the earth, as it were, into close proximity; but the writers of the Bible, by proclaiming faith in Christ, and "the new commandment which He gave," have announced principles which, when established, will not only draw all the scattered families of mankind into a state of happy union and brotherly intercourse, but reconcile all things in heaven and earth to God. The fact is, that there is no common ground on which men of genius in the literary, scientific, or political world can be compared with the sacred penmen; and that the object of the Rationalistic party, who are ready to recognise their inspiration, is not to elevate them to the first ranks of humanity, but to reduce them to a level with mere naturally able men. Besides, the sacred writers do nowhere claim the prestige of genius. With the exception of a very few, the greater part of them were men who would have passed their lives in obscurity, and left the world unnoticed and unknown, but for being called to the honourable office of proclaiming the divine will. It was not their intellectual power nor their extensive qualifications that brought them into the notice of their contemporaries, and still holds them up to the admiration of posterity, but their being the bearers of a message supported by the credentials of heaven, and the authoritative announcement of "Thus saith the Lord."

Further, this theory is founded on the erroneous assumption, that the inspiration of the sacred writers was subjective, whereas it was wholly objective. It did not spring from within, or was produced by the exaltation of the natural faculties to an unwonted pitch of energy and action: it came upon them from without, emanating from a quarter above and beyond themselves; and that source is uniformly described in Scripture to be the Spirit of God. Now the Spirit is promised equally to all the people of God; and in whatever form or degree any of them require His heavenly influences, they are bestowed. Those who enjoy them show the effects by their being led to understand the will of God as revealed in the Scriptures, to perceive it in all the analogies of divine truth, and to feel its importance and its power in sanctifying the whole tone of their characters and lives. Nay, wherever the truth is brought home to the understanding and the heart with the demonstration of the Spirit, it has also the moral power of bringing all the faculties and passions of their souls into healthful and harmonious exercise,—of not only imparting light and peace, but of giving to the uneducated, the humble, and the weak, a dignity of sentiment, a purity of feeling, and a moral energy which philosophy never gave, and never can give. The sacred writers, as good men, would enjoy those common influences of the Spirit; but that they were not all in a sanctified and saved condition, is evident from the fact that amongst the number were a Balaam, a Judas, and others, of whom our Lord declared : "Many will say unto me in that day, Lord, Lord, have we not prophesied in Thy name, and in Thy name have cast out devils, and in Thy name done many wonderful works? And then will I profess unto them, I never knew you." The inspiration of the sacred writers, then, was not a religious inspiration, the effect of transcendent piety and high-toned spiritual-mindedness. It was an inspiration not necessarily implying a regenerated character, and was amongst those extraordinary gifts which the Spirit conferred upon some who were employed in advancing the kingdom of God. Thus the Spirit of God is described as qualifying Bezaleel and Aholiab [1] for the work of erecting the tabernacle. It is the explicit doctrine of Scripture, that intellectual power or genius is derived from God (Job xxxii. 8 ; Jas. i. 17); and in reference to those two persons, it is said that even excellence in the mechanical arts is a divine gift. The statement that the Spirit of God filled, invigorated, and animated the minds of these head workmen, is so particularly made, and so often

[1] Ex. xxxv. 35.

repeated, as to convey the impression of a divine afflatus, and it is generally thought that they were endowed with the gifts and qualities necessary for their work to a degree which amounted to inspiration. In fact, the tabernacle was to an ancient Israelite nearly what the Epistles of the New Testament are to a modern Christian. Everything in it and about its apartments, and their furniture, was to possess the sacredness of a faithful exhibition of the scheme of divine grace. Nothing could have been added, subtracted, or in the least degree altered, without leading to fatal errors. To have changed the form and use of an altar, or to have confounded the furniture of the holy with that of the most holy place, would have been a corruption, the same in kind and tendency as to pervert or obliterate the most important passages of the New Testament Scriptures; and hence it was just as necessary that Bezaleel and his associate should be filled with the Spirit of God for giving a faithful transcript of the divine will in the tabernacle, as it was that the apostles should be inspired for unfolding the mind of Christ in the Epistles. The former were chosen to provide the means of religious instruction, by signs and symbols, to babes in understanding and knowledge;

while the latter were called to do it in a written form to grown-up men: and thus all Scripture, whether pictorial or alphabetic, was given by inspiration of God. The Spirit of God is described as qualifying leading men under the theocracy for the performance of public duties requiring extraordinary measures of wisdom, fortitude, and daring, as the seventy elders under Moses, Gideon, Samson, Jephthah, Saul, and others. It may be thought a Hebraism to ascribe to the Spirit of God what in our day would be called an unwonted exertion of wisdom and energy, suited to the exigencies of the occasion or the habits of the place. But if the form of expression be Hebraistic, so also were the actions themselves; for nothing like them is related in the history of any other people. But the principal work for which the Spirit of God is described as endowing men with His extraordinary gifts, is that of fitting a select few by inspiration for the delivery of divine truth to men. "God at sundry times and in divers manners spake in time past unto the fathers *by* the prophets."[1] This implies that He spoke first *to* the minds of

---

[1] The Greek original (Heb. i. 1) has ἐν τοῖς προφήταις—ἐν for διά, in for *by*; διὰ τῶν προφητῶν—as διὰ στόματος τῶν ἁγίων προφητῶν, by the mouth of the holy prophets, Luke i. 70.

the prophets, and then spoke *by* them. For this important office three things were necessary: the revelation of the truth to the chosen messenger; his apprehension, or the prepared state of his mind to receive it; and the power of imparting the revealed truth to others.

1. The revelation, or "the word of the Lord." This form of expression is a phrase of frequent occurrence in the later Scriptures, and it is almost invariably used to announce some direct communication from heaven, or the relation of a prophetic message, such as that which the seers or prophets of Israel were charged to deliver. The term naturally suggests the idea of audible and articulate sounds, by which the Lord made an oracular announcement of His will to men; and the revelation was made sometimes through the medium of a vocal address, at other times without the employment of this external agency. In the instances of Moses, when he entered the tabernacle (Num. vii. 89, viii. 1), of Nebuchadnezzar (Dan. iv. 30), of our Lord at three eventful periods of His ministry (Matt. iii. 17, xvii. 5; John xii. 28), and of Paul (Acts ix. 4), a real voice, miraculously produced, uttered sounds which were heard and understood by those to whom they were addressed; and that fact is

announced in a manner so express, that there can be no room for doubting. But the phraseology, in general, implies no external phenomena, and the *usus loquendi* of the sacred writers leads to the conclusion, that when "the word of the Lord came" (Heb. *was*) to any one, it was by a direct influence upon his mind, originating a train of ideas so far from the ordinary range of human thoughts or the penetration of human sagacity, and impressed with such unusual vividness, as was sufficient to determine it to be a supernatural communication. This is the formula with which the prophets generally introduce their communications, whether in reference to a direct special mission to individuals,[1] or to a more detailed and elaborate prediction against the nations, or to a solemn denunciation of God's judgments against the apostate people of Israel. It intimated that the *burden* or subject of their prophetic announcements was not the invention of their own minds, the result of their own observations, the fruit of their own cogitations,— not deduced from intelligence brought to them, nor

---

[1] Word of God came : 1 Sam. ix. 15, 27 ; 2 Sam. vii. 4, 27, xii. 7, xxiv. 12 ; 1 Kings xii. 22, xvii. 2, xviii. 1, xix. 9, 15, xx. 13, 14, 28, 42, xxi. 19, 28 ; 2 Kings iii. 17 ; 1 Chron. xvii. 3. The word of the Lord came : Num. xxii. 18 ; Deut. v. 5 ; 1 Sam. iii. 1, 7, xv. 3 ; 1 Kings xi. 27, xii. 24, xiii. 1, 2, 5, 9-32 ; Isa. ii. 1-3 ; Jer. i. 2, xxv. 3 ; Ezek. i. 3.

perhaps fully comprehended by the bearer of it (1 Pet. i. 10, 11),—but was a message with which the prophet was charged by God, and which bore such unequivocal evidence of its divine origin, that neither the messenger, nor the party to whom it was addressed, entertained any doubt as to its being a communication from heaven.

2. As to the way in which the word of the Lord came, it is interesting to consider the different modes employed by the Divine Being of making known himself and His will at those early periods of the world's history, when the word was in the course of being revealed, and before it was embodied in a permanent form. There is observable a gradual change from the time when, with condescending familiarity, God deigned to converse with His recently formed creature man, and to instruct him by word of mouth, down to the present age, when He no longer lets His voice be heard, and no longer commissions the prophets and apostles to make new revelations of His will to the chosen people. Having spoken to men at large by His Son, whose advent and ministry shed the full blaze of light on all that pertained to our present duty and future salvation, and the canon of Scripture being now complete under the dispensa-

tion of the Spirit, there is no necessity nor ground to look for any further knowledge or additional communication of the divine will than what we possess in the Scriptures. But in giving out the matter which was progressively embodied in a written form, God was pleased to reveal His will in different ways. Not to dwell upon that singular form called speaking face to face [1] and mouth to mouth,[2] and to enjoy which, whatever the phraseology means, was during the time of the Jewish church the distinguished and exclusive privilege of Moses, one of the most common channels by which revelation was communicated was through the medium of a dream. "If there be a prophet among you," saith the Lord, "I will speak unto him in a dream."[3] And Elihu was declaring the experience of the age of Job, when he said, "In a dream, in a vision of the night, when deep sleep falleth upon men, in slumberings upon the bed, then He openeth the ears of men, and sealeth their instruction."[4] Accordingly, it was in a dream that Jacob was promised the land on which he lay for an inheritance; and the future Saviour, in whom all the families of the earth should be blessed, was obscurely

[1] Ex. xxxiii. 11.
[2] Num. xii. 8.
[3] Num. xii. 6.
[4] Job iv. 13, xxxiii. 15, 16.

shadowed forth to him. And it was by the same means of communication that Solomon received the rare and enviable privilege of asking the best gifts of heaven.[1] Nor was it merely to His own devoted servants that God imparted a revelation of His will; but on several important occasions, even to heathen princes also: as to Pharaoh He pre-intimated the famine with which He was about to afflict the land of Egypt; and to Nebuchadnezzar the awful calamity that was impending on that proud sovereign. But in such cases there was this marked difference, that while a prophetic dream was given to heathen or ungodly men, the power of interpretation did not accompany it—they knew not what the dream meant till the interpretation was sent by some servant of the Lord; whereas the prophets and people of God received usually the interpretation along with the dream.[2] But a still more frequent method of communicating the will of God was in a vision (Heb. *bamahazeh*), Sept. ἐν ὁραμιτι. The recipient of a divine communication in this form was fully awake; but his mind, supernaturally elevated, was entirely absorbed in the contemplation of objects apart from the

---

[1] 1 Kings iii. 5.
[2] Gen. xv., xxviii., xlvi.; Dan. vii.; Matt. i. 11.

influence of material impressions, as well as unconnected with any former experience; and the supernatural scene was, by the intense excitement of his faculties, as distinctly exhibited to his mental vision as if he had obtained the knowledge through the medium of the bodily eye. It was in respect to this most frequently adopted method of revelation the prophets were called *seers;* and the scenes exhibited as *tableaux vivans* to their imagination or their senses were described as the visions of God.[1] Of such a character was the vision granted to Jacob,[2] to Moses,[3] to Elisha,[4] to Isaiah,[5] to Jeremiah,[6] Daniel,[7] and Zechariah,[8] to Peter,[9] Paul,[10] and John.[11]

There was still another way in which the will of God was intimated to His servants, viz. by immediate impulses and suggestions of the Holy Spirit, as recorded in the experience of David,[12] of Philip,[13] and of Peter.[14]

Thus, not to mention appearances of angels in human form,[15] as well as of prelusive manifesta-

---

[1] 2 Chron. xxvi. 5 ; Ezek. i. 1, viii. 3.
[2] Gen. xxxii. 24–32 ; cf. Hos. xi. 4.
[3] Ex. iii.
[4] 2 Kings vi.
[5] Isa. vi. 1.
[6] Jer. i. 11.
[7] Dan. ix.
[8] Zech. i. 8.
[9] Acts x. 11.
[10] 2 Cor. xii.
[11] Rev., *passim.*
[12] 1 Chron. xxviii.
[13] Acts viii. 29.
[14] Acts x. 19.
[15] Gen. xix.

tions of the Saviour,[1] God spake of old in divers manners to the fathers; and as "there were prophets" or inspired messengers of God "since the world began," so the mode of revealing the divine will to each was adapted with divine wisdom to the circumstances of time and place, as well as to the character and state of the recipient. By what means he was satisfied that the communication made to him was of divine origin does not always appear, although on some occasions its supernatural character was established, in the case of a dream, by its being doubled,[2] or, as in the instance of Nebuchadnezzar, by its vivid impression and portentous character; in that of a voice speaking, where there was no person present to utter articulate sounds, by its repetition;[3] and in other instances, by the hand of Providence preparing a train of circumstances, which led to the direct end of attesting the word of the Lord that the prophet had received.[4] He himself might be unable, as was frequently the case, to penetrate the hidden significance of the matter he was called to reveal, but his mind was supernaturally enlarged and invigo-

---

[1] Ex. xxxiv.; Josh. v. 13; Judg. xii. 1.
[2] Gen. xxxvii., xli. 32.   [3] 1 Sam. iii.
[4] Jer. xxxii. 6–8; Zech. xi. 11.

x

rated to apprehend the mystic truth set before him; and the extraordinary clearness of his conceptions is indicated by the formula with which the prophetic books usually open: "The vision of Isaiah,—which he *saw;*" "The words of Amos, —which he *saw;*" "The word of the Lord that came to Micah,—which he *saw.*"

3. The power of imparting the revealed truth to others. A revelation might have been given; but if the publication of it had been left to the discretion of the messenger, it might have been in some points of vital importance imperfect or erroneous, and at best it would have been a mere human testimony. Had the writers of the Bible stated what they saw and heard in the supernatural ways described above, delivering their reports from the stores of memory, and according to the dictates of their judgments,—not requiring any special assistance, and not receiving it,—what they announced as religious instruction in the name of God would so far have the sanction of divine authority; for, possessing the credentials of their prophetic office, they would claim the same confidence for the narration of what they witnessed on earth as for the voices and visions of heaven. But it would only be the substance of their in-

structions which would have a religious nature; to this only would their credentials refer; and only as it respects this could our confidence in the instructions of the Scripture conduce to our moral and spiritual improvement. The record in which they were embodied would be possessed of no authoritative character; and as its authors might have mixed up a variety of irrelevant and secular subjects with the divine communications they had received, it might be a delicate and difficult matter to separate the divine from the human, and truth from unavoidable error. The necessity, then, of the ambassadors chosen of God to reveal His will being not only qualified to *apprehend* the revelations made to them, but being endowed with the adequate power of embodying it in language, is obvious. It rendered them not omniscient,—for their knowledge was limited to the truth revealed, —but infallible, and it has stamped the record with divine authority: for we have thus a solid and comfortable assurance, not only that the word of God is in the Bible, but that the Bible is the word of God.

It was thus that all to whom God was pleased to reveal a portion of His will were qualified by the Spirit to receive and impart it; and as He was from time to time making partial revelations in all ages down to the advent of Christ, there were always some inspired messengers in the world, such as Enoch, Noah, Abraham, and his immediate descendants, Isaac and Jacob. With Moses, a new era was begun in the impartation of inspired power; for as a particular people were chosen and trained to preserve the knowledge and worship of God for many centuries amid the darkness, superstitions, and polytheism of all other nations in the world, a direct course of religious instruction and warning was always kept up through the instrumentality of divinely called and qualified ambassadors. The measure of inspiration, as well as the number of inspired messengers, was always proportioned to the exigency of the times. And hence, as an unbroken succession of prophets appeared in the later and declining ages of the monarchy, so the greatest of those messengers flourished, and some of the grandest predictions of the glorious state of the kingdom of God in the future ages of the gospel were delivered, in the darkest and most degenerate times of the Jewish church. Elijah and Elisha rose in the reign of Ahab. Isaiah continued his prophetic functions through the time of Ahaz. And during the protracted period of captivity, several eminent prophets alternately consoled, encouraged, and edified their exiled countrymen. But with Malachi inspiration ceased, and the Jews were left like other people to their own resources. The reason was, that their national character had undergone a total change; and having been completely cured of that strange fondness for idolatry, to protest against which, as a breach of the national covenant, had been the immediate occasion of the prophetic office, they no longer needed the services of those extraordinary ministers: for they thenceforth became as distinguished for their blind and bigoted adherence to national institutions, as they had formerly been for their woful departures from the law and the worship of God. The miraculous provision which had been made by the institution of inspired instructors was withdrawn or suspended for a period of four hundred years. But "as, in the material world, Providence has everywhere proportioned the means to the end, the forces being not greater than the occasion requires; so it would seem that, in His spiritual communications, extraordinary aids are only granted when ordinary influence is insufficient."[1] The advent of Messiah being the greatest

[1] Clinton's *Fasti Hellenici*, vol. i. p. 283.

and most momentous era in the world's history, demanded the renewal of miraculous aid; and accordingly inspiration, after a long suspension, was revived in the church to the apostles and evangelists, to qualify them for the extraordinary duties they had to perform in laying the foundation of the Christian church. But there is discernible a marked difference in the character of the inspiration which was imparted respectively to the ancient prophets and the apostles of Christ; and it is proper, therefore, to take a brief notice of the characteristic distinction.

The prophets, doubtless, enjoyed the ordinary influences of the Spirit in delivering their public instructions, as preachers do in modern times; but those influences were bestowed only in a partial degree; and hence, as in working a miracle a considerable time was previously spent in prayer,[1] so the illapse of the Spirit on a prophet, to whom the word of the Lord came for some special mission, was usually marked by circumstances that arrested attention. "The Spirit of God came upon the prophets." "Searching what or what manner of time the Spirit of Christ which was *in* them did signify, when He testified beforehand the sufferings

[1] 1 Kings xvii. 21; 2 Kings iv. 34, 35.

of Christ, and the glory that should follow." "It is not ye that speak, but the Spirit of your Father that speaketh in you." These and many other passages of a similar import intimate the fact of direct revelation, the result of the extraordinary influence of God acting upon the minds of the prophets and apostles, by which they were supernaturally illuminated, and had the ideas, objects, and events vividly impressed upon them, a knowledge of which they could never have acquired in a natural way, or which, without such an interposition of divine aid, they could never have been qualified to communicate to the world. These passages, viewed separately, and still more collectively, convey the impression that the recipients were wrought upon directly and immediately by the Holy Spirit, who enlightened and prepared their minds to perceive the things which they were to promulgate to others; disposed them to give earnest attention to them, to view them with intense interest; and furnished them, as the exigency of particular circumstances required, with the power of announcing in correct and appropriate language the matters which they were inspired to make known. In the nature of things, the engrossing occupation of the mind with any subject of unusual interest and importance tends to produce excitement. And how much more so, when the subject is wrapped in impenetrable mystery, and is borne upon the attention by the master-potency of the Spirit of God! At the time when the prophets were favoured with their mystic visions, their minds were commonly in a state of more than ordinary excitement. Their attention was so absorbed with the visionary scene that flitted before their fancy, as to make them totally insensible to what was actually passing around them. They were sometimes awake, but they were also sometimes in a trance; or, as it was generally in the season of deepest slumber that the prophetic afflatus came upon them, the effect was to rouse their imaginations into the most vivid exercise; and while their senses were dormant, or ceased to hold any communication with external nature, the faculties and emotions of their minds were kept in the most intense action by the strange and unknown images that were successively submitted to their eyes. Nor was this all, for sometimes violent effects were produced upon the body; and although there is no ground to suppose that the light of reason was under an eclipse, and the mental faculties were overpowered, yet the corporeal frame was sometimes subjected to so extreme an agitation, that the traces of it were felt many days after. Some indication of this overmastering power is conveyed by such statements as these: "The Spirit of the Lord came upon" the prophet. "The hand of the Lord was strong, or fell upon" him.[1] "Holy men of God spake as they were moved [2] by the Holy Ghost." The first of these expressions implies that the prophetic afflatus was usually sudden. No premonition was given of its descent, and no mental effort made to procure it; for although Elisha sought on one occasion the aid of a minstrel, previous to the utterance of a remarkable prediction,[3] that act was a personal expedient of his, to soothe and tranquillize his mind, which had been agitated by the presence of an idolatrous king. The inspiration, for the most part, was unexpected by the recipient at the time when its influence began to be felt; and sometimes that influence bore upon him with a pressure which greatly affected his physical frame. Sudden and painful intelligence frequently gives rise to such violent emotions as to agitate the

[1] Isa. viii. 11; Ezek. viii. 1, iii. 14, xi. 5.
[2] Gr. φερόμενοι, "borne along, carried forward," as a ship by the wind.—ALFORD.
[3] 2 Kings iii. 15.

bodily frame to its extremities; and is it wonderful that, when the prophets were charged with the astounding disclosures of impending judgments upon their own nation or the neighbouring countries,—disclosures of grinding famine, deadly pestilence, desolating wars and protracted exile, the fall of great monarchs, and the ruin of flourishing empires,—or, on the other hand, with the animating announcement of the glorious advent and the inestimable blessings of Messiah's reign, —the strangeness of the visions they witnessed, and the magnitude of the thoughts with which their minds were filled, were followed by nervous excitement, physical prostration, and even swooning?[1] Besides, the symbolic acts they were commanded to perform before the country— although some of them were merely ideal and visionary— were calculated by their singularity to expose the prophets to public derision and obloquy, so that they must have entered upon the discharge of the prophetic office with great reluctance. Isaiah's naming his son Maher-shalal-hash-baz (hasten-booty, speed-spoil), walking naked and barefoot three years,[2] and Hosea's marriage with

---

[1] Dan. viii. 18, x. 10, 11.
[2] Isa. xx. 2, 3, naked, *i.e.* loosing the sackcloth from his loins.

Gomer: these and the many grotesque actions and gesticulations exhibited by men of the prophetic order,—for they taught by act and sign as well as by words,—gave rise to the proverbial taunt, "The prophet is a fool, and the spiritual man (man of the Spirit) is mad." [1] Accordingly Jeremiah, with reference to the public sneers with which he was assailed by the people of his degenerate times, says, "Thou hast persuaded me, and I was persuaded; Thou wast stronger than I, and hast prevailed." [2] The reproaches that were daily heaped upon him preyed so much upon his sensitive mind, that he resolved to prophesy no more. And he did discontinue his duties for a while. It was then that the word of the Lord, which he had been commissioned to speak, became as "a burning fire shut up in his loins," and "he was weary with his forbearance;" so that he could not refrain from speaking, and he resumed his prophetic functions as formerly. Thus they "spake as they were moved by the Holy Ghost;" and they wrote also under the influence of the same divine Agent the different portions of the Scripture which they

---

[1] Hos. ix. 7, comp. 2 Kings ix. 11.
[2] Jer. xx. 7. *Pittithani*, Gr. πιιθω, *persuaded*; not *deceived*, as in the Authorized Version.

respectively contributed, some of them being prompted by the pious and benevolent motive of teaching the principles of faith and duty, others having received an express command to record the revelations made to them.[1]

That the seers themselves remained in partial or complete ignorance of the real import or character of many of the scenes supernaturally disclosed to them, appears not only from the evident bearing of several passages of Scripture, but from the nature of the case; as the objects revealed often referred to times and circumstances so far remote from their actual experience, that no explanation could have made these level to their comprehension. They were therefore, strictly speaking, reporters of what they saw, retailers of communications they had been selected as the honoured instruments of receiving from heaven. The pictures exhibited to their enraptured fancy made a deep and indelible impression, though the receivers could tell little or nothing of what their dreams portended. They could describe with the invigorated powers and from the faithful records of memory what they had seen; but they were often left in as painful

---

[1] Ex. xvii. 14, xxxiv. 27; Isa. viii. 1; Jer. xxx. 2; Hab. ii. 2; Rev. i. 11.

perplexity as to the meaning of their visions, as the people to whom their predictions were delivered. Accordingly, we read that "they searched diligently what and what manner of time the Spirit of prophecy that was in them did signify." And who does not see in this remarkable circumstance a proof of the inspiration of the prophets? Not only did the predicted events belong to periods so remotely future, and involve contingencies so many and so great, that no sagacity, however far-sighted, could have made the discovery of them; but they were wrapt up as in an unknown tongue, or in a sealed book, from the ken even of the persons employed to record them. And how, in such circumstances, could they have been the authors of a cunningly devised fable? There must have been, had they attempted to palm an imposture on the credulity of mankind, an incoherence in the parts of their story, which no ingenuity could explain or reconcile; or it would have been pervaded by a rhapsody or extravagant rant, which in the judgment of intelligent readers would have been sufficient to detect their fictitious character. But, on the contrary, when through the well-known and uniform symbols of the prophetic style one arrives at the plain meaning of the prophecies, he perceives a close connection, a beautiful harmony in their details, as well as a minute accuracy, a graphic faithfulness to historical truths, such as establishes beyond a doubt the inspiration and divine authority of the Old Testament prophets.

The inspiration that was given to the New Testament writers, though proceeding from the same Spirit, was marked by a very different character; for it was not sudden and intermittent, but permanent: it produced no violent or sensible effects upon the mind and body; for although the Holy Ghost descended, on the day of Pentecost, with " a sound from heaven as of a rushing mighty wind," [1] it was ever afterwards calm, persuasive, and gentle, invigorating their faculties, and guiding them into the knowledge and inculcation of sanctifying truth. The Spirit, which was formally and without measure imparted to Christ at His entrance into His mediatorial office, is said to be upon Him,[2] or, as it is in a parallel passage, to " rest upon Him;" [3] thus intimating a marked and most important distinction between Him and former messengers of God: for, while the Spirit fell on them only occasionally, when they were charged with some special mission, it was to continue upon

---

[1] Acts ii. 2.   [2] Isa. ix.   [3] Isa. li. 1.

Him. And as the apostles were to prosecute the ministry of the word which He had begun, He qualified them for their important work, by the extraordinary gifts and endowments of the Holy Spirit, who was to abide with them individually and collectively for ever. The history of the first plantation of the Christian church shows how fully, freely, and permanently the Spirit was with the apostles and their coadjutors.

It has been maintained by many eminent writers that the Hebrew prophets were deprived of the free and conscious use of their faculties while under the influence of the prophetic afflatus. This was the theory of Philo and the Alexandrian school, that the consciousness of the seers was entirely suspended so long as the inspiration lasted; for, as Philo expresses it, " the human understanding takes its departure on the arrival of the Divine Spirit, and, on the removal of the latter, again returns to its home; for the mortal must not dwell with the immortal." This view has had its advocates in modern times, amongst the most eminent of whom is Hengstenberg, who holds the doctrine, that a cessation of human agency and intelligent perception is necessarily connected with a state of prophetic ecstasy; and the basis on which he rests this principle is, that it was not the prophets who spoke, but God who spoke in them. He reduces them to the condition of mere passive instruments; and when he carries his hypothesis further, by maintaining that, besides losing their consciousness, the Hebrew prophets were raised to a state of furore, or raving, like that which is described by Virgil,—

> At, Phœbi nondum patiens, immanis in antro
> Bacchatur Vates, magnum si pectore possit,
> Excussisse deum, tanto magis ille fatigat
> Os rabidum, fera corda domans, fingitque premendo,—

in what respect did the inspired seers of Israel differ from the μαντις of the Greeks or the Vates of the Romans? Hengstenberg says that the heathen Pythian priestess lost her consciousness, "because the inferior part of the soul was excited to a contest against the superior part of it;" in other words, she *raved* through the influence of the vapour which issued from the fountain in her temple, or else that a great part of the maniacal excitement was the result of dissimulation and pretence. "But what an immeasurable distance," says Moses Stuart, "between a raving man or woman, uttering incoherent sentences, or (which was more common) a dissembling hypocrite, uttering cunningly and artfully and equivocally constructed sentences and poetical riddles; and a Hebrew prophet, animated by the strongest and deepest feelings of reverence for Jehovah, and a holy ardour in the cause of true piety! Is there ambiguity, flattery, self-seeking, enigmas, in the message of the latter? None. Are not all these stamped on more or less of the heathen oracles? They are. And such being the case, we would separate the Hebrew prophet from the heathen seer, not by discrepancies of a mere physiological or psychological nature, which lie beyond our ken, in case they exist at all;"[1] or rather, which involve contradictions and impossibilities; but by a rational, enlightened, holy, zealous state of mind, which raised the true seer above all false ones, and did this by making him in a high degree like to the Author of his inspiration.

Now it is doubtless true, and universally admitted, that the prediction of future events which the prophets announced was not the result of their natural sagacity, nor the conclusion of their observant minds, but was communicated to them by Him who "knows the end from the beginning," and who has all the events of futurity as well as of the present spread out as a map before Him. But if He was desirous to remove the veil that

[1] *Bib. Repository*, vol. ii. p. 231.

shrouds the distant future from the knowledge of the world, He could have done it in many ways,— though the medium of an inferior creature or inanimate thing, or by a direct utterance from heaven; and since He did not make choice of any of these methods, but employed the services of men in making such communications, it is impossible to resist the conclusion, that the consciousness and intellectual powers of rational creatures were necessary to be enlisted, as subservient to the peculiar work of prophesying. This opinion is confirmed by considering the radical import of the Hebrew as well as Greek word, prophet, which combines both an active and a passive sense, or conveys the idea of activity springing from a preceding state of passiveness; as appears from the passage in Exodus, where the Lord says to Moses,[1] "See, I have made thee a god to Pharaoh, and Aaron thy brother shall be thy prophet," or spokesman, *i.e.* should receive from Moses a knowledge of the successive demands to be made, and then communicate them to the Egyptian monarch. The Spirit of God acted upon the minds of the prophets, not by suspending or paralyzing their consciousness, but, as we formerly remarked, by enlightening and

[1] Ex. vii. 1.

invigorating their faculties; and it seems to have been in consequence of their æsthetic feelings and their imagination having been excited to an unwonted pitch by the visionary scenes presented to them, that the great majority of the prophets embodied their prophetic songs in poetry,—a far more probable hypothesis than that they first delivered them in plain prose, and afterwards at leisure wrought them into a poetic form.

It has been the opinion of many both in the ancient and modern church, that the prophets were the mere mouthpieces of the Spirit. Balaam is appealed to by Philo as an example of a humble, involuntary, unconscious instrument through whom God spoke.[1] And Josephus represents Balaam himself as apologizing to Balak on this ground: "When the Spirit of God seizes us, it utters whatsoever sounds and words it pleases, without any knowledge on our part; for when it has come into us, there is nothing in us which remains our own."[2] This mechanical view of inspiration was adopted by Justin Martyr, who considers that the mind of the prophet under the influence of the Spirit resembled a plectrum,—a mere organ, the instrument giving out particular sounds according

[1] *De Vitâ Mosis*, lib. i. t. ii. [2] *Jewish Antiq.* iv. 6. 5.

to the chord that is struck. From the Fathers this theory was handed down till the time of the Reformation, when the dogma was revived, and strenuously maintained as doing the greatest honour to the Divine Spirit. Many pious and enlightened Christians hold it still,—either supporting it by the same illustrative comparison as Justin, or representing the sacred writers as amanuenses, merely putting on record what was dictated to them by the Spirit, and having no more control over their pens than a piece of mechanism over the wheels that belong to it. This theory was ridiculed in mingled strains of eloquence, mysticism, and heresy as "a kind of spiritual ventriloquism,— a colossal Memnon's head, a hollow passage for a voice,—a voice that mocks the voices of many men, and speaks in their names, and yet is but one voice and the same; no man uttered it, and never in a human heart was it conceived."[1]

Such a theory is opposed to the constitution of the human mind; and as God, in enlisting the services of man to communicate a supernatural knowledge of His will, would undoubtedly proceed in accordance with the laws of that intellectual and moral nature with which He has endowed

[1] Coleridge, *Confessions of an Inquiring Spirit.*

mankind, His agency, in imparting the necessary inspiration to His commissioned servants, must be considered as put forth in a manner fitted alike to distinguish the divine from the human element. The influence and operation of the Spirit of God are seen, both in applying to the ends of revelation truth already known and available, and in suggesting new and hitherto unknown truth; in the wonderful harmony that reigns throughout all the successive revelations made of the divine will; in the sublime sentiments inculcated, in the holy spirit that is breathed; and in the only adequate explanation of many phenomena in the procedure of God. The influence and operation of the man also are seen in the composition and structure of the Scriptures. There are such evident and unequivocal signs of human instrumentality — of human modes of thinking, feeling, and writing,— such striking peculiarities of human temperament and disposition, and such idiosyncrasies of thought, association, and manner, distinguishing the style of the various penmen of the Scriptures from one another,—that it is impossible to ascribe these to any other cause than the free and independent, while yet infallibly guided and guarded, action of the inspired mind. Thus in the sacred volume we trace a divine and a human element. The action of both is distinct, while the union of both leads to harmonious co-operation. Further than this, in our present state of knowledge, we cannot go. In the words of Moses Stuart, " the fact that the Spirit of God did inspire the sacred writers,— that He guided, illuminated, and aided them, and preserved them from all error, is one thing : their physical or metaphysical state, while under His special influence,—the physiology, so to speak, of inspiration,—is a thing quite different from this; and as the sacred writers have not described their feelings, while none since their time have had any experience of inspiration, that, so far as I know, has never been made out." The union of the material with the spiritual is in many things that fall within our daily observation so close, and yet so mysterious, that we cannot determine the confines that separate the one from the other. Thus, for instance, in every age, the attention of thoughtful men has been directed to the great problem, how the moral freedom of man can be reconciled with the superintending direction and control of Providence; but, notwithstanding all the attainments and researches of philosophy in the present day, it is as great, as profound and inscrutable a mystery as ever. Speculatists have recently turned their inquiries into a different channel—to discover how the efficacy of prayer is consistent with the reign of material law; in other words, how the great Being whose propitious ear we invoke can grant the fulfilment of our desires, as He has promised in the Scriptures to do, without departing from the course He has apparently prescribed to Himself in the uniform operations of nature. Every Christian believes that there was a union of two natures in the person of Christ; and those natures, though perfectly distinct, were yet so intimately connected, that the sacred writers sometimes speak of Him under the name of God, as performing actions which could be done only by man.[1] Just as inexplicable as the subject either of providence, prayer, or the hypostatical union, is that of inspiration: how the Spirit of God acted upon the minds of the sacred penmen, while leaving them to act in accordance with their personal idiosyncrasies —how they were all inspired, and yet Isaiah, Jeremiah, and Ezekiel, Peter, Paul, and John, appear as distinct in their characteristic style as the writers of their respective portions of Scriptures, as these individuals were from all other men.

[1] Acts xx. 28.

LECTURE VI.

Are there different Degrees of Inspiration?—Maimonides—Rabbinical Views—Different parts of Scripture exhibit more or less of the Spirit—Job, the Psalms, the Prophets, and Apostles—Some of the Sacred Writers more prominent and copious than others — Moses, Paul — Quotations from Turretine — Some books do, others do not, bear internal evidences of Inspiration —Pye Smith's Ideas on Inspiration—Doddridge, Dr. Arnold—Things that are supposed to detract from the Plenary Inspiration of Scripture— Ezra's Interpolations — Introduction of Secular Matter — Excessive Population of the Hebrews—Spoiling the Egyptians—Life and Reign of David—Solomon —Abishag—Voluptuous and Luxurious Life—God hardening Pharaoh's heart — Command to avenge the Midianites— Bethshemites and Uzzah—The Public Execution of Saul's Descendants for the Satisfaction of the Gibeonites—Slaves—Property—Cruelties of Ancient War Practice—Alleged Errors of Apostles—Not proved—Errors in Conduct—Jonah, Judas, Peter—Line of Demarcation—Were the Words of the Sacred Writers inspired?—Words in some instances inspired—Thinking in Words—The true Theory that the Spirit prompted the thoughts of Prophets and Apostles—The Inspiration Plenary.

A QUESTION of great interest and importance remains for consideration. Admitting that the Scriptures are possessed of an inspired character, does the quality of inspiration pervade all the books of which it consists, extending even to the minutest portions of every book, and impregnating all of them in an equal degree? From the progressive manner in which the revelation of the divine will was made, some parts of the Scripture record are comparatively obscure, while the strictly local or episodical character of others exhibits a very small, indirect, and remote bearing on the great design of the sacred volume. Accordingly, there has prevailed both in the ancient and the modern church, a strong tendency to consider inspiration as communicated on different occasions with a greater or less amount of fulness; and although nothing is said in the Scripture to countenance such an idea, the hypothesis that there are certain degrees of supernatural influence easily discernible has been widely entertained. Maimonides, the celebrated Jewish writer, reckoned no less than eleven degrees of inspiration; but the rabbinical schools generally held to three, the highest being ascribed to Moses, the second to the prophets, and the third or lowest to the writers of the Hagiographa, the didactic and devotional books of the Old Testament. A similar persuasion has existed in most periods of the Christian church; and in modern times, men of piety and learning have endeavoured to classify the different parts of Scripture according to the scale on which they conceived inspiration had been imparted or was necessary. This has been done by Twesten in Germany, and by Pye Smith, Dick, Wilson, Henderson, and others in this country,—all of them believing in the general inspiration of the Bible, but not in its equal extension to every part. I do not intend to enter into an examination of the theoretical opinions which speculative writers have advanced on this subject, as to whether there are degrees of inspiration, and how many, from simple suggestion and superintendence up to plenary and verbal dictation. All these are distinctions made by men; and therefore, rejecting them all as arbitrary, partial, and destitute of authority, I lay it down as my grand and only principle, that inspiration was universal, the inspiring power being communicated to all the writers of the Bible in common. Although all Scripture was given by inspiration of God, the measure of it was vouchsafed in exact proportion to the necessity of the circumstances; while the form and extent of it was such as the nature of the case demanded, to preserve the sacred penmen from all error, and to guide them into all the truth. Let this principle be adopted, and there will be no difficulty in perceiving what estimate ought to be formed of the character and authority of every part of the Scripture. A slight acquaintance with the sacred volume will suffice to show that some of the sacred penmen appear in a more prominent character, and that their writings occupy a larger space than others, as Moses in the Old, and Paul in the New Testament. It might have been anticipated, from the varying measures of mental ability which naturally exist among men, that a similar inequality would be found amongst those whose ordinary powers were illuminated and strengthened by the supernatural influences of the Spirit; and accordingly, in looking into the sacred volume, while all the commissioned servants of God spoke and wrote under the guidance of the Spirit, there was a great diversity of spiritual gifts, some of them being endowed with miraculous gifts, with "the word of knowledge," with "the word of wisdom," and with a capacity for useful service in the church, to a larger extent than others. Thus Moses, who was instrumentally the founder of the Jewish church, partook so fully of the Spirit of God, that the posthumous record by a later hand testifies of him, "There arose not a prophet since in Israel like unto Moses." Paul, too, who took so active and influential a part in the organization of the Christian church, was by physical and mental exertions in labours more abundant than all the apostles; and through his preaching as well as his epistles, contributed beyond all his contemporaries towards the development of the doctrines and duties of the gospel. The superior services rendered by these two writers show that, while all Scripture was given by inspiration of God, it was not given to all in the same degree; and that although all the books of Scripture were composed by inspired men, they do not all declare the glory, unfold the mind, and illustrate the ways of God with equal clearness and fulness. Some parts of the Old Testament have a higher tone of spirituality; the book of Job and the Psalms, for instance, than the books of Numbers and Leviticus, which are occupied with the dry and detached statutes of the Mosaic legislation. At the beginning of the Christian dispensation there was a more plentiful effusion of the Spirit; hence the apostles gave a larger revelation of the grace of God than the prophets; and the books of the New Testament are full of brighter disclosures and a purer morality than those of the Old. In the words of an eminent divine: "As one star differs from another star in lustre, so in the firmament of Scripture some books emit more splendid and ample, and others more faint and inconsiderable, rays of light; as the exigencies of the church more or less required, and as they relate to doctrines of greater or less importance. Thus the Gospels and the Epistles of Paul send forth those radiant beams far more copiously than the books of Ruth or Esther. Yet it is certain that each of them exhibits such evidences of truth and majesty, as prove of themselves that it is divine and authentic; or, at least, nothing is found in them that can render their authenticity doubtful."[1] It is always a cause of great satisfaction, when the internal contents of a Scripture document are such as to leave no doubt of its divine origin and authority; and when a reader, instead of appealing to external evidences of its truth, can reply somewhat like what was done to the woman of Samaria by her fellow-townsmen: "I believe, not because of thy saying, but because I have read the book myself, and know that it is of God." But there are some books of such a character, that they do not contain internal evidences of inspiration. In this class must be ranked the genealogies which, embodied in the Chronicles and other parts of the historical books, were probably copied from the

[1] Francisco Turretine, *Institutio Theologiæ*, vol. i. p. 71.

national registers; and a few other books, which appear so unlike in form as well as spirit to the other books of Scripture, that some men of piety and undoubted reverence for revelation have hesitated to recognise them as parts of the word of God. "Whether," says Dr. Pye Smith, "the whole of the Chetubim or Hagiographa, though of undoubted genuineness and authenticity as historical documents, can be considered as indited by the Holy Ghost, and as forming part of the rule of faith, is by no means so clear as to warrant our demanding an unqualified assent and agreement from all Christian men. Our canon may possibly include books not inspired."[1] Dr. Doddridge has expressed similar sentiments on the book of Esther,[2] and Dr. Arnold on some portions of Daniel. The opinions of such men as Dr. Doddridge, Pye Smith, and Dr. Arnold are worthy of respect even by those who may entirely differ from them; and though it were true, as they allege, that these books may be excluded from the sacred record without affecting one doctrine of faith or one precept of duty, yet as the book of Esther details

---

[1] *Eclectic Review*, 1826.
[2] Doddridge's *Dissertation on the Inspiration of the New Testament*.

a remarkable interposition of Providence for the preservation of His ancient church, as the Song has been signally useful in fostering the devout affections of multitudes of spiritually-minded Christians, and the authenticity of Daniel has been established on the most solid basis, we feel it impossible not to recognise such testimonies to the divine character of these books.

Not only are there some books whose title to inspired authority has been called in question, but there are numerous isolated portions in various books both of the Old and New Testaments which have been thought to vitiate the claim of Scripture to plenary inspiration. These are the interpolations of Ezra in Genesis, and others of the early historical books; and besides, there are other insertions, incorporated with the sacred text, of such a nature as plainly indicates their human origin: viz., the poetry of Lamech, the song of the well, the edicts of Nebuchadnezzar and Cyrus, the letter of Claudius Lysias to Felix, the speech of Tertullus, the account of the disastrous voyage from Alexandria, the detailed conversations of bad men, and even of Satan himself. Now Ezra was an inspired man, who acted under divine guidance; and when, in his revision of the Scriptures, he inserted explanatory notes referring to the obsolete name of a place or to a people who were unknown, because they had become extinct in his day, he was influenced by the same Divine Spirit which indited the Scriptures at first; so that his interpolations must be considered as equally inspired with the original text. With regard to the snatches of popular ballads, the legal documents of foreign countries, and the other purely secular matters which have been referred to as finding a place in the sacred volume, they have been made use of by the writers of the Scriptures because they were necessary to elucidate the history, or served to promote the cause and interests of religious truth. They are not to be considered, therefore, as a mere setting to adorn the pearl of great price, or like the mass of worthless earth in which precious ore being embedded, has to be detached from it as an unsightly encumbrance, but as historical facts enlisted by the superintending direction of the Spirit in the service of revelation, and therefore as forming an essential part of the inspired word. Still further, there are statements interspersed throughout the historical books of what purport to be facts, but which have been pronounced in certain quarters to be monstrous exaggerations, that tend seriously to affect the plenary inspiration of the record in which they are made. As some of those writers professedly believe that the Scriptures contain the word of God, they do not lay the responsibility of such statements on divine inspiration. But they deny that the passages which contain those statements are inspired, and ascribe them to the interpolation of later editors, who, being led by national vanity to magnify the prosperity of Israel from the earliest times, have blended popular traditions with the facts of sober history to such an extent as to render the sacred books no longer documents of reliable truth and authority. Foremost in this class of objections is the vast increase of the Israelites, who, consisting only of seventy persons,—all, it is alleged, that emigrated with Jacob,—rose within the space of 198 years, the duration of the sojourn in Egypt, to the prodigious amount of more than three millions. Such an excessive population in so short a time, and from so small a stock, is justly pronounced to be, on natural principles, and according to the ordinary rate of calculation, altogether incredible.[1] But a careful examination of the Scripture record shows that nothing like the alleged statement is made by

[1] Colenso on the Pentateuch.

the sacred historian. The immediate descendants of Jacob, who went down with him to Egypt, did indeed amount only to seventy souls; but along with them was a large number of home-born servants or retainers belonging to the pastoral tribe of which he was the acknowledged chief. The conjunction of these different parties was intimated by Joseph, when he spake of "his brethren" and his "father's house," *i.e.* servants;[1] and how numerous these were, may be inferred from what is said of Abraham[2] and of Isaac.[3] The rapid increase of the Hebrew population is indicated by the fact that "the land," *i.e.* of Goshen, "was filled with them;"[4] but the subsequent history shows that they were dispersed in vast numbers throughout the Delta or Lower Egypt, as artisans or tradesmen, and that by their energy, wealth, and extensive influence, they wielded almost the whole powers of the country. This amazing increase excited the jealous fears of the new king of Egypt, who devised a persecuting policy to check it. Notwithstanding this, contrary to all natural expectations, they "grew and multiplied," till, at the Exodus,

---

[1] Gen. xlvi. 31; cf. Gen. xxx. 43, xxxii. 5, 7, 16, xxxvi. 7, xxxiv. 25.
[2] Gen. xii. 16, xiv. 14.   [3] Gen. xxvi. 13-16.
[4] Ex. i. 7.

those that were of an age fit for war amounted to 600,000 men. Assuming, what is now ascertained by statistical tables, that the number of males above that age is as nearly as possible the half of the whole number of males, the entire male population of Israel would amount to 1,200,000; and adding an equal number for women and children, the aggregate number of Israelites who left Egypt would be 2,400,000.[1] The calculations of Colenso and others, who object to this vast amount of population as a legendary tale, have been founded upon the genealogical list of Jacob's descendants, which was constructed on the principle of recording only the heads of families, the ancestors of the Israelitish nation born in Canaan, and omitting all others. No mention is made in that register of the servants who certainly accompanied the patriarch into Egypt;[2] and although it is impossible to specify their numbers, yet, considering that Jacob inherited the tribal property and honours of his father and grandfather, they may be reckoned at upwards of a thousand. Such retainers are usually considered, according to Oriental custom, as forming parts of their masters' families. It is a fact that they were incorporated with the patriarchal families; for,

[1] Ex. i. 7; Ps. cv. 26.   [2] Gen. xlvi. 6, 32.

having become Hebrews, included in the covenant by the rite of circumcision and the participation of the passover, they constituted a portion of the Hebrew tribe equally with the natural descendants of Jacob. And along with these servants, "a mixed multitude went up also with them." On these grounds, then, it appears that an egregious mistake is committed by those who found their conclusions solely on the catalogue of Jacob's descendants, as if they comprised the entire emigrants to Egypt, instead of making their estimates on the broader basis of the numerous body who had become, in accordance with divine directions, incorporated with Israel.

Another circumstance connected with the time of the Exodus has been considered as inconsistent with the idea of inspiration. God is described as saying to Moses, "I will give this people favour in the sight of the Egyptians: and it shall come to pass, that, when ye go, ye shall not go empty: but every woman shall borrow of her neighbour, and of her that sojourneth in her house, jewels of silver, and jewels of gold, and raiment: and ye shall put them upon your sons and your daughters; and ye shall spoil the Egyptians."[1] It is utterly impossible,

[1] Ex. iii. 22, xi. 2, 3.

it is alleged, that God could have inspired such actions as these words describe; the ascription of which to Him is an insult to His majesty, degrading to His justice and goodness, and outraging the purity of His perfect character. The word which our version renders *borrowed*, signifies properly to *demand*, or *ask;* and the circumstances were these: The Israelites, having received little or no wages for all their laborious service in the house of bondage, were very poor. They made a demand for adequate remuneration for all their toil; and it was paid in light but valuable articles of wearing apparel and personal ornament. The demand, however, was not made only at the last moment, as if it had been extorted to ensure their departure; for the order was issued, and doubtless acted upon, previous to the infliction of the last plague.[1] But the effect was, that the accumulated earnings of so many years' unrequited labours proving so heavy a demand all at once, the Egyptians were impoverished, and the Israelites were enabled to leave the country like a victorious army laden with spoil.[2]

A part of the Old Testament history which has provoked more scoffing ridicule on the Scripture

[1] Ex. xi. 2.   [2] Ps. cv. 37; Ezek. xxxix. 10.

as an inspired book than most other parts, is that which relates to the son of Jesse. The life and reign of David, it is said, were full of deceit and intrigues, of grossly immoral and criminal conduct, of inhuman cruelty to his enemies, and of a vindictive spirit even to the close of his days. And yet this king, whose memory is blackened by such flagrant offences both against God and man, is prominently held forth by a commissioned prophet of the Lord as "a man according to God's own heart." But it must be observed, that it was in his youth, before he was anointed to the royal dignity and elevated to the throne of Israel, that he was specially designated. This honourable testimony is borne only once in the Old Testament, and once in the New in allusion to the former;[1] and it was given long before his adultery with Bathsheba, or his murder of Uriah. It was not meant to indicate him as a person of spotless purity and virtue in his private character and conduct; but one who as a king of Israel would act in the spirit of the constitution, promoting the grand objects for which the nation had been selected by God, and securing the good which lay within the scope of the nation's reach at the period. Solomon imitated, it is said,

---

[1] 1 Sam. xiii. 11; Acts xiii. 22.

the deceitfulness of his father; for while he pretended to condone his brother Adonijah for his natural ambition as an elder brother to attain the crown, he betrayed his smothered resentment on the paltry occasion of that brother wishing to marry Abishag. And yet Solomon was endowed, through the special favour of God, with the highest gifts of wisdom. There is no ground for charging Solomon either with cruelty or precipitation in this case. According to Oriental usage, he that obtains the former king's wives has a claim upon the throne. Solomon penetrated the artful scheme of Adonijah; and, considering this new attempt was rebellion against the viceroy appointed by the Divine King, resolved on condemning him to the punishment of treason. These, not to speak of the polygamous excesses and the luxurious splendour of Solomon, are represented as enormous exaggerations,—as betokening, in the whole tenor of the Jewish history and the current of national events at that period, a desire to embellish the narrative, and aggrandize the character of their nation. They have been introduced, it is alleged, by later writers as interpolations on the simplicity and unpretending plainness of the original writers, and thus have so vitiated the present historical books, that they are no longer trustworthy records. But for this allegation these sceptical critics have no ground whatever but their own fancy, which is father to the thought; and that the accounts of Solomon's unconstitutional reign are quite true, and have been recorded to show that they led to the decline of the Hebrew monarchy, was shown in Lecture II.

Incidents of another kind are dwelt upon, as tending even in a stronger degree than those already noticed, to detract from the plenary inspiration of Scripture. God is described as saying to Moses, "I will harden Pharaoh's heart," and after the interview it is recorded that "Pharaoh's heart was hardened."[1] This declaration, it is said, is so utterly unworthy of God, and opposed to His holy, benevolent character, that it cannot have been uttered by Him, or given by inspiration in this record. But God is often said to do a thing which, in the natural course of His providence, takes place. The hardening of Pharaoh's heart would be the *result;* but the divine message through Moses would only be the *occasion*, not the cause, of the king's determined obduracy. Most assuredly God did not harden the Egyptian monarch by any

[1] Ex. vii. 3, 13.

direct influence upon his mind. But the circumstances in which the applications of Moses and Aaron were placed, operating along with his constitutional impetuosity of temper, would produce the effect anticipated, and lead to his assuming an attitude of stern and immoveable hardihood. Similar incidents, representing the divine character in a still more offensive light, are recorded in the historical books; as the command of God to " avenge the children of Israel upon the Midianites."[1] This was a very special case, calling for the direct interference of God to punish an infamous scheme for the destruction of the chosen people. Though the Moabites and Midianites had leagued together in inviting Balaam to curse the Israelites, the latter had taken the lead, if not acted alone, in practising the detestable art of idolatrous licentiousness; and therefore they were singled out as the objects of condign punishment by Him "to whom vengeance belongeth." It is observable that, in the command of God to commence hostilities against the Midianites, no order was issued for the slaughter of the women, and in ancient warfare they were usually reserved for slaves. But the Midianitish women had been the chief actors in the scheme of

[1] Num. xxxi. 2-18.

seduction, and therefore they had forfeited all claims to mild or merciful treatment. This was to be a war of extermination,—for the Midianites, like the Canaanites, were enormously wicked sinners, and therefore the only class to be spared were young girls, who would be treated according to the humane rules prescribed to the Hebrews for their conduct to female captives.[1] A third instance of this kind is sneered at—the excessive severity ascribed to God for so trivial an offence as that of the Bethshemites[2] looking into, and of Uzzah touching, the ark.[3] The sanctity of the ark was so strictly guarded, that not even the Levites who carried it were permitted to behold it uncovered;[4] and as this jealous care which God took of His symbol was well known in Israel, it was an unwarrantable and presumptuous act of the Bethshemites to look into it. In the case of Uzzah, who died in a moment by the visitation of God, there was a noticeable peculiarity. He was a Levite, and the whole proceedings connected with the removal of the ark were contrary to the express regulations of the law. Instead of being carried on the shoulders of the Levites, the ark was con-

---

[1] Deut. xxi. 10–14.
[2] 1 Sam. xv. 32, 33.
[3] 2 Sam. vi. 6, 7.
[4] Lev. xvi. 2 ; Num. iv. 5, 6.

veyed in a wheeled vehicle. Instead of being enveloped in its coverings, and thus concealed, it was kept exposed to the rude gaze and profane curiosity of a crowd. Uzzah, as a Levite, should have known and prescribed the order of removal according to the law. There is observable a gradation in the severity of punishments for profaning the ark, proportioned to the opportunities of knowledge possessed by the offenders. The Philistines, who were ignorant heathens, suffered by diseases from which they were afterwards relieved. The Bethshemites, who were prompted to look into it thoughtlessly, and through the impulse of curiosity, suffered also from a pestilence severely, but, as many think, not fatally; while Uzzah, who, being a Levite, headed the procession, and ought to have been dutiful, was struck with sudden death, because he was flagrantly transgressing in the public view of the people.

The painful episode of the Gibeonites and the descendants of Saul[1] appears an outburst of such fierce superstition, that it has been unhesitatingly pronounced a legendary tradition, inconsistent with the character of an inspired history. The circumstances were these:—A famine which occurred

[1] 2 Sam. xxi.

early in the reign of David, of protracted duration and unusual severity, was regarded as a judgment inflicted for national sins; and the king, having in his anxiety inquired of the Lord, was informed by the oracle, that it was "for Saul and his bloody house, because he slew the Gibeonites." There is no record of the origin or design of the persecution of that people. There is reason, however, to believe that, while it occurred in the course of Saul's sudden fit of fanatical zeal to extirpate the remnant of the ancient Canaanites in the land, he was actuated by a grasping ambition to seize their possessions for the aggrandizement of his family. By the slaughter of this people, a solemn covenant made with the heads and representatives of the nation had been broken; and the offence was the more outrageous, that the Gibeonites, renouncing idolatry, had been since the days of Joshua attached to the service of God in the sanctuary. There is ground to believe, also, that the younger members of Saul's family, who were his "captains of hundreds" and "captains of thousands," had been active and zealous agents in executing his sanguinary orders. Guilt had been incurred by them as well as by him; and therefore it is said that the famine was "for Saul and his bloody house." In consequence of the massacre having been authorized by the highest officer in the kingdom, the surviving Gibeonites had submitted in silence. But by the answer of the oracle to David, they had been constituted Goëlim, or blood-avengers; and as, by the Hebrew law, a pecuniary compensation for murder, though accepted by many people in the East, was an unlawful commutation, there was no alternative but to demand satisfaction in blood, *i.e.* the death of the nearest kinsman of Saul; and as the massacre stimulated by his authority had been of a wholesale description, a full reparation was required and given by the execution of seven males of his royal line, seven being a complete number. Now it is observable, that while the divine oracle announced the moral cause for which the calamity of famine was inflicted, it issued no instructions respecting the mode of expiation. Nor did David make any suggestions on that point. The sacrifice of Saul's sons was the spontaneous demand of the Gibeonites, who, though they had formally renounced idolatry, still retained the lingering influence of Hivite superstition. The entire responsibility of this revolting execution lay on the Gibeonites. God did not command nor sanction it. But He in His *providence permitted* it as an act of justice, not only to ensure equitable usage to the Gibeonites, lest they might be threatened with future oppression, but to remove the flagrant dishonour brought on His church and people by the guilty infraction of a solemn national treaty. There is no approval of the transaction expressed by the sacred historian, who simply relates the painful incident as it occurred; and the king gave his assent to it, as the only appointed means of purging the land from blood.[1]

Another passage of a similar kind is objected to, on account of the degrading view in which it is supposed to represent the Divine Being: "If a man smite his servant or his maid with the rod, and he die under his hand, he shall be surely punished. Notwithstanding, if he continue a day or two, he shall not be punished; *for he is his money.*"[2] This enactment occurs in the midst of many other regulations, pervaded by a humane and considerate spirit, to provide for the protection of the poor and the dependent; and such enactments were indispensably necessary in a country where slavery was tolerated, in order to secure male or female slaves from the oppression of tyrannical

---

[1] Num. xxxv. 31-34; Deut. xxi. 1-9.
[2] Ex. xxi. 20, 21.

masters. The punishment of undue severities, especially such as terminated in a fatal result, was left to the discretion of the magistrate on a full consideration of the circumstances. But where the slave who had been severely dealt with survived the harsh treatment for a while, no proceedings were to be instituted against the master, as it was presumed that an owner would not willingly injure a slave who *was his property*. It was this expression, *he is his money*, which, according to Dr. Colenso, proved so revolting to the mind of a simple Zulu, and from reflecting on which that writer was first led to the conclusion that the Pentateuch was unhistorical. For it asserts, as he alleges, " the horrid idea, that the great and blessed God, the Father of all mankind, would speak of a man-servant or a maid as mere 'money,' and allow an execrable crime to go unpunished, because the victim of his brutal usage had survived a few hours." A more strange and complete misconception of the meaning of this clause in the act can scarcely be imagined. Every reader of ordinary intelligence, whose mind is free from prejudice, must perceive that it is a reasonable consideration, based upon the principle that it was clearly against the master's interest to destroy his property; and that, so far from detracting from the sacred character of the book in which it stands, it furnishes one of the minor evidences of its divine origin, as it was a merciful provision for mitigating the evils of slavery, and a provision utterly unknown in the legislative code of any other nation before the Christian era.

Even more unworthy of a place in this book, which claims to be all given by inspiration of God, has been declared by many critics the eulogy pronounced by the prophetess Deborah on the unnatural, treacherous, and cold-blooded conduct of Jael to Sisera. She certainly rendered a service of the greatest importance to Israel. She would be regarded by admiring contemporaries as a heroine, and her deed celebrated in future ages, as effecting one of the most signal deliverances which the ancient church and people of God experienced. But the real character of this daring act cannot be appreciated, unless it is viewed in the light of the Sinaitic covenant, to the obligations and privileges of which Jael and her tribe had been admitted. She and her husband had been incorporated with the people of God, and were bound by a command paramount to all other considerations to extirpate idolaters. In this light the words of Deborah must be viewed; and the eulogy on Jael must be considered as pronounced not on the moral character of the woman and her deed, but solely on the public benefits which, in the providence of God, would flow from it. Remarks to the same purport may be made on a similar passage in the Psalms, where the sacred writer, predicting the sacking of Babylon, exclaims, " O daughter of Babylon, who art to be destroyed; happy shall he be that rewardeth thee as thou hast served us. Happy shall he be that taketh and dasheth thy little ones against the stones."[1] Such horrid cruelties were perpetrated in ancient warfare; and the sacred writer prophetically declared that the same atrocities which the Babylonians had perpetrated in Jerusalem, would be re-enacted in their capital by the victorious enemy who should sack it. The Psalmist does not indicate *any joy of his own* in anticipating this massacre of the helpless infants. He merely announces the fact that the Medo-Persian invaders would be jubilant amid those scenes of blood, as all victors do exult when they have laid a proud and formidable foe prostrate in the dust. And the little infants are particularized as a class of the inhabitants whose

---

[1] Ps. cxxxvii. 8, 9.

sufferings were sure to be conspicuous spectacles in the predicted scene of desolation.

These passages, and others of a similar import, which have often been paraded by scoffing critics hostile to the Scriptures, are, when rightly understood, in no way inconsistent with its character as an inspired book. Instead of presenting false or perverted views of the Divine Being, as has been alleged, they declare the will of God, and His method of dealing with men as they were able to bear it, in the early imperfect state of the church; and although many enactments of the Mosaic law, as well as many incidents recorded in the sacred history, appear coarser and harsher than what is agreeable to modern ideas, refined and elevated by the pure spirit of Christianity, it must be borne in mind that the Hebrew statutes, where it was impracticable at once to extirpate inveterate evils, contained many elements of improvement upon the laws and usages of all ancient nations.

Objections to the plenary inspiration of the Scriptures have been raised on a totally different ground, viz. the supposed errors of the sacred writers. "They were fallible men," says Dr. Williams, in *Essays and Reviews;* " and they have committed mistakes in history, chronology, geography, and other departments, like other authors." It is admitted that they were men of like passions and infirmities as others, and in their private conduct as individuals did occasionally do things which were wrong. Moses, for instance, was betrayed into undue heat of temper; Nathan, through mistaken zeal, committed an error in judgment, by encouraging David in his contemplated project of erecting a temple; Jeremiah was hurried, through the pressure of suffering, to curse the day of his birth; Jonah was querulous and discontented; Peter dissembled; Paul was intemperate in speaking to a magistrate; he and Barnabas rose into fierce contention respecting John Mark. Besides, in the ordinary intercourse of life they possessed no greater knowledge than their natural sagacity or memory enabled them to acquire; and hence we find them using such vague statements as Paul,—" hoping to come *about* winter;" " not knowing the things which were to befall him in Jerusalem;" he " baptized the household of Stephanas; besides, he knew not whether he baptized any other;"—these, and many other things that are incidentally mentioned in the Epistles, show that in the common familiar intercourse of life they were left to act for themselves, as others.

But there is observable a broad line of demarcation between the conduct of the prophets and apostles as men, and their procedure as the commissioned servants of God and witnesses for Christ; for while they were betrayed through constitutional weakness or violence of temper into occasional errors in private life, they were infallible in the discharge of apostolic offices. It is alleged, indeed, that the apostles did err through imperfect knowledge at first, as when the evangelists, in accordance with the reigning notions of their age and country, recorded that demons entered into the bodies of men and animals, and that the coming of Christ was close at hand. In regard to the former, it has been the belief of all sound interpreters in every age of the church, that in the time of our Lord there were such formidable calamities as demoniacal possessions, several incidents in the evangelical narrative being absolutely unintelligible except on that hypothesis. And as to the apprehension which prevailed in some of the early Christian churches of the second coming of Christ, it probably arose from a mistaken interpretation of some expressions which were used by men who, themselves living under the powers of the world to come, and viewing the future with the telescopic eye of faith, spoke of them as near at hand. But they fell into no error in expecting the immediate end of the world; and Paul expressed his own uniform conviction, as well as that of his brother apostles, when he wrote to the Thessalonians, "that they should not be shaken in mind, or be troubled, neither by spirit nor by word, nor by letter as from us, as that the day of Christ is at hand. Let no man deceive you by any means; for that day shall not come except there come a falling away first, and that man of sin be revealed, the son of perdition." In short, although discrepancies and apparent inconsistencies are found in many parts of the sacred writings, they are all capable more or less of explanation and reconciliation. No serious error has ever been proved;[1] and the Scriptures, possessing plenary inspiration, must be regarded as an authoritative and infallible rule in all matters of faith and duty.

We consider that this conclusion has been established by the arguments adduced in the preceding lectures, independently of the admission or rejection of the dogma of verbal inspiration. By verbal inspiration is meant a suggestion not merely

[1] Note I.

of ideas and sentiments, but of the very words in which these are expressed. Now there can be no doubt that there were cases in which the Spirit of God put the precise and actual words into the mouths of the inspired persons who uttered them. Thus, for instance, when the prophets predicted future things of which they had no knowledge, and others spoke in languages they did not understand, it is obvious that the expressions must have been supplied to them. Besides, there were cases in which arguments of the greatest importance are founded on the precise use of a single word. Thus, when our Lord said, "Before Abraham was, I am," is it not evident that the change from the past to the present tense in this declaration has great doctrinal significance? Our Lord Himself argued from the use of a word; for He proved the reality of a future state from the words addressed to Moses at the burning bush, "I am the God of Abraham, of Isaac, and of Jacob." "God," He concluded, "is not the God of the dead, but of the living." The apostles also founded on the use of a word; as a weighty inference is drawn from the use of the word "seed" in the singular, and not in the plural;[1] another is dependent on the word

[1] Gal. iii. 16.

"all,"[1] and a third on the words "once more,"[2] as employed by the prophet Haggai. But although in rare instances, as those just specified, the importance and even necessity of verbal inspiration must be conceded, the *theopneustia*, which the apostle claims for all Scripture, indicates a rational influence on the mind of the sacred writers, rather than a mechanical control of the lips; and as it is usual and natural for men to think in words, so the action of the Spirit of God on the minds of apostles and prophets would, in accordance with the principles of their mental constitution, prompt and stimulate them to the adoption of such words as would most exactly express the divine mind they were commissioned to make known. Thus the sacred writers were left each of them to speak and write in his own natural manner,—some in a plain, prosaic, and humble, others in a poetical and embellished, highly rhetorical, and argumentative style; and a satisfactory explanation is obtained of the phenomena of inspiration.

The plenary inspiration of the Scriptures renders that book the supreme standard of authority in religion. This conclusion cannot be affected by objections that have been brought either from

[1] Heb. ii. 8. [2] Heb. xii. 27.

within or from without the sacred volume. The multiplicity of various readings cannot affect it: for they do not invalidate a single doctrine or statement; and their existence affords the prospect that enlightened criticism will ere long establish a perfect text. Nor is the authority of Scripture endangered by the dogmas of scientific men. Science is progressive, and many of its once favourite doctrines, as the nebular theory and others, she has been compelled to abandon. Let the students of the Bible and the students of science prosecute their independent courses, and we have a confident assurance, that through a sound exegesis of Scripture, and a patient study of nature, there will be found a perfect harmony between the works and the word of God.[1]

[1] Note K.

NOTES.

Note A.—Philo, who was a contemporary of Josephus, says that "the Jews would rather have suffered a thousand deaths, than that anything should be once altered in all the divine laws and statutes of the nation."

(Philo Judæus ap. Eusebii *prepar. Evang.* lib. viii.)—The Jews were extremely fond of arranging their sacred books, and even several minute portions of them, in accordance with the letters of the Hebrew alphabet. It was on this account that the canonical books of the Old Testament, which really amount to 39, were reckoned at the reduced number of 22. The twelve minor prophets were considered as forming one book. But that the twenty-two books comprehended the whole thirty-nine is proved to a demonstration, by a comparison of our present list with that drawn up and published by a succession of early Christian writers: by Melito, Bishop of Sardis, in the second century, who travelled to the East in order to make the relative inquiries into the state of the Old Testament canon, as known in that quarter of the world; by Origen in the third century, who enumerates the twenty-two books; by Athanasius in the fourth, who also gives the names of the twenty-two books, which were recognised by the universal church of that age as forming the canon of the Jewish Scriptures. This list is confirmed by the subsequent testimonies of Gregory Nazianzen and Jerome, and it is established by the Council of Laodicea in 363. Collateral evidence of the same point is furnished by the Septuagint translation, by the Targums or paraphrases of the said books, and by the steady, uniform adherence of the modern Jews to the canon as acknowledged and held by the church of their fathers. The *Chetubim* or *Hagiographa* include the whole of the Psalms, the book of Job, Proverbs, Ecclesiastes, Canticles, 1 and 2 Chronicles, Ezra, Esther, and the prophecies of Daniel. The triple distinction of the Jews is quite fanciful. Moses, *i.e.* the Pentateuch, was of course the first division. Under the "prophets," or second division, are included Joshua, Judges, Ruth, 1 and 2 Samuel, 1 and 2 Kings, 1 and 2 Chronicles, Ezra, Nehemiah, and Esther, besides all the prophets, except Daniel. This shows, in our Lord's real classification, the historical books ought to be included under the prophets, having been written by prophets. "When our Saviour," says Bishop Marsh, "spake of the Old Testament as composed of three parts,—the *law of Moses*, the *prophets*, and the *Psalms*,—He gave an exact description of the *Hebrew Bible*. It is true that our Saviour did not enumerate the books of each class; but it may be easily shown that the three classes comprehended the *present books* of the Hebrew Bible, and *no more*. For the first class was devoted exclusively to the writings of Moses, and the second class admitted the writings only of those whom the Jews denominated *the prophets*. Neither the first nor the second class, therefore, ever could have contained the productions of later writers, whom the Jews could not *possibly* regard in the same light as their ancient prophets. Nor could even the third class have contained any of those books which we call Apocrypha. For *most* of them were Greek in their very origin, and consequently were incapable of admission into the

Hebrew canon. And with respect to the few among them which may have been written in that kind of Hebrew which was spoken in *later times* by the Jews in Palestine, it would have been quite inconsistent with the veneration of the Jews for their ancient Hebrew Scriptures to have admitted *whole books* written in Chaldee, though they did not exclude the works of Ezra and Daniel on account of some parts of them being Chaldee."[1]

Note B.—It is well known that Biblical scholars have long been divided in opinion as to the proper translation of 2 Tim. iii. 16. In the original Greek there is no verb; and the insertion of the substantive verb ἐστι being left to the reader's discretion, its position at the beginning or the end of the sentence must affect the import of the passage. Its introduction in the early part of the text, so that the words stand, "All Scripture is given by inspiration of God, and profitable," etc., asserts the inspiration of all parts of the sacred volume; whereas, if it is deferred to a remoter place in the verse, the meaning of the passage is materially altered: "Every writing, divinely inspired, is also profitable," etc. But this rendering is objectionable on various grounds. 1. Because γραφή has here a special meaning, defined by the ἱερὰ γράμματα of the preceding context, which cannot be expressed by "writing." It denotes Scripture, according to the use of the term in the New Testament; and γραφή being without the article, and standing absolute, it is evident that the Scripture referred to was not limited to the Jewish Scriptures, but comprehended the whole of the revealed word of God. But the translation, even as amended, "All Scripture,

[1] *Comparative View of the Churches of England and Rome*, p. 102; see also Cosin on the Canon, pp. 94, 95.

divinely inspired, is also profitable," etc., is open to various objections. It evidently implies that some parts of the Scripture are not divinely inspired. Besides, it makes the conjunction καί, *and*, serve as an emphatic instead of a merely connecting word. And it tends to weaken the import of the statement, that "all Scripture is divinely inspired," by transferring the emphasis to the affirmation of its being profitable, which no one needs to be informed that Scripture is. It can scarcely be supposed, therefore, that the apostle would make so trivial a statement, nor that it could enforce the counsel which he had addressed to Timothy. The weight of critical authority in modern times, from De Wette to Tregelles, is in favour of the first translation. Dr Pye Smith, particularly in the last edition of his *Scripture Testimony*, supports the second rendering; as does Alford also, although he acknowledges that he does so with great hesitation. Our Authorized Version has adopted the first, along with the Ethiopic version. The Syriac, the Arabic version, and the English Bible of 1549, and other English versions, lend their countenance to the second. Although the Clementine Vulgate has *est* after *utilis*, and totally omits the καί, giving this meaning, "All Scripture, divinely inspired, is useful for instruction," the Vulgate itself has the same reading as the Greek, *Omnis Scriptura divinitus inspirata, et utilis ad docendum.* (See Findlay's *Vindication.*)

It has been considered by some, that the statement of the apostle was limited exclusively to the Old Testament Scripture, under the persuasion that, during the youth of Timothy, no part of the New Testament could have been written, or at least been generally published. But this is to overlook the established facts of the history. The words occur in the Second Epistle to Timothy, which was the last that he wrote, and that in the year 66, when already the Gospels of Matthew, Mark, and Luke, as well as the Acts, had appeared, together with almost all the other Epistles, besides those of Paul. Now the Epistles were regarded by Paul from the first as Scripture, for he gave orders that they should be read publicly in the churches (1 Thess. v. 27), and to be exchanged one with another, so that all might participate in the privilege of hearing their instruction (Col. iv. 16). And hence it may be concluded, that he, as well as Peter, ranked all his own with those of the other apostles amongst the "all Scripture that is given by inspiration of God."

In regard to the Pastoral Epistles, they have been subjected to a series of severe attacks in modern times, begun by Schleiermacher in 1807 upon the First Epistle of Timothy, and extended by Eichhorn, De Wette, and Baur against the two Epistles to Timothy and that to Titus,—all of which Davidson has marshalled in full array. But able defenders appeared in vindication of these Epistles; and while their authenticity and genuineness have been fully established on critical grounds, their full recognition by the church before the close of the second century has been proved by the strongest testimony of ecclesiastical history. In fact, the discovery of the work of Hippolytus has overthrown the theories and arguments of those critical sceptics.

NOTE C.—It has been alleged that the majority of expositors have found the Messiah in too many prophetic passages. We do not think so; but most assuredly Rationalistic writers, who eliminate altogether the Messianic element, have gone to the opposite extreme, and have maintained their theories on very slender, often untenable ground. We take Dr. Williams, who has retailed the opinions of the German critics in his famous contribution to *Essays and Reviews*, and from that work we cull a sample or two of their interpretations of prophecy. Thus, "the child born" (Isa. ix. 6) he refers to Hezekiah,—an interpretation to which the objections are insuperable. No one single feature of the prophecy corresponds with the life and reign of Hezekiah. The very lowest meaning which German rationalism or Jewish unbelief can give to such words as "Mighty God," are as inapplicable to Hezekiah as the highest. If it would be blasphemy in the prophet to designate him by this appellation in the full sense of the words, it would be equally low, unworthy flattery, to style him "Mighty God" in the sense of Godlike Hero or Divine Warrior; for Hezekiah, though a good man, was in no conceivable sense a hero. Such a word as "mighty" can hardly be associated with the name of one who, when his land was invaded, made abject submission in such words as those which he sent to the king of Assyria: "I have offended; return from me: that which thou puttest upon me I will bear" (2 Kings xviii. 14).

With as little propriety can he be styled "Wonderful Counsellor;" for Hezekiah, though a good, was a very weak, man. He had to lean for counsel on others, and God gave him a counsellor of surpassing excellence in Isaiah. In fact, if applied to Hezekiah or any of his successors till the destruction of the monarchy, this most astonishing of prophetic utterances is utterly meaningless. If applied to the Virgin-born, it is a glorious anticipation of the Christian faith; and every one of these attributes is seen to be a distinguishing characteristic of the Redeemer, as displayed in the government of the church. If the Holy Ghost spoke by Isaiah at all, He does so in this prophetic utterance, which refers solely to Him of whom, at His conception, it was announced that "the Lord shall give unto Him the throne of His father David, and He shall reign over the house of Jacob for ever." Another sample of Dr. Williams' interpretations is that put upon Isa. iv. 2, which he translates and explains most incorrectly, making "the Branch of the Lord," *i.e.* the Messiah, into "*Jehovah's budding,*" *i.e.* a better generation of sons and daughters.

The grand attempt made to destroy the predictive character of the prophetic writings is by the division of the book of Isaiah into two parts, the latter part being written at an interval of two hundred years after the former by a younger prophet of the same name, who was personally acquainted with Cyrus, and hence the reference to him! The fifty-third chapter of Isaiah, in which the last sufferings of the Messiah are so graphically described, is represented as a historical summary of the life of Jeremiah. The ground on which this elaborate effort of criticism to expunge the predictive element from the Hebrew prophecies rests, is the use of Chaldaic forms of the Hebrew verb *Hiphil*, the introduction of the name of Cyrus, and the adoption of the Chaldaic word *Sagan* for prince. See *Replies to Essays and Reviews;* Birk's *Bible and Modern Thought;* Davison's *Use, Intent, and Inspiration of Prophecy.*

NOTE D.—The prophets were men to whom God communicated a knowledge of future events, long before the causes of them had begun to develope themselves, so as to make them discernible by human sagacity. It might be supposed that the prophecies of Christ and of the kingdom of God would be the result of a sagacious mind, full of pious aspiration in times of great revival, when men's minds were animated by more than usually devout feelings. But some of Isaiah's prophecies, and those the most spiritual, were uttered or written in the reign of idolatrous kings, when idolatry was rampant. The prophets all predicted something of Christ. Jacob had said, Christ's advent should be before the sceptre departed from Judah, or a lawgiver from between his feet; Haggai and Malachi, that He should come when the second temple yet stood; and Daniel had foretold the very year, eighteen centuries ago, in which He would appear,—a prediction which appeared so unprecedentedly minute, as to excite doubts and suspicion respecting the credibility of this prophet. "But this has now been established on a solid basis of proof, and scepticism on the book of Daniel been dispelled. The prophetic declaration as to the exact time of Messiah's advent did not rest on mere circumstantial evidence, but was capable of mathematical and absolute demonstration. Interpret the seventy weeks in what way we will, and put the period of their commencement backward and forward, it is evident to all that the time must have expired, and Messiah the Prince have come."

Note E.—The vernacular language of our Lord's contemporaries—ancient Hebrew having not survived the captivity—was, though still called "the Hebrew tongue,"[1] Syro-Chaldaic, or Aramaic. But throughout the Roman Empire, Greek was a universal medium of communication. Not only in Greece and its colonies, in Asia Minor and Egypt, but in Rome itself, the prevalent use of the Greek tongue was a remarkable feature of the age; and that Palestine was no exception is proved by many considerations. The common use of the Septuagint in the synagogues, and the quotations from the ancient prophets made by our Lord and His apostles from that version; the composition of the Gospels and

[1] Luke xxiii. 38; Acts xxvi. 40.

Epistles in that language, for the use of the resident inhabitants of Palestine as well as of the Hellenistic Jews of the Dispersion; the fact of there being only two New Testament books which were said to have had Hebrew originals, of which, however, no record exists, and which have never been seen by any but in their Greek form; the testimony furnished by the writings of Philo and Josephus; the Sermon on the Mount, addressed to a mixed multitude, comprising people from Tyre and Sidon,[1] who spoke the Greek language, and from the Decapolis;[2]—these and various other circumstances afford evidence that cannot be gainsaid, that Greek was known to, and familiarly spoken by, all classes in Palestine during the first age of Christianity.—Roberts' *Discussions*, Part I.

NOTE F.—Mr. Froude (*Short Studies on Great Subjects*, p. 254) says: "Though extremely probable, it is not absolutely certain, that those passages in the Acts in which the writer speaks in the first person are by the same hand as the body of the narrative. If St. Luke had anywhere directly introduced himself,—if he had said plainly that he, the writer who was addressing Theophilus, had personally joined St. Paul, and in that part of his story was relating what he had seen and heard, there would be no room for uncertainty. But so far as we know, there is no other instance in literature of a change of person introduced abruptly, without explanation." In answer to this expression of doubt, several of the early Christian Fathers,—Irenæus, Clement of Alexandria,[3] towards the close of the second century, Ter-

---

[1] Luke vi. 17.   [2] Matt. iv. 25.
[3] *Adver. Hæres.* lib. iii. ch. 14 and 15; *De Jejunio*, ch. 10; *De præscrip. Hæres.* ch. 22; *Adver. Marcion*, lib. v. ch. 2 and 3, etc.; *Stromat.* lib. v.

tullian in the beginning of the third,—bear concurrent testimony to the book of the Acts and the authorship of Luke. And Eusebius[1] has placed it amongst the sacred books that were universally acknowledged as of canonical authority by the churches.

NOTE G.—Mr. Matthew Arnold's idea of inspiration is given in his last work, *Literature and Dogma*. According to his view, it is a mystic something that inspires the mind with awe, sometimes even to "cruel terror," or a "timid religiosity," which exerts a powerful influence on the imagination. "This," in his view, "was what moved the men who wrote the Bible." When the sacred books were produced, a secret but strong influence beyond themselves acted upon the Israelitish people, and inspired them with awe,—an influence from which they got a sense of righteousness, and were stimulated to do right. This mystic tendency, which was "not themselves, but beyond themselves," was what they meant to express under the name of *Jehovah*, which, untranslated, gives the name of a mere mythological divinity, and which our translators have erroneously rendered by the word *Lord*, conveying the idea of an exalted man. In short, Arnold's representation of this mystic influence is, that it is an innate power which, like that operating upon the impulses of men to self-preservation and reproduction, prompts them to righteousness. We are accustomed to speak of God guiding and governing men. But Mr. Arnold rejects the idea of a personal God, and says it is something which he calls "not ourselves." The stimulus of this secret influence, he says, was the whole inspiration of the Hebrew writers; and when they declared their

---

[1] *Hist. Eccl.* iii. 25.

emotions of joy or sorrow, and their consciousness of sin, they thought not of a personal God, but meant only to express the idea of righteousness. "God is simply the stream of tendency by which all things fulfil the law of their being. And this was Israel's consciousness, out of which the grand, solemn statements of Moses, the passionate affections of David, and the lofty imaginations of Isaiah sprang." If there be any meaning lying hid in this conglomerate of hyperbolical expressions, it has baffled all our efforts to penetrate it; and the conclusion to which we are forced to come is, that although Mr. Arnold's work professes to be a guiding light towards a better apprehension of the Bible, we feel that we are left totally in the dark as to what this strange work means to teach.

NOTE H.—The following excellent remarks on the internal proofs of the supernatural in the Scripture, from the pen of the eloquent Dr. Harris, President of Bodwoin College, form an appropriate sequel to the sentiments contained in the latter half of this chapter:—

"Naturalism must account for Jesus as the necessary outgrowth of His age. It must affirm of Him, as of all great men, that His individual force is of slight account: all that was in Him was but the outgrowth of His age; if He had not lived, the spirit of the age would necessarily have found utterance through some other. But Jesus cannot be accounted for as the natural outgrowth and product of His age. His age was, of all the ages, the most barren of spiritual life: polytheism had decayed into epicurean scepticism; Judaism had degenerated into the formalism of the Pharisee and the unbelief of the Sadducee. Jesus was in all particulars unlike His age, and contrary to it; not only so, but He introduced into it a new life, and commenced its transformation into His own likeness. The world was like a barren field,—nothing visible but the blackened cinders of scepticism, and the scorched and hollow stalks of empty profession. Jesus came, and life, verdure, and fruit appeared. There went forth from the very publicans, Matthews, and from the very Pharisees, Pauls; from that ungodly age there went forth godly men and women, confessors and martyrs,—a living church of God, a power of faith and love, which have been the admiration of all succeeding ages. Demonstrably, here was not a life spontaneously developed out of humanity, but a life coming down upon humanity from above,—an energy of God's redeeming grace, as a new and renovating power into the history of man."

NOTE I.—Many of those passages which have been singled out as containing errors and contradictions, admit of a satisfactory explanation. Thus, Num. iii. 39 states the total number of the Levites as 22,000; whereas the aggregate amount of the different summations given in other parts of the same chapter makes the whole as 22,300. It is supposed that the sum-total is given, as in former instances, in round numbers, or that the 300 in excess were themselves first-born, who could not on that account be substituted for other first-born. The small number of the first-born males may be ascribed to one or other of the following causes: either that there was no notice taken of families in which the eldest child was a daughter, or that the first-born was counted after the law was promulgated. 2 Chron. xvi. 1 records that " in the six-and-thirtieth year of the reign of Asa, Baasha king of Israel came up against Judah ;" whereas it is alleged, from 1 Kings xv. 33, that Baasha had apparently died in the twenty-seventh year of Asa's reign; so that there is a flagrant contradiction between the two statements. If, however, the chronology here be reckoned, as it is believed it should be, not from the commencement of Asa's reign, but from the disruption of the kingdoms, the thirty-sixth year from that epoch would agree with the sixteenth year of that monarch's reign; and this was in all probability the chronology adopted in the national register, from which the sacred historian drew his materials. Again, it is said that 2 Chron. xxii. 2 makes Ahaziah forty-two years old when his father died; whereas xxi. 20 states that his father himself was but forty years of age at his death. It is evident, from the nature of the case, that the text in the parallel passage 2 Kings viii. 26 is the correct reading; most commentators are accustomed to remove the difficulty by suggesting that the letter *Caph*, whose numerical power is *twenty*, was substituted for *Mem*, whose numerical power is forty. We prefer the explanation given by Dr. Lightfoot, which is this: that Ahaziah began to reign in the twenty-second year of his own age, but in the forty-second of the reign of the Omri dynasty,—a powerful and disastrous dynasty to the kingdoms both of Israel and Judah, and therefore most likely to form an epoch in the eyes of a Hebrew writer. 2 Chron. xxv. 7, 8, have been pronounced contradictory and unintelligible. It must be admitted that the passage is obscure as it stands; but many critics of eminence have suggested that the particle "not" has in the course of transcription been dropped out of the text, and that the insertion of this little word will restore the clearness and sense of the prophet's advice to Amaziah. It has been noticed that there is a contradiction between 2 Chron. xxiv. 14, which states that "spoons and vessels of gold and silver were made of the surplus money collected by Jehoiada;" and the parallel passage in 2 Kings xii. 13, where it is said "there were *not* made for the house of the Lord bowls of silver, etc., of the money that was brought into the house of the Lord." It may be that the word "not" has dropped also out of the text in the former passage; otherwise there is here a direct contradiction. But it is in a matter of very trivial importance, and errors of this kind are very apt to occur in the course of frequent transcription. Various errors also have been noticed in regard to numbers; as in the story of the Bethshemites it is said, "God smote fifty thousand threescore and ten men" (1 Sam vi. 19). Bethshemesh being a small village, the numbers must be erroneous. The verse should be rendered: "He smote fifty out of a thousand." God, instead of decimating, according to an ancient usage, slew only a twentieth part, *i.e.*, according to Josephus, 70 out of 1400 (see Num. iv. 18–22). Such errors were inevitable, unless there had been a constant miraculous superintendence of transcribers. But the errors are comparatively unimportant. Prof. Rawlinson describes the Pentateuch as "a history absolutely and perfectly true," but as having "accidental corruptions of the text, a few interpolations, glosses, which have crept in from the margin."[1] Mr Birks considers that "the inspiration and authority of the Scriptures are not synonymous with entire freedom from the intrusion of the slightest error."[2] And Messrs. Webster and Wilkinson express themselves in the following manner: "It will be understood that an inspiration which may be truly characterized as direct, personal, independent, and plenary, is consistent with the use of an inferior or provincial dialect, with ignorance of scientific facts and other secular matters, with mistakes in historical allusions or references, and mistakes in conduct, and with

[1] *Bampton Lect.* p. 77.
[2] *The Bible and Modern Thought*, p. 208.

circumstantial discrepancies between inspired persons in relating discourses, conversations, or events." [1]

NOTE K.—Although the Scriptures were given to instruct mankind in religious truth only, yet, considering their divine origin, it might be expected that, wherever mention is made of the material world, there would be no opposition to the principles of true science. The sacred writers speak of physical nature in popular language, and it is evident that in no other way could they have been understood by the generality of mankind in any age. But their statements are far-reaching in all they have said upon this subject. The idea of creation, the bringing the matter of the universe out of nothing, could have been derived only from divine inspiration; for all pagan writers speak of the world as formed from pre-existent matter. The second and third verses of the first chapter of Genesis are quite in accordance with all the cataclysms and revolutions to which geology has shown the pre-Adamite earth was subjected. The subsequent account which the historian gives of the preparation of the world for the existing economy of providence, — of the animal creation, beginning with the formation of the simplest animals, and ascending in the scale of organized structures, in exact accordance with the modern zoological arrangement established by Cuvier,—of the distinction of species, and the succession of species both of plants and animals from parent species,—of the natural supremacy of rational man, the descent of the human race from a single pair, and the antiquity of man,—is confirmed by the testimony of the most enlightened observation and the conclusions of true science. Nor is there less confidence to be attached to the Mosaic account of the Flood—partial,

[1] *Introduction to the Greek Testament,* p. 46.

indeed, in superficial extent, as the Scripture use of the word "all" frequently warrants, but universal in the destruction of mankind, with the exception of a single family. A similar remark may be made as to the introduction of diverse languages, which, as has been most satisfactorily proved by Sir H. Rawlinson and others, must have occurred in the place and time which the Bible history assigns to it. The allusions which are occasionally made to the sun, moon, and stars, to all objects beyond the earthly scene, are extremely guarded, and described only as objects of sight. In other respects, great progress has been made in illustrating obscure points of Scripture history through the Assyrian and Egyptian monuments. Pharaoh Sesonch (Shishak) is represented dragging a group of captives to the temple of his gods — each having his breast labelled with an inscription telling his country; and amongst them is Rehoboam, king of Judah, with the name *Jaudh Malk*, "Judah Melek," king of Judah, in a cartouche over him (see Lepsius' *Letters*); also it has been proved that the immense number of Egyptian monarchs enumerated by Manetho do harmonize with the Biblical chronology; for there were three dynasties —before Upper and Lower Egypt were united—ruling contemporaneously. The researches at Nineveh have also thrown great light on Scripture history, particularly on those historical puzzles,—the promise made by Belshazzar that Daniel should be "the *third* ruler in the kingdom:" for it is now fully ascertained that that young king was reigning conjointly with his father Nabonadius; and also the existence of Merodach Baladan, king of Babylon, who had revolted from Assyria (Isa. xxxix. 1).

MESSRS BLACKWOOD & SONS

HAVE RECENTLY PUBLISHED :—

THE PARISIANS.

By EDWARD BULWER, LORD LYTTON. Author of 'The Coming Race,' &c. To be completed in Four Volumes. With Illustrations by SYDNEY HALL. Vols. I. and II. are published, 6s. each.

KENELM CHILLINGLY.

HIS ADVENTURES AND OPINIONS. By EDWARD BULWER, LORD LYTTON. Second Edition. 3 vols. crown 8vo, £1, 5s. 6d.

THE COMING RACE.

Eighth Edition, crown 8vo, 6s.

MIDDLEMARCH.

By GEORGE ELIOT. A New Edition. 4 vols. fcap. 8vo, £1, 1s.

A TRUE REFORMER.

3 vols. crown 8vo, £1, 5s. 6d. (Originally published in 'Blackwood's Magazine.')

"This will probably prove the most successful political novel that has appeared in England since 'Coningsby,' and it deserves to be so. . . . A carefully-elaborated scheme of national defence is so ingeniously interwoven with stirring accounts of Parliamentary struggles and triumphs, and so enlivened by amusing sketches of prominent statesmen, that it might well make an army reformer of a girl of eighteen, while the love story on which the debates and arguments are threaded is touching enough to flutter the pulses of a chairman of committee."—*Pall Mall Gazette.*

FRENCH HOME LIFE.

By "an English Looker-on, who has lived for a quarter of a century in France amidst ties and affections which have made that country his second home."—*Preface.*

Contents :—SERVANTS. — CHILDREN. — FURNITURE.— FOOD.—MANNERS.— LANGUAGE.—DRESS.—MARRIAGE. In Octavo, 10s. 6d.

"The present book of essays, which might in justice be called a guide-book to the French mind, will tell the reader all that he ought to know by this time, and certainly does not know, about French ways. Less amusing than M. Taine's work on England, it is deeper and in the main truer. The writer, indeed, does not aim at being amusing; he seeks to give philosophical analyses of the customs which constitute home life on the other side of the Channel, and he quite succeeds. . . . If, however, we dissent from some of the optimist conclusions drawn from French customs in this book, we cannot give it too high praise for its force and accuracy as a whole."—*Pall Mall Gazette.*

SKETCHES AND ESSAYS.

REPRINTED FROM THE 'SATURDAY REVIEW.'

Contents.—FASHIONABLE SCRAMBLES IN COUNTRY HOUSES.—THE RETURN OF THE TOURISTS.—THE END OF THE HOLIDAYS.—DINNERS IN THE PROVINCES, ETC.—WEDDINGS AND WEDDING PRESENTS.—SOCIAL LADYBIRDS.—THE INFANT'S PROGRESS.—PLATO IN PETTICOATS.—MOHOCKS AND THEIR LITERATURE.—SCHOOLS. In crown 8vo, 5s.

INCIDENTS IN THE SEPOY WAR OF 1857-8.

Compiled from the Private Journals of General Sir HOPE GRANT, G.C.B.; together with some Explanatory Chapters. By Captain H. KNOLLYS, R.A., Author of 'From Sedan to Saarbruck.' 8vo, with Maps and Plans.

MYSIE'S PARDON.

A Novel from Australia. By JAMES WALKER HAY. Three vols. crown 8vo, £1, 5s. 6d.

NEW POEM BY MR AUSTIN.

ROME OR DEATH.

Crown 8vo, uniform with 'Madonna's Child,' by the same Author.

A HANDBOOK OF WEATHER FOLK-LORE:

Being a Collection of Proverbial Sayings in Various Languages relating to the Weather, with Explanatory and Illustrative Notes. By the Rev. C. SWAINSON, M.A., Vicar of High Hurst Wood.

POEMS.

By the late ISA BLAGDEN. With a Memoir, by ALFRED AUSTIN. Fcap. 8vo.

FROM PATMOS TO PARADISE;

Or, LIGHT ON THE PAST, THE PRESENT, AND THE FUTURE. By the Rev. JOHN CUMMING, D.D., F.R.S.E., Minister of the Scotch National Church, Crown Court, Covent Garden, London. Crown 8vo, 7s. 6d.

PICCADILLY:

A Fragment of Contemporary Biography. By LAURENCE OLIPHANT. With Eight Illustrations by RICHARD DOYLE. Fourth Edition, 6s.

LUCIAN.
By the REV. W. LUCAS COLLINS, M.A. In crown 8vo, 2s. 6d. Being Vol. XVIII. of 'Ancient Classics for English Readers.'

HISTORY OF THE LODGE OF EDINBURGH.
(MARY'S CHAPEL) No. 1. Embracing an Account of the Rise and Progress of Freemasonry in Scotland. By DAVID MURRAY LYON. With Twenty-six Facsimiles of Ancient Statutes, Minutes of various Lodges, Seals, and Orders, &c., and Authentic Portraits and Autographs of Sixty eminent Craftsmen of the past and present time. In Imperial Octavo, bound in gilt cloth richly ornamented, £1, 11s. 6d. Published under the Patronage of H.R.H. THE PRINCE OF WALES, K.G., Patron of the Order.

FAIR TO SEE.
By LAURENCE W. M. LOCKHART. A New Edition, in One Vol., 6s.

THE MAID OF SKER.
By R. D. BLACKMORE, Author of 'Lorna Doone.' A New Edition, in One Volume, 7s. 6d.

WORKS OF GEORGE ELIOT.
Cheap Edition.

ADAM BEDE. 3s. 6d.	SILAS MARNER. 2s. 6d.
THE MILL ON THE FLOSS. 3s. 6d.	FELIX HOLT. 3s. 6d.
SCENES OF CLERICAL LIFE. 3s.	

OUR POOR RELATIONS.
A PHILOZOIC ESSAY. By COL. E. BRUCE HAMLEY. With Illustrations, chiefly by ERNEST GRISET. Crown 8vo, cloth gilt, 3s. 6d.

CHRONICLES OF CARLINGFORD.
By MRS OLIPHANT.
SALEM CHAPEL. 2s. in boards, or 2s. 6d. cloth.
THE PERPETUAL CURATE. 2s. in boards, or 2s. 6d. cloth.
MISS MARJORIBANKS. 2s. in boards, or 2s. 6d. cloth.
THE RECTOR and THE DOCTOR'S FAMILY. 1s. sewed, or 1s. 6d. cloth.

JOURNAL OF THE WATERLOO CAMPAIGN:
Kept throughout the Campaign of 1815. By GENERAL CAVALIE MERCER, Commanding the 9th Brigade Royal Artillery. 2 vols. post 8vo, 21s.

THE OPERATIONS OF WAR EXPLAINED
AND ILLUSTRATED. By EDWARD BRUCE HAMLEY, Colonel in the Royal Artillery, Companion of the Bath, Commandant of the Staff College, &c. 3d Edition, 4to, with numerous Illustrations, 28s.

THE SYSTEM OF FIELD MANŒUVRES

Best adapted for Enabling our Troops to meet a Continental Army. Being the Wellington Prize Essay. By LIEUTENANT F. MAURICE, Royal Artillery, Instructor of Tactics and Organisation, Royal Military College, Sandhurst. Crown 8vo, 5s.

THE SUBALTERN.

By G. R. GLEIG, M.A., Chaplain-General of Her Majesty's Forces. Library Edition. Revised and Corrected, with a New Preface. Crown 8vo, 7s. 6d.

RECREATIONS OF CHRISTOPHER NORTH.

By PROFESSOR WILSON. In Two Vols. New Edition, with Portrait, 8s.

THE NOCTES AMBROSIANÆ.

By PROFESSOR WILSON. With Notes and a Glossary. In Four Vols. crown 8vo, 16s.

DRAWING-ROOM DRAMAS FOR CHILDREN.

By W. G. WILLS, Author of 'Charles I.,' &c., and the HONBLE. MRS GREENE. Crown 8vo, 6s.

GOETHE'S FAUST.

Translated into English Verse by THEODORE MARTIN. Second Edition, post 8vo, 6s. Cheap Edition, fcap., 3s. 6d.

SONGS AND VERSES:

Social and Scientific. By an OLD CONTRIBUTOR TO 'MAGA.' A New Edition, with Music of some of the Songs. Fcap. 8vo, 3s. 6d.

CHARLES THE FIRST.

AN HISTORICAL TRAGEDY IN FOUR ACTS. By W. G. WILLS, Author of 'The Man o' Airlie,' 'Medea,' &c. 8vo, 2s. 6d.

A MANUAL OF ENGLISH PROSE LITERATURE,

Biographical and Critical: designed mainly to show characteristics of style. By W. MINTO, M.A. Crown 8vo, 10s. 6d.

THE GENESIS OF THE CHURCH.

By the RIGHT REV. HENRY COTTERILL, D.D., Bishop of Edinburgh. Demy 8vo, 7s. 6d.

MEMOIR OF COUNT DE MONTALEMBERT.
A CHAPTER OF RECENT FRENCH HISTORY. By Mrs OLIPHANT, Author of 'Life of Edward Irving,' &c. In Two Vols. crown 8vo, £1, 4s.

COUNT DE MONTALEMBERT'S HISTORY
OF THE MONKS OF THE WEST, FROM ST BENEDICT TO ST BERNARD. 5 vols. 8vo, £2, 12s. 6d.

HISTORICAL SKETCHES OF THE REIGN OF
GEORGE SECOND. By Mrs OLIPHANT. Second Edition, in One Vol., 10s. 6d.

HISTORY OF RATIONAL THEOLOGY AND
CHRISTIAN PHILOSOPHY IN ENGLAND IN THE SEVENTEENTH CENTURY. By the Rev. JOHN TULLOCH, D.D., Principal of St Mary's College, St Andrews, and one of Her Majesty's Chaplains for Scotland. 2 vols. 8vo, £1, 8s.

ARCHÆOLOGICAL SKETCHES IN SCOTLAND: KINTYRE.
By CAPTAIN T. P. WHITE, R.E., &c., of the Ordnance Survey. With 138 Illustrations. Imperial folio, £2, 2s.

THORNDALE; or, The Conflict of Opinions.
By WILLIAM SMITH, Author of 'A Discourse on Ethics,' &c. Second Edition. Crown 8vo, 10s. 6d.

GRAVENHURST; or, Thoughts on Good and
EVIL. By WILLIAM SMITH, Author of 'Thorndale,' &c. Crown 8vo, 7s. 6d.

THE ROYAL ATLAS OF MODERN GEOGRAPHY,
IN A SERIES OF ENTIRELY ORIGINAL AND AUTHENTIC MAPS. By A. KEITH JOHNSTON, F.R.S.E., F.R.G.S., Author of the 'Physical Atlas,' &c. With a complete Index of easy reference to each Map, comprising nearly 150,000 Places contained in this Atlas. Imperial Folio, half-bound in russia or morocco, £5, 15s. 6d. Each Plate may be had separately with its Index, 3s.

THE HANDY ROYAL ATLAS.
45 Maps clearly printed and carefully coloured, with GENERAL INDEX. By the Same. Imperial 4to, £2, 12s. 6d., half-bound morocco.

LAYS OF THE SCOTTISH CAVALIERS, AND
OTHER POEMS. By W. EDMONDSTOUNE AYTOUN, D.C.L., Professor of Rhetoric and Belles-Lettres in the University of Edinburgh. Twenty-second Edition. Fcap. 8vo, 7s. 6d.

THE BALLADS OF SCOTLAND.
Edited by PROFESSOR AYTOUN. Fourth Edition. 2 vols. fcap. 8vo, 12s.

THE BOOK OF BALLADS.
Edited by BON GAULTIER. Eleventh Edition, with numerous Illustrations by DOYLE, LEECH, and CROWQUILL. Gilt edges, post 8vo, 8s. 6d.

THE SPANISH GYPSY.
By GEORGE ELIOT. Fourth Edition, crown 8vo, 7s. 6d.

WISE, WITTY, AND TENDER SAYINGS,
In Prose and Verse. Selected from the Works of George Eliot. By ALEXANDER MAIN. Handsomely printed on Toned Paper, bound in gilt cloth, 5s.

MADONNA'S CHILD: A Poem.
By ALFRED AUSTIN. Crown 8vo, 7s. 6d.

GRAFFITI D'ITALIA.
By W. W. STORY, Author of 'Roba di Roma.' Fcap. 8vo, 7s. 6d.

NEW AND CHEAPER EDITION.

THE HISTORY OF SCOTLAND.
By JOHN HILL BURTON, Historiographer-Royal for Scotland. Continued in this Edition down to the extinction of the last Jacobite Insurrection.

In Eight Volumes, crown 8vo, 7s. 6d. each, bound in cloth.

MARY QUEEN OF SCOTS
AND HER ACCUSERS. By JOHN HOSACK, Barrister-at-Law. This work contains the 'Book of Articles' produced against Queen Mary at Westminster, which has never hitherto been printed. A New and Enlarged Edition, with a Photograph from the Bust on the Tomb in Westminster Abbey. 8vo, cloth, 15s.

OUTLINES OF NATURAL HISTORY,

For Beginners; being Descriptions of a Progressive Series of Zoological Types. By H. ALLEYNE NICHOLSON, M.D., D.Sc., F.R.S.E., F.G.S., &c., Professor of Natural History and Botany, University College, Toronto; formerly Lecturer on Natural History in the Medical School of Edinburgh. Fcap. 8vo, pp. 114, with 46 Engravings, 1s. 6d. cloth.

A MANUAL OF ZOOLOGY,

For the Use of Students. With a General Introduction on the Principles of Zoology. By the same Author. The Third Edition, revised and enlarged. Crown 8vo, pp. 706, with 280 Engravings, 12s. 6d.

"It is the best manual of zoology yet published, not merely in England but in Europe."—*Pall Mall Gazette.*

"The best treatise on zoology, in moderate compass, that we possess."—*Lancet.*

A MANUAL OF PALÆONTOLOGY,

For the Use of Students. With a General Introduction on the Principles of Palæontology. Crown 8vo, pp. 620, with 400 Engravings, 15s.

"This book will be found to be one of the best of guides to the principles of palæontology and the study of organic remains."—*Athenæum.*

THE SIX OF SPADES:

A Book about the Garden and the Gardener. By S. REYNOLDS HOLE, Author of 'A Book about Roses,' &c. Crown 8vo, 5s.

A BOOK ABOUT ROSES, HOW TO GROW

AND SHOW THEM. By S. REYNOLDS HOLE, Author of 'A Little Tour in Ireland.' Fourth Edition, Enlarged. Crown 8vo, 7s. 6d.

THE HANDY BOOK OF FRUIT CULTURE

UNDER GLASS. By DAVID THOMSON, Author of 'Handy Book of the Flower-Garden,' 'A Practical Treatise on the Culture of the Pine-Apple,' &c. In crown 8vo, with Engravings, 7s. 6d.

HANDY BOOK OF THE FLOWER-GARDEN:

Being Practical Directions for the Propagation, Culture, and Arrangement of Plants in Flower-Gardens all the Year Round. Embracing all classes of Gardens, from the largest to the smallest. With Engraved and Coloured Plans, illustrative of the various Systems of Grouping in Beds and Borders. By DAVID THOMSON. A New and Enlarged Edition, crown 8vo, 7s. 6d.

BOOKS IN THE PRESS.

FABLES IN SONG.
By ROBERT LORD LYTTON.
AUTHOR OF 'POEMS BY OWEN MEREDITH.'
Two vols. crown 8vo.

MR KINGLAKE'S
FIFTH, OR "INKERMAN VOLUME,"
OF
THE INVASION OF THE CRIMEA.

THE PHILOSOPHY OF HISTORY IN EUROPE.
Vol. I., CONTAINING THE HISTORY OF THAT PHILOSOPHY IN FRANCE AND GERMANY.
By ROBERT FLINT,
Professor of Moral Philosophy and Political Economy, University of St Andrews.

ECONOMIC GEOLOGY.
By DAVID PAGE, LL.D., F.G.S., &c.
Professor of Geology in the Durham University College of
Physical Science, Newcastle.

THE SECOND VOLUME OF
MARY QUEEN OF SCOTS AND HER ACCUSERS.
EMBRACING A NARRATIVE OF EVENTS FROM THE DEATH OF JAMES V. IN 1542,
UNTIL THE DEATH OF QUEEN MARY IN 1587.
By JOHN HOSACK, Barrister-at-Law.
Containing a Variety of Documents never before published.
(This Volume will complete the Work.)

ADVANCED TEXT-BOOK OF BOTANY.
FOR THE USE OF STUDENTS.
By ROBERT BROWN, M.A, Ph.D., F.R.G.S.
Lecturer on Botany under the Science and Art Department of the Committee of the
Privy Council on Education.
Crown 8vo, with numerous Illustrations.

THE INSPIRATION OF THE HOLY SCRIPTURES
BEING THE BAIRD LECTURES FOR 1873.
By the Rev. ROBERT JAMIESON, D.D.
Crown Octavo.

WILLIAM BLACKWOOD & SONS, EDINBURGH AND LONDON.

www.ingramcontent.com/pod-product-compliance
Lightning Source LLC
Chambersburg PA
CBHW022119290426
44112CB00008B/728